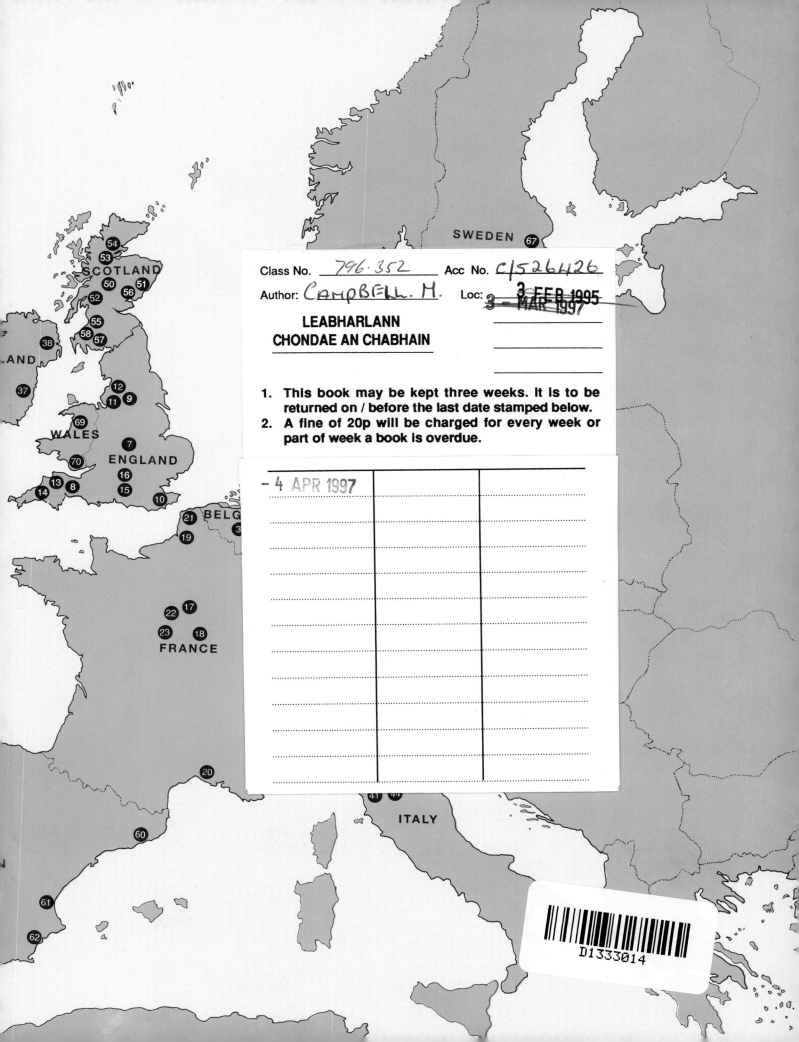

Class No. _796.352_   Acc No. _C/526426_

Author: _CAMPBELL. M._   Loc: 3 FEB 1995

3 — MAR 1997

LEABHARLANN
CHONDAE AN CHABHAIN

1. This book may be kept three weeks. It is to be returned on / before the last date stamped below.
2. A fine of 20p will be charged for every week or part of week a book is overdue.

- 4 APR 1997

D1333014

E U R O P E A N
GOLF COURSES

EUROPEAN
GOLF COURSES

The 70 best courses for golfing breaks in
Europe and the British Isles

Malcolm Campbell
with photographs by Brian Morgan

Foreword by Peter Alliss

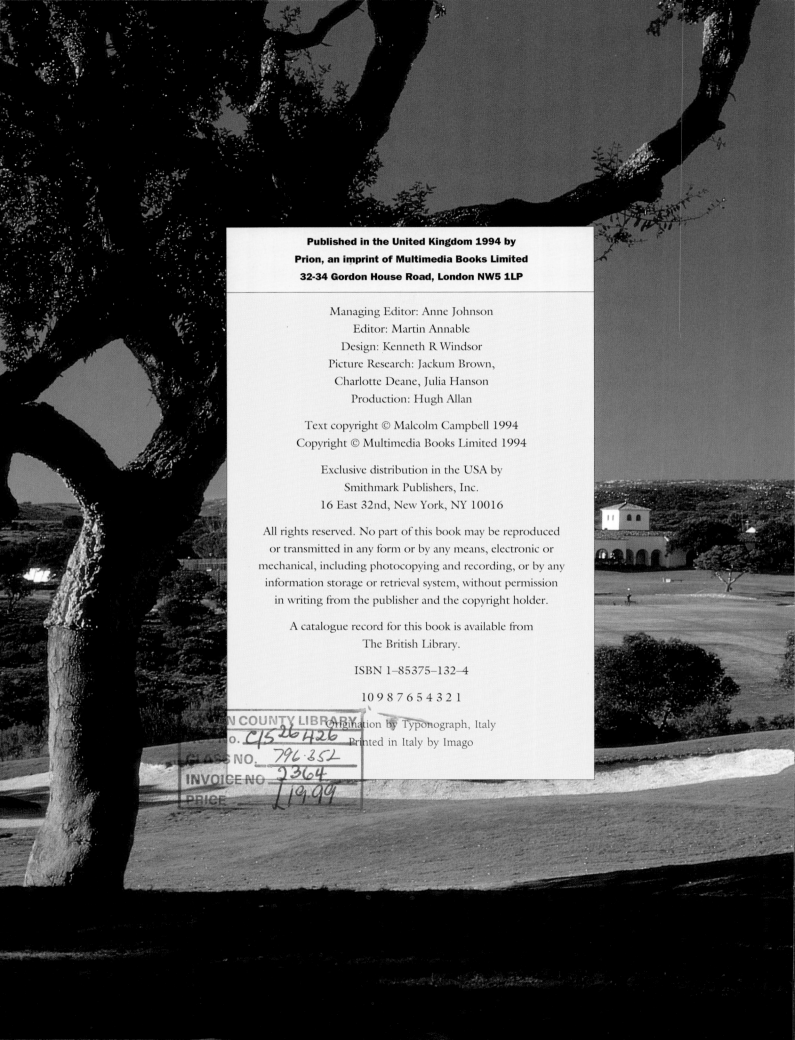

Published in the United Kingdom 1994 by

Prion, an imprint of Multimedia Books Limited

32-34 Gordon House Road, London NW5 1LP

Managing Editor: Anne Johnson
Editor: Martin Annable
Design: Kenneth R Windsor
Picture Research: Jackum Brown,
Charlotte Deane, Julia Hanson
Production: Hugh Allan

Text copyright © Malcolm Campbell 1994
Copyright © Multimedia Books Limited 1994

Exclusive distribution in the USA by
Smithmark Publishers, Inc.
16 East 32nd, New York, NY 10016

All rights reserved. No part of this book may be reproduced
or transmitted in any form or by any means, electronic or
mechanical, including photocopying and recording, or by any
information storage or retrieval system, without permission
in writing from the publisher and the copyright holder.

A catalogue record for this book is available from
The British Library.

ISBN 1–85375–132–4

10 9 8 7 6 5 4 3 2 1

Origination by Typonograph, Italy
Printed in Italy by Imago

N COUNTY LIBRARY
o. C/5 26 426
CLASS NO. 796·352
INVOICE NO 2364
PRICE £19.99

Contents

Foreword

B Y

P E T E R A L L I S S

The growth of European golf over the last 25 years has been quite staggering. In the 1960s, to travel anywhere to play golf, whether on holiday or professionally, was something done by the very few.

It wasn't until the mid-1960s that the first new golf courses appeared on the Costa del Sol – and what great excitement they caused. Robert Trent Jones, one of the world's most famous architects, was called in to design and construct courses along American resort lines, and what a splendid job he did at Las Brisas and Sotogrande. Atalaya Park was next on the agenda, designed by German architect Bernard von Limburger.

These dates are well burnished on my memory because I was fortunate enough to take part in the opening ceremonies on all three of those very different courses. Since then the Costa del Sol, Costa Brava and Costa Blanca have become dotted with golf courses. Developments spilled over into the Algarve and worked their way up to Lisbon and further north.

Many courses have been built in France and although there was depression in the late 1980s and '90s, those developments continue at a fair old pace.

Switzerland and Austria enlarged their list of golfing venues and the Swedes moved along at a remarkable pace, extraordinary really when you consider that the long winters make their summers so short. Given the Swedish keenness for golf, I've often wondered why their neighbours, Norway, have never really got involved in the game.

Golf is also on the move in Denmark; and Belgium, Italy and Greece all have major developments under construction.

Unfortunately golf on the Continent in some locations is still looked upon as an elitist sport. This is hard to comprehend, particularly as there has been a wave of top-class Continental players, both professional and amateur, men and women, making their presence felt.

For Germany, Bernhard Langer, one of the world's great professionals; for Spain Seve Ballesteros and José Maria Olazabal; for Sweden Joakim Haeggman, Jesper Parnevik for Sweden, are all making – and will leave – their indelible mark.

The number of golf courses built has been remarkable. Sometimes you wonder if the courses are being developed to attract visitors or just for local membership.

One of the problems with northern Europe is its winter. It doesn't have equatorial advantages so, although golf can be played all the year round, there are a number of months when the game is played under miserable conditions.

However, if you've never contemplated golfing in northern Europe I urge you to try. There are some beautiful courses to be discovered.

Historically there is so much to ponder and learn. The Dutch, for example, have always vied with the Scots as to where the game really began. For my money, the Scots have it by a distance, but your arguments tend to creak and groan when a new Egyptian tomb is unearthed and the carvings on the wall depict figures looking strangely like golfers, wielding sticks attempting to hit an object from a strange lie wearing a style of clothing popular in 2020 BC!

Golf takes us to many beautiful places and its variety is probably its greatest charm. It is a game that can

Golfers ready for a change of scenery now have a huge choice of courses, including the Alps.

be enjoyed alone. Of how many other sports, apart from snooker and darts, can that be said? The camaraderie, the friendship, the courtesy, yes, courtesy, displayed even in the heat of battle and never taken as a sign of weakness, are all part of this great game of ours.

Golf has been my life and it was preordained that it should be that way; that I should follow in the steps of my father Percy, one of the major participants in the world of professional golf from the early 1920s through to his retirement in the 1980s. It was through him that I developed my appreciation of golf plus the joys, the pain and, sometimes, the discomforts the game brings.

This book is a veritable golfing magic carpet and I recommend it to you. I only wish I were a few years younger and starting out all over again.

Introduction

Gathering together a selection of the great golf courses of Europe in one volume is a *tour de force* which is not only an exercise in total subjectivity but clearly exposes the arbiter to charges of partiality against which there can be little defence.

The purpose of this book, therefore, is not to attempt to identify the 'best' golf courses in Europe, but rather to embark on a golfing voyage of discovery identifying en route some of the game's outstanding European venues where the visitor will find exceptional and pleasurable golf and, equally importantly, a warm welcome besides.

In the selection which follows there are famous challenges where great deeds have been done and championships won; there are remote courses of incredible splendour; ancient links where the very beginnings of the game were established; and hidden gems which are cherished like golfing talismans.

The growth in the popularity of golf in Europe since the beginning of the 1980s has been of truly phenomenal proportions. Today the game is emerging from the second great golf course building boom in a century, with the signs of a slowing down process only now being seen.

In the last two decades of the last century there was a similar course building boom when the organized game spread from Scotland across the border into England, to Europe and indeed to the rest of the world. The Scots were the pioneers, both in terms of their ability to play the game and in laying out a series of memorable courses upon which to display their skills.

Golf course design at the turn of the century was something less than the multi-million dollar industry it has become a hundred years on.

Several of the courses featured in this volume were the work of the legendary Tom Morris of St Andrews – Old Tom as he became known. At the height of his powers as a golf course creator, Old Tom commanded a fee of £1 per day plus expenses. If the task of laying out the course detained him for more than four days it was a rare event indeed and more likely to have been the result of extended hospitality than the need to solve technical problems.

Today the master craftsmen – or golf course architects as they are now known – command fees for a single 18-hole layout which might easily parallel the national debt of some of the developing countries.

But of course the game has changed since Old Tom's day. Where once upon a time a few thousand took their pleasure on the links with basic implements and balls ill-suited to the task, today there are millions with the finest equipment modern technology can devise. The demand for courses upon which they can play mounts inexorably and the modern Tom Morris must be able to provide courses which will not only survive the mass of play to which they are now subjected but also be capable of simple and economic maintenance.

The game has changed dramatically and so too have the players. Only in Scotland, where it had its genesis and developed over centuries, has the game of golf truly been one for all the people. Elsewhere in Europe it has, for most of its history, been the preserve of the well-to-do or, indeed, in some countries, only the very wealthy.

However, Kings have played golf with commoners across the decades; European monarchs have captained clubs and played in national amateur championships. Golf has provided the common ground to make such things possible, and today it is played by a much broader spectrum of the population than ever before.

The game's great contribution has undoubtedly been its ability to cut across the social and economic divide in a way that very few other forms of human endeavour have been able even to contemplate.

Across the length and breadth of Eur-ope the royal and ancient game has gathered momentum. In France and Germany, in particular, the golf course building pro-gramme has been intense and there are now many more fine courses to explore in these countries than ever before. Scandinavia continues to lead the way in developing young players, with the Swedes now pro-ducing top-line golf players in much the same way as they have been doing so suc-cessfully with tennis players for a decade longer.

In the British Isles new courses continue to be built to meet the ever-growing de-mand. Many of them are very fine layouts to complement the traditional venues like the Old Course at St Andrews which remains

The R&A Clubhouse at St Andrews – the home of golf.

the Mecca for all who put club to ball in the accepted fashion.

But all over Europe there is great golf to be found. From the wild and remote links of Royal Dornoch to the beautiful surroundings of the Corfu Golf and Country Club in Greece, there is something to satisfy even the most discerning golfer's taste.

This volume presents a selection intended to be representative of the great golfing delights of Europe together with suggestions on where the travelling golfer might rest his head between rounds along with tourist attractions for the non-golfing compan-ion. Constraints on space demand that it can be no more than broadly representative of all three, but if it gives even a taste of the wonderful menu of golf courses and ancillary delights which Europe can set before the travelling golfer and those who travel with him or her, then I will be well pleased.

Malcolm L. Campbell
Auchinloch, Scotland

Austria

Far better known for its skiing and winter sports than for golf, Austria is nonetheless a country with a strong golfing heritage. The magnificent Alpine settings are perfect in the summer for pursuit of the royal and ancient game and the country has upwards of 70 courses from which the visitor can choose.

The season is rather short by comparison with other European neighbours but from April to October it would be hard to find a more glorious setting for holiday golf. The wonderful mountains, forests and lakes add their own unique atmosphere of tranquillity to the game.

Development of new courses continues all the time. Much of that development has come as a direct result of the interest generated in golf in Germany and Austria in the wake of the success of Germany's double US Masters Champion, Bernhard Langer. Langer's meteoric rise to the very pinnacle of world golf, along with that of Severiano Ballesteros of Spain, brought a much wider awareness of the game to Continental Europe.

Like Germany, Austria has been a golfing nation for many decades, but the game was always the preserve of the wealthy until the golf boom of the 1980s began to change all that. Many of Austria's golf clubs are venerable institutions which have been catering to an elite membership since the 1920s. Semmering and Karntner are two of that vintage while the oldest club in Austria is the Golfclub Wien in Vienna which dates back to 1901. The club is located in the famous Vienna park, the Prater.

One of the engineering marvels of Europe, the magnificent Brenner pass links Austria to Italy.

A spate of new golf course building saw more than 20 new courses completed within half a dozen years in the 1980s, including the splendid Golf and Country Club, Gut Altentann near Saltzburg.

It was the first course built by Jack Nicklaus in Europe and confirmed the commitment of the Austrians to the modern trends in the game. It is golf in the cultural atmosphere of one of Austria's great cities, the birthplace of Mozart .

By contrast, the beautiful holiday course of Innsbruck at Igls is set high in the mountains in the famous alpine ski resort. Together Innsbruck and Gut Altentann represent the two differing aspects of golf in the country where the sound of the cow bell is better known than the solid crack of ball on club.

Golf Club Innsbruck-Igls

FOUNDED 1956

GOLF IN THE ALPS

For those who appreciate holiday golf which is challenging without being too difficult and is accompanied by some of the most magnificent views in Europe, the course of the Innsbruck-Igls Golf Club is very hard to match.

Located only a few kilometres from the famous Innsbruck alpine resort, the course is surrounded by magnificent mountains and breathtaking panoramas. The club has two courses, the 18-hole layout at Igls built in 1977, and a further nine-hole course a few kilometres away at Lans dating back to 1956.

Both are renowned for their scenery rather than their challenge although there is certainly enough of that for the majority of players, particularly on the 18-hole course.

In mountain terrain more suitable for skiing than golf, the Igls course is as much a challenge of physical strength as golfing prowess.

THE COURSE

There is much to enjoy about this G & G Hauser designed layout as well as the magnificent scenery.

Several of the holes wind their way around and through a heavily wooded area where the fairways have been cut through tall fir trees. The trees present a major obstacle for winter skiers but they are less of a hardship for the golfer.

The fairways are generous enough and only a wildly struck shot should find trouble in the woods.

The front nine is longer than the back by more than 200 metres, much of that due to the two par 5s in the first half.

The 5th, particularly, is worthy of closer scrutiny. It is the longest hole on the course at 523 metres from the back tees. A double dogleg with a hilly fairway, it has a pond which makes the approach to the green very awkward. Even in the thinner alpine air where the ball flies much further, this is still a hole out of range for all but the very longest hitters.

The 7th, the second of the par 3s, is another testing hole on the front nine at more than 192 metres from the back tee. There is some respite at the next, a modest par 4 of 330 metres, before you have to tackle the second of the big par 5s.

At close to 500 metres, the 9th will not yield a par let alone a birdie easily, and again it is out of range most of the time for the average player.

On the back nine, at 433 metres, the 13th is the longest of the par 4s, but the 11th is only slightly shorter and certainly matches it for difficulty.

In some ways Igls saves the best for last with three good finishing holes, although par should not be too difficult to achieve.

> **Golf Club Innsbruck-Igls**
>
> *Oberdorf 11, 6074 Rinn*
>
> ◆
>
> Location: 10km
> from Innsbruck
>
> Tel: (43) 52 23 8177
>
> Course: 18 holes, 5910m,
> par 71
>
> Visitors: Welcome at any time.
>
> Course closed November
> to March
>
> Green fees: 400-500AS

Sometimes Innsbruck resembles any run-of-the mill rural British course – until the clouds clear and the Alps reveal themselves.

FACILITIES

The Innsbruck club has excellent facilities with a bar and restaurant and a driving range at both of its clubhouses.

At Igls there is always equipment available for hire. Caddies are available on request but there are no golf carts for hire.

THE REGION

Innsbruck is an alpine holiday resort with all the associated attractions of mountain climbing and hill walking in the summer.

There are few better places in the world to pursue either. But there are other attractions for the visitor to savour as well.

In the town of Innsbruck, on the most beautiful of the old town's arboured streets, the Herzog-Friedrich-Strasse, there are several splendid bay windows and painted house fronts. The 'Golden Roof' attracts many visitors to this area of town.

Two of the holes, the 16th and the 18th, are par 5s with the former the more difficult because of its length. At 473 metres it is a good test but should be a comfortable three-shot hole.

The last is much shorter and only just a par 5 at 438 metres. If you feel intoxicated with the heady atmosphere of the mountains and the clear and clean alpine air, you may feel you can reach the green in two shots in search of a memorable finish. Many who have tried have succeeded.

The two par 5s are separated by a charming little par 4 which requires only a modest drive and a short pitch to reach the green.

The other Innsbruck course at Lans is a much older layout having been built in 1956. It is a charming course and well worth playing, but quite short with a par of 33.

The comfortable Sporthotel Igls offers transfer facilities between the hotel, airport and golf course.

It may not be the most taxing golf you'll ever find when you're playing in Europe, but there can be few more dramatic backdrops to a course anywhere in the world.

St James' Cathedral, the most important baroque church in the Northern Tyrol, preserves at the high altar 'Mary's help' – the famous miracle-working image by I. Cranach.

The Tyrol Regional Museum Fernandeum has a fascinating collection of historic art, including original reliefs of the 'Golden Roof'.

Also worth a visit is Bergisel, the site of the Tyrolian struggle for freedom in 1809 under the leadership of Andreas Hofer.

ACCOMODATION

Being an internationally famous alpine resort, there is no shortage of accommodation for visitors to this part of the Tyrol.

The Hotel Europa Tyrol in Innsbruck provides first-class amenities and service as a tourist base for the area while the Sporthotel Igls is ideally placed for the golf course.

The Sporthotel Igls also offers transfer facilities between the hotel, airport and golf course.

Golf and Country Club Gut Altentann

FOUNDED 1986

ALPINE MONSTER THAT JACK BUILT

When Jack Nicklaus was called in to design the Gut Altentann course at Henndorf am Wallersee he was in no mood to compromise. It was his first design venture in Europe and he built a layout which will test any player.

The site is a wonderfully scenic piece of ground only a few kilometres from Salzburg, the town of Mozart.

Nicklaus incorporated the natural characteristics of the area and the original contours of the land into a spectacular design which features lakes and streams in a typically American layout.

Gut Altentann has an interesting history. As far back as 785 the ground was given over to the Mondsee monastery. Up to the 17th century the manor house in which the archbishops and curators lived was gradually expanded into a magnificent castle. In 1860 the manor was destroyed by fire.

THE COURSE

This site was chosen for the new Golf and Country Club Gut Altentann and the course opened for play in 1986.

> **Golf and Country Club Gut Altentann**
>
> *5302 Henndorf am Wallersee*
>
> ◆
>
> Location: 11km from Salzburg
>
> Tel: (43) 62 14 6026
>
> Course: 18 holes, 6180m, par 72
>
> Visitors: Weekdays only but pre-booking is essential.
>
> Course closed from November to April
>
> Green fees: 800AS

There are several dogleg holes in the Nicklaus layout and water comes into play on many of the holes. An easy par 4 of just over 300 metres gets the round underway. A tough par 5 follows, and an even tougher par 4 of 398 metres after that is an early indication of what Nicklaus has in store.

The two par 3s on the front nine, the 4th and the 9th, are very fine holes and nicely balanced.

On the back nine Nicklaus again offers a tempting start with a short par 4 of 328 metres but immediately follows it up with a tough par 4 at the 11th.

The short 12th is not too demanding but requires care before Nicklaus builds the challenge to a crescendo of which Mozart himself might well have been proud.

The food and service – as well as the view – from the clubhouse are almost out of this world.

American knowhow and Austrian scenery – an unbeatable combination.

THE REGION

This part of Austria has a magic that is all its own. The mountains are never far away and the Austrians offer a unique hospitality to visitors unmatched elsewhere in Europe. The cultural delights of this part of Austria are renowned all over the world. Salzburg offers a host of attractions for the discerning visitor with wonderful culinary delights to be enjoyed en route.

In the last four holes there is only one par 4 – a tough 388-metre affair which is extremely demanding. The 15th is the longest hole on the course and the short 16th has been the graveyard for many a score. In the 1992 Austrian Open, Mark James needed thirteen strokes before he finally walked off the green an older and a wiser player on this 170-metre dice with death.

At more than 470 metres with a sea of sand in front of the green and a lake behind, the final hole is nothing short of a monster. This course is no place to take your game unless it is in anything but the best order.

FACILITIES

Being a new country club complex, Gut Altentann has every facility the visiting golfer could wish for.

There is a welcoming bar and a first-class restaurant. The club has its own swimming pool and tennis courts and, in common with all Jack Nicklaus layouts, a very good driving range and practice area.

The 17th-century Salzburg Cathedral, with its splendid marble façade, rich stucco decoration and valuable treasures, is quite magnificent.

The annual Salzburg Music Festival celebrates the city's most famous son, Mozart, and attracts thousands of visitors, as does his birthplace in Getreidegasse. There are also several magnificent castles to visit, including Hellbrunn Castle with its famous water-gardens.

ACCOMMODATION

Apart from the accommodation available at the country club itself, there are many hotels to choose from in the area.

In Salzburg the Hotel Osterreichischer Hof offers excellent accommodation, a fine restaurant and wine list.

Also ideal for golfing visitors is the Hotel Goldener Hirsch which offers transfers between the hotel, airport and golf course.

2

Belgium

In much the same way as England, Belgium owes much of its golfing development to the interest shown in the game by its Royal Household.

King Baudouin was a player of international standard, and over many decades there have been royal connections with many of the country's clubs.

Belgium shares with Spain the distinction of having a monarchy which follows the practice of conferring royal titles on selected golf clubs. They are the only two countries in continental Europe where this is the case.

Belgium has 10 royal clubs in all and the royal connection goes back as far as 1903 when King Leopold II saw the benefits of trade to his country by providing golf facilities for visiting businessmen. Clubs were set up in the royal parkland on the outskirts of Brussels and on Crown land made available at Ostend.

The King was not a player himself, but the clubs he was instrumental in setting up still flourish today along with six other royal clubs in the country. Other members of the Belgian royal family, however, have been highly accomplished players.

King Baudouin's father, King Leopold III, was also a first-class player quite capable of holding his own in amateur championships in Belgium and France. In 1939 he played in the Belgian Amateur at Zoute and remains the only reigning monarch to have played in his own national championship. He also reached the last eight of the French Championship in 1949.

Belgium has its own unique character shown here at springtime on this peaceful canal in the heart of Bruges.

The two best-known of Belgium's many fine courses are perhaps the Royal Club de Belgique, a truly spectacular course set in magnificent surroundings just east of Brussels, and Royal Waterloo where part of the Lion course overlooks the old battlefield.

Today, Belgium boasts upwards of 50 golf courses, many of them built in the recent past as the country embraced the great golf boom of the 1980s.

Often Belgium is overlooked as a destination for the itinerant golfer. This is unfortunate for there are many fine courses where it is easy to find a tee time and where the visitor will receive a warm welcome.

Access could not be easier. North Sea Ferries run a first-class overnight service to Zeebrugge which can put the travelling golfer on the first tee very early in the morning after an excellent dinner, a good night's sleep and breakfast on board.

The country's road system puts Britain's to shame and there is much of interest in Belgium for the non-golfer to enjoy.

Royal Waterloo

FOUNDED 1923

IN THE FOOTSTEPS OF THE MAESTRO

In 1934 the late Sir Henry Cotton, probably the finest British player after Vardon, Braid and Taylor, won the first of his three Open Championships.

Shortly afterwards he left Britain to become the professional at the Royal Waterloo Golf Club, just outside Brussels. It was an unprecedented move which Cotton always claimed was made to benefit his health but was resented by some in Britain who took the view that the Open Champion had sacrificed his country on the altar of a not inconsiderable retainer.

However, if it was Britain's loss it was Belgium's gain, for Cotton took with him a style and panache which sat very well with the members at this fine old Belgian club. He remained as professional until 1938, the year of his second Open victory at Carnoustie.

Today Royal Waterloo remains one of the finest clubs in Europe with close to 2000 members enjoying 45 holes in splendid surroundings close to the site of the old battlefield at Waterloo.

The club was founded in 1923, at Rhode-Saint-Genèse, and five years later work was completed on a splendid clubhouse built in the English style. However, the club suffered badly during the Second World War when the course was turned over to horse pasture by the forces of occupation. After the war the club prospered again but it ran into a major problem in 1958. The expansion of Brussels, and the need for development land, forced the club to move from its original site.

THE COURSES

A new site was found at Ohain south of the city and close to the old battlefield.

Fred Hawtree, who had designed the original 18-hole course and an additional nine holes, was called in to build a new 36-hole layout.

On 1 January 1960 the Royal Waterloo Club officially opened the new layout together with a magnificent, modern-style clubhouse enjoying spectacular views from its terrace.

Hawtree laid out La Marache as the principal of the two courses, and, since its official opening, the course has hosted many important professional championships. These include the Belgian Open, the Volvo Mens Open and the Trophée Laurent Perrier, as well as a host of leading amateur events.

La Marache winds its way through rolling fairways and great stands of trees which have matured since they were planted by Hawtree more than three decades ago.

There are some wonderful holes on this layout. The double dogleg 3rd for example is a superb ex-

> **Royal Waterloo Golf Club**
>
> *Vieux Chemin De Wavre*
>
> *50, 1380 Ohain, Belgium*
>
> ◆
>
> Location: Off the N253 south of Brussels
>
> Tel: (02) 63 31 850
>
> Courses: La Marache – 18 holes, 6211m, par 72.
> Le Lion – 18 holes, 6224m, par 72. Le Bois Heros – 9 holes, 2143m, par 33
>
> Visitors: Welcome
>
> Green Fees: BF1800-3000

ample of strategic design. At 489 metres from the back tee, it plays downhill for half its length, but to get home in two requires a long drive turning right to left to get round the corner. From there the long hitter should manage to get home with an iron club but accuracy is at a premium.

Any drive left out to the right means that you will need a long shot over the dogleg and a copse of tall trees. However, there are few who succeed in making that carry.

In 1983 the club brought in architect Paul Rolin to build a new American-style 18-hole layout which would supersede the shorter course laid out originally by Hawtree.

The Lion course presents a marked contrast to La Marache and at 6224 metres is a stiffer test. Le Lion is flatter and more open and has views of the old battlefield. The short nine-hole layout, Le Bois Heros, is an interesting test which again puts the

premium on accuracy.

The Royal Waterloo Club is widely regarded as one of the top 10 clubs in continental Europe and with every justification.

In addition to the late Sir Henry Cotton, the club has boasted several eminent players as club professionals, including Aubrey Boomer, Donald Swaelens, Flory van Donk and, until 1993, Ryder Cup player, George Will.

FACILITIES

Royal Waterloo has outstanding facilities for the benefit of members and guests – try to avoid playing on Mondays when you will find them closed. There is a fine restaurant and bar and there are first-class practice facilities as well.

Visiting players are welcome except at weekends during the season. However, it is advisable to pre-arrange a tee time.

The battlefield at Waterloo is a must for all visitors, yet it is strange to reflect how the fate of two armies was decided so dramatically in 1815 at such an ordinary venue.

The approach to the 9th at La Marache. At first sight, it looks simple enough, but dangers await the unwary in the form of four bunkers jealously guarding the pin.

The Region

Royal Waterloo lies a few kilometres outside the Belgian capital, Brussels. The monument on the site of the famous battlefield where Napoleon lost an empire and the fate of Europe was decided by sword and field artillery, is a must for visitors to the area.

Accommodation

Brussels is a busy city and, like the rest of Belgium, has an infinite variety of attractions for the visitor. There are plenty of stylish hotels and fine restaurants to suit every variety of taste.

The Copthorne Hotel on the Avenue Louise close to the city centre offers first-class accommodation in a beautifully appointed hotel. Guests will be warmly welcomed by manager Denis Heskin, a member at Royal Waterloo, who has been away from his native Limerick for 20 years and is renowned as a prodigious hitter and a fine host.

The hotel has its own underground garage – an important consideration in a congested capital city –

and boasts a first-class restaurant offering international cuisine.

Those looking for something away from the city centre might like to try Le Dernièr Cri restaurant close to the Royal Waterloo club which offers fine food, an excellent wine list in intimate surroundings.

The Copthorne offers first-class accommodation, wonderful cuisine, good parking facilities and – in manager Denis Heskin – the most genial of hosts.

3

Denmark

For golfers anxious to get away from their native heath in search of an alternative golfing destination, Denmark has probably not figured too seriously so far in their plans.

But that will undoubtedly change as more golfers discover just how much this country has to offer to the itinerant golfer. There are spectacular courses, nearly 40 of which have been built within the past 20 years. And, with a population of only five million, nowhere ever seems to get crowded – least of all the golf courses.

To drive on Danish roads is to experience a quietness and serenity more reminiscent of remote Scottish glens than of a modern European community with a standard of living which it is hard not to envy. And if you remain under the illusion, as many still seem to do, that because Denmark is in Scandinavia it is covered in snow for most of the year, you should be disabused of this erroneous notion immediately.

Denmark never fails to please – the warmth of the welcome and the wonderful climate are an unbeatable combination.

Denmark enjoys a much better climate than most parts of the British Isles with long, hot summers and light evenings when play is possible until a couple of Carlsbergs short of midnight.

Most clubs are open throughout the year and, generally, all the courses in the country enjoy summer greens from March right through to November.

Add to that the fact that you can get there in your own car in about the time it takes to drive from London to Dornoch and it becomes clear why Danish courses are becoming as popular as the lager which sells three bottles abroad for every one consumed at home.

And if you don't think that amounts to much, you don't know much about the consumption of the Danes!

From Denmark's oldest club, the Kobenhavn Golf Club in the Royal Deer Park outside Copenhagen which dates back to 1898, to the wonderful new layout at Royal Oak in Jutland, there is a huge variety of courses from which to choose.

The great links of Holstebro is widely regarded as among the best in the country in its very British heathland setting, while there are majestic courses through forests and beside fjords in Funen and Sealand. The Nordbornholms Golf Klub on the Baltic island of Bornholm is a gem and even has its own airport.

It's all there in Denmark for the golfer – if he can tear himself away from Legoland. And it would be hard to find a friendlier place to play.

Esbjerg Golfklub

FOUNDED 1921

CHALLENGE IN THE FOREST

This famous Danish course is set in an undulating landscape amid great stands of pine and spruce on the outskirts of the Maebaek forest.

Laid out in 1975 by Copenhagen architect Frederik Dreyer, it is one of the best courses in Scandinavia. Like Holstebro further to the north, there is more than a hint of the best Scottish inland golf about this course which can be stretched to almost 6500 metres from the championship tees.

From the back tees it is an awesome challenge and ranks as one of the toughest par 71 layouts to be found anywhere in Europe. The SSS from the back tees is 74.

Most visitors will find it as much challenge as they need from the regular tees at just over 6000 metres. But even from these more forward tees it remains a testing par of 71.

Because it is close to the sea, the wind is a vital element in the challenge of Esbjerg, although in no way could it be likened to a links course.

Accurate driving is the key to success here and, although the fairways are generous in width, they demand the greatest respect from the tee. A missed fairway offers very little chance of recovery and, with large rolling greens, any wayward approach shots put a very severe strain on the putter.

Esbjerg Golfklub
Sonderhedevej, Marbaek, 6710 Esbjerg
◆
Location: Off B447 north-west of Esbjerg
Tel: (45) 75 26 9219
Course: 18 holes, 6434m, par 71
Visitors: Welcome at any time
Green fees: DKr180

THE COURSE

Although there are undeniably shades of Scotland about this long-established course, it remains very traditionally Danish.

The challenge is set out from the very beginning with an opening par 4 of 366 metres played uphill to a huge green. Two bunkers threaten the drive on the right and a long, dangerous bunker protects the

This is golf at its most civilized. After the awesome challenge you will have faced earlier, the sanctuary of this 18th green will be very welcome.

Could there be a more picturesque hole in all of Scandinavia than the 4th at Esbjerg? There are shades of Scotland among the pines.

right side of the green. Two good shots are required here from the back tee.

The long par 5 5th merely confirms that this Esbjerg course will give the player no respite. A monster 500-metre dogleg from the back tee, it has water crossing the fairway twice with out-of-bounds down the length of the hole on the right. A good drive and a careful lay-up short of the water are required here.

The 16th is perhaps the pick of the holes on the back nine. It is a beautiful dogleg left protected by a bunker on the right of the fairway. From the more forward tee it presents less of a problem. The green is narrow in front and two long and dangerous bunkers put great pressure on the approach shot.

The Region

Esbjerg is one of Denmark's major ports and a town with a lively night life. There are splendid sandy beaches nearby on Jutland's west coast and plenty of attractions for the non-golfer.

Esbjerg is also the main North Sea ferry port from the UK and this is an ideal way to travel to Denmark for the golfer. The quiet roads make motoring a pleasure and a car is really an essential for anyone intent on coming here.

Car hire rates tend to be heavy but, with good ferry connections from Europe through Sweden and Copenhagen, it is very easy for the golfer to drive his own car to Denmark.

Accommodation

There are many types of accommodation available in the region.

The Hotel Hjerting is one of many fine hotels in Esbjerg offering first-class and reasonably priced accommodation. It is also situated within easy reach of the golf course.

Another gem is the Hotel Ansgar. Situated in the centre of town, it is a traditional, family-run hotel enjoying an excellent reputation for its facilities and service and for its restaurant.

Holstebro Golfklub

F O U N D E D   1 9 7 0

HEATHER AND A HINT OF SCOTLAND

There is very much an air of good old-fashioned British heathland golf about the fine Holstebro Golf Club in Jutland. The course has been widely regarded in Denmark for many years as the finest in the country and one of the very best in northern Europe.

The club lies a few kilometres south-west of the town of Holstebro, one of the main trading areas and the cultural heart of West Jutland.

Built on classic heathland and pine forest and heather, the Forest Course conjures up images of the great courses of Blairgowrie in Scotland or of Sunningdale in England, and has been host to many international events.

That it is very much a thinker's course is confirmed by Roy Howett the club's English professional from Croydon. 'If you don't work out how to get it round here then the course becomes very difficult indeed,' he says with just a hint of dogmatism.

And there can be no argument about that.

THE COURSE

The premium is very much on accurate driving and positional play to open up many of the holes which are doglegs. Thick heather and trees await those who forget or are not up to the task.

The greens are usually superb once they have emerged from their winter hibernation and the season is a long one in this part of Denmark. There is a very strong feeling of traditional values about this styl-

ish club which was founded in 1970. Since then it has quickly gained an enviable reputation both for the quality of its golf and for its friendliness.

The challenge of the Forest Course is obvious from the very first hole. It is a demanding par 4 of 372 metres which doglegs sharply to the right. A long and accurate drive is needed to open up the green for a difficult second shot.

The par 5 2nd gives a little respite before the picturesque 3rd. A modest 148 metres in length, it demands careful club selection for the shot through a beautiful avenue of pines.

However, it is only after this opening trio of holes that the full assault on Holstebro really be-

Holstebro Golfklub
Rasted, 7570 Vemb
◆
Location: 5km south-west
of Holstebro off A16
near Idom
Tel: (45) 97 48 5155
Course: 18 holes, 6199m,
par 72
Visitors: Welcome at any time
Green fees: DKr180 per
day midweek; DKr200 at
weekends

gins. Accurate driving is the key to survival. Apart from the great stands of pines there is little in the way of semi-rough to prevent a wayward shot reaching the heather. In bloom it adds a great splash of colour to this beautiful golf course but, like heather everywhere, it is a nightmare to play from. 'Make sure you get it out' is old advice, but nowhere is it more apt than here is western Jutland.

The 6th and 7th, the former a stiff par 5 and the latter an equally stiff par 4, almost form a semicircle

The greens at Hostelbro are of the very highest order once the winter months are over. The club deserves its reputation as one of the finest in northern Europe.

between them so tight are the doglegs. Position from the tee is absolutely vital and neither hole concedes a par very easily.

The 9th is the stroke index 2 hole and another tough dogleg par 4 which brings the player back to the clubhouse. The green is defended by a big bunker on the right at the side of the green and by another short of the green to the left.

The immensely long 16th is arguably the best hole on the back nine demanding again both length and accuracy from the tee. A missed tee shot here virtually puts paid to any chance of a par and even a good drive will have to be followed by a second of similar quality to keep in play on a narrow, uphill fairway.

The course is generally undulating, although not hilly, and extremely pleasant to walk. Wildlife abounds and with the fresh smell of the pine forest and

the clear air, Holstebro it is one of the most pleasant places to play golf anywhere.

A new nine-hole layout, The Park Course, was opened in 1993. Several changes had to be made to the Forest Course to accommodate the new layout. However, these have not detracted in any way from the original course.

FACILITIES

Holstebro is very much a golf club rather than a leisure complex. It provides excellent facilities for its members and visitors with good locker rooms and a friendly club bar. There is also a fine restaurant.

The club, like most in Denmark, is keen on promoting junior golf. It has no waiting list for juniors and has a strong programme to encourage youngsters who start at seven or eight years of age.

THE REGION

Denmark is a relatively small country with excellent roads almost free of traffic. Travel around the country

This is the 16th, possibly the most challenging hole at Hostelbro. However, the picture belies the very narrow long fairway and even the top players do well to make par here.

This is the 1st of the nine-hole course which looks deceptively straightforward. Beware the bunker to the front of the green.

is, therefore, very straightforward and there is much to see and do.

In Jutland the wonders of Legoland fascinate youngsters and adults alike and this world-famous park is within an hour's drive of Holstebro. The activity parks of Sommerland West and Varde, and the Lion Park at Givskud, are also within easy reach.

Water sports are widely available on the Danish fjords with windsurfing high on the popularity list. Fine restaurants, shops and pubs abound, where the Danes seem to consume the entire national output of Carlsberg.

In summer the evenings are long and warm in Jutland and the region boasts a very high annual sunshine count.

ACCOMMODATION

There are few countries with a wider range of accommodation for visitors. Holiday apartment hotels are very popular and the Bork Haven Holiday Hotel is typical of many in the region.

Here, the fjord is a windsurfer's paradise. Other facilities include tennis, badminton and sailing. The solarium and sauna are standard in the vast majority of Danish hotels.

For those who prefer more formal surroundings, the Royal Hotel in the centre of Holstebro has much to recommend it. The hotel straddles the River Stora which runs through the town. The Prismet Restaurant serves international cuisine, has an extensive wine list, and enjoys a first-class reputation.

Royal Oak Golf Club

F O U N D E D   1 9 9 2

IN A LEAGUE OF ITS OWN

The Royal Oak Golf Club at Jels in southern Jutland was opened in 1992 but it is already established as one of the outstanding golf courses in Scandinavia, and certainly has the potential to become one of the best in Europe.

The course was the dream of Danish businessman Andreas Schou. He became so frustrated by having to wait for a weekend tee time at the club where he was a member that he decided to solve the problem by building his own course amid the forests and lakes of the Jels countryside.

He brought in Danish architect Jens Malling to design the course in conjunction with three-handicap player, Per Gundtoft, who supervized construction. Gundtoft remains as the Royal Oak green superintendent.

And what a marvellous golf course the pairing put together. It is an unashamedly American design, spread across open countryside and alongside a lake.

The 18-hole layout with wonderful practice facilities is the first in Denmark to be built to full USGA specifications. It features large greens which are firm and fast and a joy to putt on. The practice ground matches the best American standards and the six-hole practice course is extensively used.

Royal Oak Golf Club

Golgvej, Jels, DK-6630 Rodding

◆

Location: 30km south-west of Kolding

Tel: (45) 74 55 3294

Course: 18 holes, 6425m, par 72

Visitors: Welcome at any time

Green fees: DKr250 weekdays or weekends

THE COURSE

The long par 5 5th is one of several outstanding holes. The second shot to this 528-metre challenge is threatened by the lake which eats into the fairway around 70 metres from the green. The water is hidden by the slope and a strip of rough runs across the fairway at this point.

A careful lay-up with the second shot is sound advice here. Only the longest and bravest are able to carry the trouble.

The 10th is another fiercely challenging hole. A long par 3 of 190 metres, it features a lake short of the green on the left and a dangerous bunker on the right.

The 2nd is an example of Scandinavian golf at its very best; water to the right and a green that is very difficult to hold with the approach.

The thatched clubhouse at the Royal Oak is one of the very best in Denmark. The food and wine lists are first class and the welcome and service are simply Scandinavian.

A very long iron is required in the prevailing wind to reach a green which is cleverly contoured.

The club is named after the 'Royal Oak' tree which stands alongside the 12th fairway. It was so named after King Christian X and Crown Prince Frederik who decided to rest themselves and their horses there during the Royal Review at the manor of Jelsgard in October 1935.

FACILITIES

Just as spectacular as this magnificent layout which can be stretched to nearly 6500 metres for championship purposes is the Royal Oak clubhouse. It has a justifiable claim to be the most beautiful clubhouse in Denmark and has facilities to match.

A team of thatchers from Austria was drafted in to construct the roof of the building, and they have done such a fine job that this modern clubhouse

looks as if it might have stood in splendour on the same spot for a century.

Royal Oak has an award-winning chef in house and the club's restaurant is quite simply outstanding.

The club also offers full conference facilities for those who wish to combine business with a great deal of pleasure. Royal Oak prides itself on being able to provide tee times for visitors at the weekend. A limit is placed on Saturday and Sunday events to keep the course available for visitors during what would normally be the club's busiest time.

Visitors are made very welcome and there is a 50 per cent discount for juniors.

THE REGION

The area around the Jels lakes offers spectacular scenery. The Jels lower lake is circled by forest on the one bank and the golf course on the other. The town

The 8th is plain sailing provided you're only messing about in a boat. Overhit your approach and you'll find a watery grave just like thousands have done before you.

has an interesting church and mill and an open-air theatre which provides the setting for the nationally renowned Jels Viking plays.

A Viking longboat adds a reminder of the country's adventurous past to the view across the lake from the 5th green.

Apart from golf the area offers excellent facilities for yachtsmen and anglers. For those made of sterner stuff there is an open-air swimming pool in Jels.

The cities of Kolding and Haderslev are only a 15-minute drive from the course and the major west coast port of Esbjerg is less than an hour away.

Kolding has much to offer the visitor. The historic castle of Koldinghus and the Trapholt Art Museum attract many tourists throughout the year and the town has its own Geographical Gardens with more than 2000 plants from all over the world.

The reception at the Hotel Koldingfjord is guaranteed to restore your spirits – whatever your score.

You'll need to pitch with care but there are compensations. For this is one of the most majestic and beautiful settings for a golf course anywhere in the world.

There can be few more pleasant places for the golfer – or non-golfer – to stay than the 115-room Hotel Koldingfjord.

ACCOMODATION

There are numerous hotels in the area offering first-class accommodation and with a relatively small population. Booking ahead is less of a problem than in most other European cities.

The Hotel Koldingfjord is situated about 30 kilometres from the Royal Oak course. In Denmark, with its traffic-free roads, this presents few problems for the golfing tourist. It is an ideal base from which to explore the area.

Set in the heart of cultivated forest, this magnificent hotel offers 115 bedrooms, all with spectacular views over the fjord, an indoor swimming pool, sauna, solarium and billiard room. It also has its own tennis courts and a wonderful fjordside restaurant and café. You are virtually guaranteed to enjoy a memorable stay.

4

England

I t was the Royal connection with golf that took the game from Scotland across the border to England and made it a respectable pursuit. It was probably the Union of the Crowns in 1603 that had the most influential effect on the development of the game in England, although it is known to have been played there much earlier.

There is a reference to golf by Catherine of Aragon, the first of Henry VIII's six wives, in a letter to Cardinal Wolsey in 1513. It is claimed that a golf club was founded at Blackheath outside London in 1608, but there is no documentary evidence to support it. The earliest date that can be substantiated is 1766. In that year a silver club was donated to the golfers of Blackheath bearing the inscription 'August 16, 1766, the gift of Mr Henry Foot to the Honorable Company of Golfers of Blackheath'. Royal Blackheath stands, therefore, as the oldest golf club in England.

When the Royal Households of England and Scotland were united under James VI of Scotland when he became James I of England, the game became fashionable. There is some argument as to whether the king introduced the game to the neighbourhood of Greenwich or to Blackheath but there is no dispute that golf was played later at Molesey Hurst and at Westminster. The royal connections are obvious. St James's Palace was close to Westminster and Molesey Hurst was little more than a stone's throw from Hampton Court.

Although the game was established in small pockets in England in the 18th century, it was to be another hundred years before there was a really significant spread across the country.

The Royal North Devon Club at Westward Ho! is the oldest existing golf course in England. The club was formed in 1864 and it was upon its famous links that the great J. H. Taylor learned to play as a boy before he became a member of the legendary Triumvirate of Vardon, Braid and Taylor who between them won 16 Open Championships over the space of 20 years.

The most important club in the development of golf in England is the Royal Liverpool Club, better known as Hoylake. It was here that the Amateur Championship was born and here, too, that the great amateur players like John Ball, Harold Hilton and Charles Hutchings made their impact on the game.

It was at Hoylake, too, that the greatest amateur player of them all, Bobby Jones, won the Open Championship in his historic Grand Slam year of 1930 when he was victorious in the Amateur and Open Championships of both the United States and Great Britain.

Today there are more than 1400 golf courses in England ranging from the great championship links of Royal Birkdale, Royal Lytham and Royal St George's to small clubs with only nine holes but equally enthusiastic memberships.

The Belfry

FOUNDED 1977

RYDER CUP BATTLEGROUND

The Belfry is an unashamedly American-style golf course. When Peter Alliss and Dave Thomas were given the remit to build 36 holes on the site near Sutton Coldfield, later to become the headquarters for the PGA, they were asked to produce a course for 'target' golf.

The order of the day was to provide undulating and randomly-shaped greens that could be cut to make them lightning fast and provide corners to tuck the pins in to make them difficult to get at.

But there were problems early on in the construc-

tion. The hot and dry summer of 1976 didn't help and the constructors ran into difficulties with the irrigation system which cost the best part of £100,000 to install.

The Ryder Cup was scheduled to be played here in 1981 but it was decided that the course wasn't fully prepared and the match was switched to Walton Heath.

However, over the years improvements were made and The Belfry hosted its first Ryder Cup match in 1985. It was a good week for Europe and won huge publicity for the complex.

The Belfry
Wishaw, North Warwickshire, B76 9PR
◆
Location: Two miles north of M42 Junction 9, off A446
Tel: 0675-470301
Courses: The Brabazon – 18 holes, 6975yds, par 73. The Derby – 18 holes, 6127yds, par 70
Visitors: Welcome at any time
Green fees: Brabazon £50 (Apr - Oct), £35 (Nov - Mar) Derby £25 (Apr - Oct), £17.50 (Nov - Mar)

There was little doubt that the Ryder Cup would return to The Belfry in 1989. Some improvements were made to the course and more spectator mounding was built for the huge crowds.

The drawn match meant that Europe retained the trophy after their historic victory at Muirfield Village in 1987 and once again The Belfry basked in the reflected glory.

However, there was controversy over the decision to take the Ryder Cup there for the third consecutive time in 1993. The Ryder Cup Committee was split

There's a deceptive calm here but this is the 18th, which has provided three of the most memorable Ryder Cup showdowns of all time.

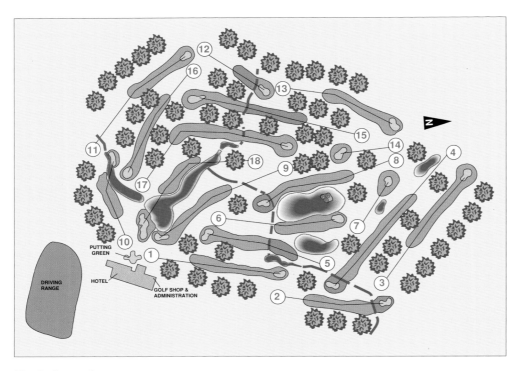

The Brabazon Course

particularly when the wind is against you.

A new tee was introduced at the 16th to straighten the hole and two bunkers which were thus taken out of play were removed. A new bunker 270 yards from the championship tee eats into the fairway on the left.

The long par 5 17th also underwent some dramatic changes in the run-up to the 1993 Ryder Cup. Another tee was introduced and the fairway was also tightened up by repositioning the left fairway bunker and increasing the size of the bunker in the corner of the dogleg.

over the decision on the venue and the casting vote of PGA President Lord Derby took the event back to The Belfry again.

The Belfry, in association with the PGA is developing a new national training academy due to open in September 1995 and a third golf course due to open in early 1996.

THE COURSE

Co-designer Peter Alliss rates the run of holes from the 6th to the 10th among his favourites. For the 1993 matches more improvements were made to the course. The 9th underwent some alterations including an enlarged fairway bunker on the left side and remodelling of the bunkers which protect the spectacular three-tiered green. The green was also extended slightly to allow for even more dramatic pin placements for the second shot over the lake.

The short 10th hole is the 'signature' hole at The Belfry, tempting the professionals to try to drive the green across the burn which runs in front. And there can be no doubt of the power of the long par 5 15th,

The 7th where American design meets old England. There can be few more imposing bunkers than this one guarding the front of the green.

The 18th again – but this time as the player sees it on his or her way home. And for those lucky enough to be staying there, The Belfry awaits in the background.

The 18th is a terrifying finishing hole – particularly in the heat of Ryder Cup battle, and must be considered one of the great final holes in championship golf. It has certainly been the scene of high drama in the three Ryder Cup matches played to date.

FACILITIES

Visitors to The Belfry will find every possible facility to make their stay as enjoyable as possible. The Hotel has 8 bars and restaurants plus a leisure centre and nightclub. There are also first-class practice facilities with a floodlit driving range to complement the two 18-hole courses.

THE REGION

The Belfry is only a few miles from England's second biggest city, Birmingham, with its famous Bull Ring. The National Exhibition Centre is close by and it is an ideal base from which to explore the Midlands.

There are many fine alternative courses in the area, too, including Little Aston to the north and Fulford Heath and Kings Norton to the south. The fine parkland course at Edgbaston is also within easy reach.

ACCOMMODATION

It is first-class all the way at The Belfry Hotel which gained its international reputation through the successes of the European Ryder Cup team.

This four-star hotel was created from a beautiful country manor set in the heart of the Warwickshire countryside. It has 219 bedrooms, all with excellent facilities. There is a leisure club with indoor swimming pool, squash courts and saunas and, for those still feeling energetic after a day's golf, the Bel-Air Nitespot offers the opportunity to dance the night away. The hotel is also popular as a conference centre.

Manor House Hotel and Golf Course

F O U N D E D 1 9 2 9

ECHOES OF THE BASKERVILLES

Hard on the very edge of Dartmoor, where the presence of Sherlock Holmes in canine pursuit is almost tangible, lies one of the great unsung courses of the south-west of England.

The Manor House Hotel and Golf Course, just outside Moretonhampstead, dates back to the days long before the country club concept came into vogue. The course was built in 1929 in the grounds of the magnificent Jacobean-style mansion house built for the family of W.H. Smith.

It joined the chain of British Transport Hotels with golf courses attached, which at one time included Gleneagles, Turnberry and the Old Course Hotel at St Andrews.

Today, it is owned by Principal Hotels and offers excellent facilities – and an extremely fine golf course – to its guests.

THE COURSE

In many ways this is the ideal holiday golf course. Not too long at just over 6000 yards, it presents an interesting and varied challenge of which it would be hard to tire.

Manor House Hotel and Golf Course

Moretonhampstead, Devon, TQ13 8RE
◆

Location: Two miles from Moretonhampstead

Tel: 0647-40355

Course: 18 holes, 6016yds, par 69

Visitors: Welcome at any time

Green fees: £22.50-£28

The magnificent views from the hotel high up above the course, the great splashes of colour of the rhododendrons and azaleas, and the calmness and serenity all combine to make this a rather special place to play golf.

The course opens with a beautiful short par 4 played from a tee hard against the gable of the grand hotel itself. The fairway drops away steeply to the River Bovey as it meanders its way through the course. At the 1st it runs down the left side and across the front of the green.

Passing gorillas may have tried to drive the green from the highly elevated tee; mere Homo sapiens content themselves with a modest iron shot and delight in the sight of the ball falling from the sky and down a magnificent backdrop of ancient oaks.

The Bovey River dominates the centre of the course and makes the approach to the 2nd, a stiff par 4 of 375 yards, very dangerous indeed. The river runs diagonally across the fairway towards the green leaving no margin for error.

It is there again at the next, the short 3rd which is a delightful par 3. The hole is only 151 yards at its longest and the river threatens down the right while overhanging bushes cramp the opposite side. Thick rhododendron bushes consume any shot that is marginally too long.

The late Sir Henry Cotton rated the long par 4 7th hole at Manor House one of his all time favourites. The river winds its way across and down the right

This is as perfect a setting for a golf and country club as you could find anywhere with its delightful blend of English refinement and west country hospitality.

side of the fairway and impenetrable woodland threatens on the left. Two of anyone's best shots are required to reach the sanctuary of the green.

At 450 yards, the 11th is the longest par 4 on the course. Played from an elevated tee, the drive must skirt tall trees down the right to leave a clear view for a long approach. The hole is bracketed by two interesting par 3s, the second of which must be carefully judged for length to avoid thick woodland immediately behind the green.

The Manor House finish is testing indeed and only slightly marred by the second shot to the long par 4 18th which is played blind. The fairway runs sharply to the right and the green nestles in a corner amid mature trees, conveniently placed only a few steps from the main hotel entrance.

Most players will do well to get a par here and even a 5 should send you into the wonderful surroundings of the 19th bathed in a glow of achievement.

FACILITIES

There are few clubhouses in the world of golf with a grander watering hole to greet the intrepid player than at Moretonhampstead. This wonderful manor house has a charm and air of refinement not readily found elsewhere.

The facilities are, quite simply, first-class. Club hire is available at the professional's shop and the hotel has a small fleet of golf carts for those who prefer not to walk.

THE REGION

The haunting and sinister images of Conan Doyle's Dartmoor are easy to conjure up in this secluded but gloriously beautiful part of Devon. The granite tors and rolling countryside of this wilderness, now a national park, attract thousands of visitors each year.

There are dramatic viewpoints at Hayton Rocks and Hound Tor out on the moor while, nearer civilization, there are charming little inns

You'll need to drive carefully at the 1st. That little ditch which looks so innocuous is the River Bovey which you will encounter again and again throughout the course.

The game is over and you want to reflect, perhaps in the South Terrace lounge at the Manor House Hotel. Once there, it would be difficult to imagine staying anywhere else!

where a glass of scrumpy can soon wash away the cares of the course – not to mention the imbiber if he is not very careful.

Places with names that trip off the tongue like Lusleigh and Bovey Tracy are reached by way of the high-banked lanes that turn the countryside into a motorist's maze.

ACCOMMODATION

With such superb facilities available at the Manor House Hotel, thoughts of alternative accommodation can be instantly cast aside. Excellent food, an exquisite cellar and a grand dining room beckon.

On a warm Devon day, with a cool glass of wine taken on the veranda overlooking the course and gardens, it would be hard to find a more delightful spot to be.

Royal Birkdale Golf Club

FOUNDED 1889

MAN-SIZED BUT NOT A MONSTER

Royal Birkdale has been the setting for more than 30 championships since it first staged the Amateur Championship in 1946.

Hardly a year has gone by since then without an important event being staged over this famous Southport links, making it the most prolific venue for tournament golf since the Second World War.

Former Open Champion Peter Thomson once described Birkdale as 'man-sized but not a monster' and that is a fair description. The course is one of a group set among the great sand dunes that dominate the landscape along the coast of Lancashire.

Although Royal Birkdale came to prominence in relatively recent times as a championship course, it is a club boasting a long history. It celebrated its centenary in 1989 although the present course is not the original. The first layout of nine holes was about a mile away from the present course, but it survived for only eight years until the land was taken over for building and a new site had to be found.

Mr C. J. Weld-Blundell agreed to lease 190 acres of sandhills on his estate to the club for a peppercorn rent for the first two years and £100 a year thereafter. The club brought in George Low from Royal Lytham and St Annes (next door to Birkdale) to supervise the layout of the new course.

He threaded the fairways through the valleys between the giant sand dunes rather than over the top of them, with the result that Birkdale has many more of the characteristics of an inland course than a traditional links. The turf is softer than pure linksland although there is no denying Birkdale's seaside credentials.

In 1931 Fred Hawtree and the legendary J. H. Taylor, then in partnership and internationally known as golf course architects, were asked to redesign and reconstruct the course. Part of the redevelopment was the famous white clubhouse built in a more central position. Today this famous building is

Royal Birkdale Golf Club

Waterloo Road, Birkdale, Southport, Merseyside PR8 2LX

◆

Location: Two miles from the centre of Southport off the A565

Tel: 0704-567920

Course: 18 holes, 6703yds (medal), par 72

Visitors: Welcome from Monday to Friday

Green fees: £50-70

The 7th offers a fair-sized green, but you'll need to select the club for your approach with due care and consideration. These bunkers aren't just there for show.

one of the most recognizable of all golf clubhouses.

The Open Championship has been played at Royal Birkdale on six occasions since it was first staged there in 1954. It had been scheduled to host the Open in 1940, the year after the new Hawtree-Taylor layout had been used for the English Amateur Championship, but the Second World War intervened.

In 1951 King George V1 conferred 'Royal' status on the club and it was proud to claim that no major changes had to be made to the course before the first Open was played there three years later.

A clubhouse for the 1990s and beyond. Don't be misled by the modern façade, for behind this exterior a traditional Lancashire welcome is still to be found.

THE COURSE

There is no escaping the severity of the Birkdale challenge. There is an abundance of willow scrub which grows in wild profusion on the great sand dunes. In many ways it presents a much more punitive threat than heather and is as unyielding as gorse.

After the 1991 Open there was some criticism levelled at the Birkdale greens and a major improvement scheme was put in hand after the event.

Work involved some major surgery to replace the subsoil on the greens to return them to more traditional linksland turf. A long period of heavy fertilization and irrigation had contributed towards a change in the character of the greens.

There have been many memorable championships

at Birkdale but none more significant than when Arnold Palmer played what he considered to be the best 'short burst' of golf of his illustrious career.

He played the first six holes in three-under-par at the start of the second round of the 1961 Open and did it in a fearsome gale. It was the championship which many believe restored the course to its premier position among the world's great courses.

FACILITIES

The Royal Birkdale Golf Club offers its members and guests first-class clubhouse facilities. It is a very warm and friendly club to visit with an excellent dining room and a splendid lounge with views across the links.

THE REGION

This part of Lancashire is pure golfing country with several fine clubs along what locals call 'The Line' which stretches from Liverpool to Blackpool.

Southport has long been a favourite English holiday town with its refined image, grand buildings and exclusive shops. It is an ideal centre from which to visit the north of England or to experience the glitz of Blackpool with its famous tower, funfair and illuminations.

ACCOMMODATION

Being a holiday town there is no shortage of accommodation to suit every taste and budget in Southport.

Perhaps the best of the hotels close to the Birkdale links are the Scarisbrick Hotel and the Prince of Wales, which have long-standing reputations.

There are very adequate alternatives at the Tree Top Motel and the Blundells Hotel only a mile away from the course.

Royal St George's Golf Club

FOUNDED 1887

SOLITUDE AND A DRIVER'S PARADISE

The first 33 years of the Open Championship were very strictly a Scottish preserve. The world's greatest golf event rotated around Prestwick, St Andrews, Musselburgh and, on one occasion, Muirfield until 1894 when the Royal and Ancient Golf Club decreed that the event should be played for the first time in England.

It was a major departure for the Open and a significant one too for it was won for the first time by an English professional, the legendary J.H. Taylor, who returned a four-round total of 326. This score was achieved from a record entry of 94 players and marked the start of the domination of the Championship for the next 20 years by the great Triumvirate of Vardon, Braid and Taylor.

The 16th looks wilder and more desolate than you'd expect in the Home Counties of England. The bunker to the left, by the way, is a killer.

The Royal St George's with its towering sandhills and rumpled fairways has a long and distinguished history in English golf dating back to the mid-1880s. Dr Laidlaw Purves, a Scot who had come down from Edinburgh and was a member at Wimbledon, set out in search of a suitable seaside site for a course to serve the needs of London golfers. At that time inland courses were not highly thought of and Dr Purves wanted to create a links course inspired by the fine examples that he had left behind in his native country.

It is said that he surveyed the links of Sandwich from the tower of St Clement's church and declared it perfect for his purpose. In 1887 he formed the Sandwich Golfing Association and plans were drawn up for an 18-hole course with the assistance of a certain Scottish greenkeeper named Ramsay Hunter.

Since then there have been changes, most recently by the respected architect, Frank Pennink, largely to keep pace with the development of the game. Essentially, however, the layout remains much as it was in the beginning.

Royal St George's Golf Club
Sandwich, CT13 9PB
◆
Location: One mile east of Sandwich, Kent
Tel: 0304-613090
Course: 18 holes, 6534yds, par 72
Visitors: Welcome with certain restrictions
The handicap limit for men is 18 and 15 for ladies
Green fees: On application

The 6th typifies classic English links golf at its best, with the sea in the background and three bunkers guarding an undulating green. The dunes complete the picture.

Sloping lies on the fairways are a common factor on the undulating ground and have prompted several famous players to criticize the Kent links as unfair. But this is harsh criticism, for St George's is a classic seaside links.

If there are fewer flat lies in the fairway than on other Open Championship courses, then the traditionalists would say it is none the worse for that since that is the way the game developed originally anyway.

THE COURSE

The late Sir Henry Cotton who won the first of his three Open titles at Sandwich was a great lover of this famous links. He once remarked: 'The turf at Sandwich gives lies one dreams about, the ball is always "lying a treat" so, with larks singing and the sun shining on the waters of Pegwell, it is a veritable golfer's heaven.'

The picturesque thatched starter's hut at Royal St George's is one of the memorable features of this great links, but the first hole over which it stands

sentinel is an instant reminder of how difficult is the test that lies ahead.

At 445 yards from the back tee it needs two comprehensive blows to reach a green with a big bunker right in front. If the drive is not long enough, the second will be played from a hollow in the fairway known as 'the Kitchen'. From there it is a testing shot indeed to reach the green.

In the celebrated Open Championship of 1949, Irishman Harry Bradshaw was leading the field when he found his ball lying inside a broken beer bottle behind the 5th green. He elected to play the ball as it lay and smashed it out. But he ran up a six as a result of his misfortune and was eventually beaten by Bobby Locke in a play–off.

The 14th is known as 'Suez' because the second shot on this tough par 5 has to carry a canal. It was here in 1934 that Henry Cotton pulled his game together after a disastrous start to the final round of the Open and went on to break the domination of the Americans in the event. He had started with three great

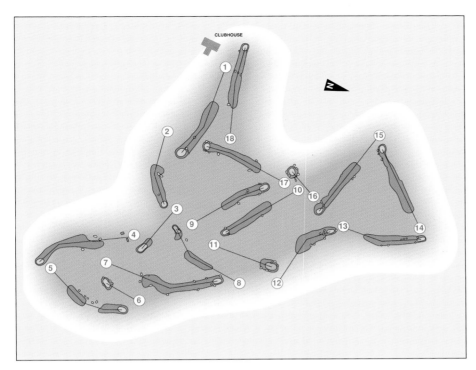

The Royal St George's Course

But the 'garden of England' county has many other delights to offer the visitor.

The desolate lands of Romney Marsh, in which the Royal Military Canal was cut as a defence against Napoleon, lie to the south-west, while in the south is the Weald, once densely wooded countryside.

Kent's chalk downs end in the famous white cliffs of Dover. Tunbridge Wells to the west is noted as a health resort and four of the Cinque Ports – Dover, Romney, Hythe and

rounds including a 65 – in memory of which Dunlop named a famous golf ball – but took 40 to the turn in the last round and seemed to be heading for defeat.

However, he produced two majestic strokes at the 13th to steady himself with a par and then birdied the 'Suez' hole on his way to a famous victory.

FACILITIES

There is a very traditional and conservative air about the clubhouse at St George's and it has changed very little over the years. The leather furnished smoking-room is a timeless symbol of times gone by and a tankard of real ale, drawn from the cask, remains a highlight of any visit.

The dining room is first-class as befits a club of such international standing. The club also has good practice facilities and caddies are available by prior arrangement.

THE REGION

St George's lies at the heart of that corner of Kent where the golf is as fine as anywhere in England.

There's a deceptive calm about the 1st tee at Sandwich which gives little hint of the rigours and challenges to come.

Sandwich – belong to Kent. And the cathedral city of Canterbury lies only a few miles from St George's and attracts thousands of visitors each year. It is a must for anyone visiting the area.

HOTELS

The area around Sandwich is not particularly well supplied with hotel accommodation. The Bell Hotel is usually the choice for a few day's stay at Sandwich. It is a comfortable hotel and enjoys a good reputation for its food and service.

Royal Liverpool Golf Club

F O U N D E D 1 8 6 9

HISTORY AND CHALLENGE

The Royal Liverpool Golf Club is historically the most important club in England. It is here at Hoylake on the coast of old Cheshire that many of the most significant events in English golfing history have taken place.

Hoylake, as the club is better known, is steeped in history and tradition. The Amateur Championship – the oldest event of its kind in the world – had its origins here in 1885 and the first international match between Scotland and England was played at Hoylake in 1902.

The first match between amateur teams representing Great Britain and the United States – the precursor to the Walker Cup – was played at Hoylake, also in 1902.

The club was also one of the earliest arbiters of amateur status in the game. When Thomas Owen Potter, the honorary secretary of the club, suggested that an open amateur tournament be held at Hoylake in 1885, an entry was received from a Scotsman by the name of Douglas Rolland who, the previous year, had finished second in the Open Championship.

His application was rejected but it left the club with a dilemma. John Ball, who was to become the club's greatest player and one of the game's greatest amateurs, entered too. But in 1878, at just 15, he had tied for fourth place with Bob Martin of St Andrews in the Open. Ball lost the play-off for fourth place the following day, but there was a money prize due to him from the purse.

There is some discussion as to whether the sum involved was a sovereign or a half sovereign, but Jack Morris advised the young John Ball to put the money in his pocket. It was this incident, recalled all these years later, that came back to haunt Ball when he wanted to enter the Amateur Championship.

However, a diplomatic way was found round the problem. The age limit for receiving cash prizes was

Royal Liverpool Golf Club

Meols Drive, Hoylake, Wirral,

Merseyside

◆

Location: 10 miles south

of Liverpool

Tel: 051- 632 3101

Course: 18 holes, 7110yds,

par 74

Visitors: The club welcomes

visitors but not before

9.30am or between 1.00pm

and 2.00pm, and only a

limited number at weekends

Green fees: £40-55

On a clear day you could play for ever. And all this just ten miles from the hurly-burly of Liverpool.

At least this bunker guarding the 18th green is the last challenge you'll need to face before you take a well-deserved drink in Hoylake's historic clubhouse.

fixed at sixteen and John Ball did not forfeit his amateur status. He went on to win the Amateur Championship eight times.

The Royal Liverpool Club was the home not only of John Ball but also of that other great amateur of the same era, Harold Hilton, the first player to hold the amateur title on both sides of the Atlantic in the same year.

There is little in the way of great scenic splendour at Hoylake, although there are views of the hills of North Wales towards the middle of the round and Hilbre Island rises out of the vast expanse of sand banks in majestic solitude.

THE COURSE

Hoylake has one of the most fearsome opening shots in championship golf. The practice ground runs along the entire right side of the hole, turning sharply right in the landing area for the drive and continuing all the way to the green. It is the most unnerving start either with or against the wind.

The short 7th known as 'Dowie' was, until 1994, a fine example of the problems of Hoylake. Flanked on the left by a low turf wall (beyond which is out-of-bounds) the shot had to carry 200 yards to the green with absolutely no margin left for error. The hole was remodelled for the 1994 season but remains a daunting challenge.

The short 11th, among the dunes at the far end of the course from the clubhouse, is a superb one-shot hole. Aptly named the 'Alps', it requires a prodigious blow, sometimes with a wooden club, to reach the sanctuary of the remote, oblong green.

The next, the dogleg 12th, is an even more severe

The green at the 12th looks serene enough, but you'll need to beware of overclubbing. Most golfers wouldn't wish this heather on their worst enemy.

test. It demands a long, straight drive into the neck of a tight landing area between two groups of savage bunkers. A visit to any of them virtually guarantees the loss of a stroke.

The long second shot must steer well clear of a pair of bunkers set on the edge of the fairway just short of the green, while the pin is protected by another on the right.

The five holes to the finish are as difficult as can be found anywhere, with the 17th generally regarded as the toughest of them.

The Open Championship has been played at Hoylake 10 times, the last occasion being in 1967 when the popular Argentinean player, Roberto de Vicenzo, was the winner. Hoylake was removed from the Open rota after that – quite why it is difficult to say – and many believe that the Championship is poorer as a result.

FACILITIES

The magnificent old clubhouse, with its traditional club room on the first floor, is an Aladdin's cave of historical golf artefacts which it is well worth taking the time to investigate.

Full catering facilities are available in the clubhouse but full lunch and dinner are normally only available to parties of 20 or more.

Caddies are available by prior arrangement and the club has excellent practice facilities. Visitors need to have an official handicap certificate.

THE REGION

'The Line' of courses, which starts at Hoylake and runs north to Royal Lytham and St Anne's, is a Mecca for visiting golfers. However, there is a host of attractions in the area other than golf.

The Wirral, upon which Hoylake is located, is a

low-lying, oblong peninsula with the River Dee on one side and the River Mersey on the other. It is historically part of Cheshire, but has been shared with Merseyside for some 20 years since 1974.

The Lancastrian soap king, William Hesketh Lever who founded Unilever and became the first Lord Leverhulme, built Port Sunlight on the Wirral as a model company suburb in the 1890s. The suburb was named after Sunlight soap and there are several interesting attractions there. The Lady Lever Art Gallery, built to house Leverhulme's famous art collection, is particularly worth a visit.

A large collection of canal boats, working steam engines and memorabilia of life on the canals is on display at the Boat Museum in Ellesmere Port at the terminus of the Shropshire Union Canal. And trips on a horse-drawn narrow boat are always popular.

Ness Gardens, the botanical gardens of Liverpool University, outside Neston, are also very popular. They feature exotic trees and plants and are renowned for their collection of flowering cherries.

ACCOMMODATION

The three-star Leasowe Castle Hotel at Moreton is only a few minutes from the Royal Liverpool course and is an ideal base. This 16th-century castle has a health club, sauna and solarium among its first-class facilities. The hotel also offers special golf breaks.

An alternative is the independently owned Bowler Hat Hotel in Oxton, Birkenhead, which is set in its own gardens overlooking the Wirral peninsula. It is only two miles from the course.

The Bowler Hat enjoys an excellent reputation for its cuisine and service.

A wild and windy setting with the Welsh hills looming in the background. The greatest challenge at the 3rd comes from the weather which is never predictable.

Royal Lytham
and St Annes Golf Club

FOUNDED 1886

OPEN CHALLENGE IN AN URBAN SETTING

The great links at Royal Lytham and St Annes has witnessed many memorable events in its long history, none more so than Tony Jacklin's famous victory in the 1969 Open Championship when he was to become the first British winner for 18 years.

> **Royal Lytham
> and St Annes Golf Club**
>
> *Links Gate, Lytham and St Annes,
> Lancashire, FY8 3LQ*
> ◆
> Location: One mile from St Annes
> Tel: 0253-724206
> Course: 18 holes, 6673yds,
> par 72
> Visitors: The club welcomes
> visitors between 9.30m and 12.00
> and 2.30pm and 4.00pm, but
> not before lunch on
> Tuesdays or at weekends
> Green fees: £45-60

It was also at Lytham that Bobby Jones won the first of his three Open titles in 1926, the year the club first hosted the event.

Although it is not now as much a seaside links in character as it once was, and is unlikely ever to win a contest as the most attractive course in the game, the splendid layout of Royal Lytham remains one of England's greatest and, certainly, most difficult championship courses.

It is the last of the great line of courses along the edge of the Irish Sea, which begins at Hoylake and is strung out northwards along the Lancashire coast. Over the years it has changed in character. Perhaps it has mellowed, for it is now a little softer and more lush than it once was.

Recalling his first visit there for a professional tournament in the 1920s, three-times Open Champion Henry Cotton likened the greens, burned brown by the hot summer, to 'putting on ice'. Anyone who has played on traditional British golfing turf at the height of a drought when no water was available to temper the speed will know exactly what he meant.

Certainly the arrival of modern watering systems has despatched the days of the ice-like greens to the history books, but the fine Lytham greens can still be keen enough in dry conditions. The course has managed to retain the fine links grasses which so many of the great courses have lost through overzealous use of the sprinkler.

The roll call of champions at Royal Lytham is a veritable Who's Who of the game's greatest players and a tribute to the quality of the challenge that the course presents. In addition to Jacklin and Jones, Peter Thomson, Bobby Locke and left-hander Bob Charles from New Zealand all survived dramas to win Opens there.

In 1974 Gary Player played his final shot to the last green left-handed using the back of his putter after he had run through the green with his approach and the ball had lodged against the clubhouse wall.

Alexander Doleman, a school teacher from Musselburgh in Scotland, was the driving force behind the formation of the club in 1886. The club leased ground from the St Annes-on-Sea Land and

Building Company and built an 18-hole course with an additional nine holes for ladies. However, it was a short lease that the company were not keen to extend and the club, with a membership of some 400, decided to move to its present location in 1897.

The members built the magnificent clubhouse, which still stands so proudly today, at a reported cost of £8500. George Lowe is credited with the design of the original course on the present site, but such notable architects as Harry Colt, Herbert Fowler and G.K. Cotton have all left their mark.

The Course

Over the years the course has become more hemmed in and now has a distinctly urban setting with three sides of the boundary overlooked by houses, and the fourth

On a calm clear day the 7th purrs like a pussycat – the low handicap player can expect to reach it in two. But when the wind blows it's a very different story.

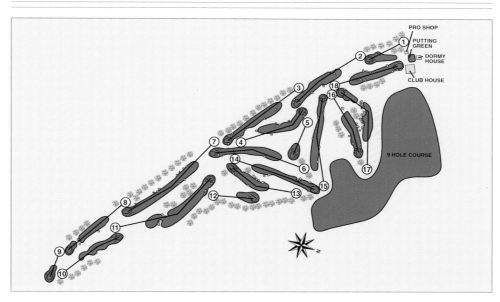

The Royal Lytham and St Annes Course

running alongside the railway line. There are none of the great sandhills of Birkdale here but, although it is now some way from the sea and is greener than it once was, it still retains many of the qualities of the true links.

Royal Lytham is unique on the Open Championship rota in that it is the only course with a par 3 opening hole. At 208 yards it is a testing rather than a tough opening shot but it is played from a tee protected by trees. Correct judgement of the wind here is critical.

Lytham has another idiosyncrasy in that it has consecutive par 5 holes – a rare distinction among the courses in use for the Open Championship.

The second of them is the 551 yard 7th where the dunes are wild and the drive must be kept well clear of a sea of bunkers on the right. The green is defended by menacing dunes and hidden by a bank in front. In calm conditions, however, the top professionals can usually get home with as little as a medium iron for their second shot.

FACILITIES

Royal Lytham has a magnificent and very traditional old clubhouse. The bar is warm and inviting and the club has an excellent dining room.

There is a first-class practice facility but the club does not employ caddies. Club professional, Eddie Birchenough, has a well stocked shop. Golf clubs, however, are not available for hire.

THE REGION

There are many attractions on the Lancashire coast around Lytham St Annes. The seaside resorts of Blackpool and Morecambe were developed to meet the needs of in-dustrial Lancashire and remain as popular now as they always have.

To the east lies the wild countryside of the Forest of Bowland, an almost treeless area of moorland and fell, which is sandwiched between the Lake District on one side and the Pennines on the other.

Those seeking a little solitude away from the resort towns could do worse than take a drive up through the Trough of Bowland on the unclassified road from Marshaw. The road climbs to more than 1000 feet to the very heart of the fells and there is not

A superb clubhouse awaits you after your round. But beware as you approach the 18th green – the bunkers say it all.

Rooms with a view. There certainly are for those residents who are lucky enough to have a home overlooking the magnificent 9th.

an amusement arcade within at least 40 miles!

Preston is not far from Lytham for those who prefer something a little more urban, and the city of Lancaster is only a few miles to the north.

This handsome city was once a great port and boasts a perfectly preserved 18th-century waterfront at St George's Quay in the area down by the Lune.

ACCOMMODATION

St Annes has plenty of good hotel accommodation but popular among golfers are the Clifton Arms Hotel and the Chadwick Hotel on the waterfront.

There is a wide choice of restaurants close to the course with Bennett's Bistro always a popular choice – particularly with fish lovers.

St Mellion Golf and Country Club

FOUNDED 1976

THE COURSE THAT JACK BUILT

When Martin and Hermon Bond, two of golf's most affable characters, decided to build a second course to complement the one they had already constructed in a remote corner of Cornwall called St Mellion, they

Championship golf in an idyllic West Country setting with Plymouth only a few miles down the road. No wonder the top players flock here year after year.

brought in none other than Jack Nicklaus.

When Jack was finished they had a monster of a course ready to put the fear of death into the most tournament-hardened professional. And if the cost of it all put the fear of death in the brothers Bond they certainly were too much in the way of gentlemen to say so – even if they thought it.

Jack moved a greater part of Cornwall to build the 'stadium' course and rumours of £100,000 a hole were rife while he was about it. Be that as it may, it is a remarkable course.

THE COURSES

The original course was built in 1976 and is a pleasant if sometimes wildly undulating layout. Some changes were forced on it when construction began on the Nicklaus course but it has not suffered unduly.

The new layout is unashamedly American in its concept. It is tough, uncompromising, and as much a test of endurance as it is for shotmaking for even the best players.

And never was it more difficult than on the day Jack Nicklaus, Tom Watson, Sandy Lyle and Nick Faldo played a challenge match to open the course officially. It might have been the middle of July but it was as cold as a Cornish winter. A gale was blowing and the rain lashed across the course in horizontal and penetrating sheets.

That the course remained playable and the match was finished was a tribute not only to the quality of the construction but to the determination of the players who were followed all the way by an invited audience.

Since then St Mellion has gained national recognition as the venue for the Benson & Hedges

---

St Mellion Golf and Country Club

Saltash, Cornwall PL12 6SD

◆

Location: Five miles
north-west
of Saltash

Tel: 0579-50101

Courses: Old – 18 holes,
5927yds, par 70.

Nicklaus – 18 holes,
6626yds, par 72

Visitors: Welcome at
any time

Green fees: On application

International, along with a reputation as one of the toughest venues ever to stage a European Tour event. There are no easy holes on this golf course. There is simply a progression of ever more difficult ones.

The 3rd, with its high slope on the left and a ravine on the right, and the 5th, where the drive must carry

The picturesque and tranquil setting of the short 11th belies the watery grave that awaits the uninitiated.

a lake and a stream threatens thereafter all the way to the green, are two that spring immediately to mind.

There is more water at the 10th, the 11th and the 12th. The second of the trio is a short hole where water threatens on the left side while, at the next, a pond has to be carried from the tee and a ditch runs across the hole short of the green.

There are those who fervently believe Nicklaus was inspired by the 13th at Augusta when he built this par 5. Yet this could never be regarded as anything other than an English course.

The Nicklaus challenge round St Mellion ends with a monster par 4 of 472 yards from the back tee. The pond which was originally built to the right of the green has been moved to the opposite side of the fairway and is as troublesome there as it was before.

FACILITIES

St Mellion is not just a golf club, it has all the facilities of an American-style country club. There is a range of bars and restaurants and a veritable plethora of other sporting activities.

The Nicklaus course was designed for golf carts and they are available and certainly advisable. Many of the greens and following tees are widely separated as befits a tournament venue and there is a deal of climbing to be done.

THE REGION

St Mellion is an ideal base for exploring the many attractions of the beautiful county of Cornwall. The country club is only a few miles from historic Plymouth where the Pilgrim Fathers embarked for America in 1620 and from where Drake set sail against the Spanish Armada.

The Cornish coast is a maze of little estuaries and chocolate box harbours. Brunel's Royal Albert railway bridge, which has carried trains from Plymouth into Cornwall since the last century, remains a masterpiece of engineering and a popular attraction for visitors. It is best seen from the Tamar road bridge which is built alongside and was opened in 1961.

Prehistoric remains abound in the Duchy while more recent relics of Cornwall's past survive in the chimneys and outbuildings of the old tin mines.

The legacy of a now declining fishing industry can be seen in the charming little villages of Mousehole and Mevagissey, reminders of more romantic days.

ACCOMMODATION

Visitors to St Mellion need look no further than the country club itself when it comes to accommodation. A fine hotel with every possible facility stands alongside the 18th green.

In addition, there are 30 high-class lodges available for rental. And there is no place that extends a more genuine or friendly welcome.

Sunningdale Golf Club

FOUNDED 1900

CLASSIC HEATHLAND GOLF

The famous Old Course at Sunningdale is a classic heathland layout quite rightly regarded as the finest inland course in England.

It may not be so demanding as some of the great seaside links but if there is a more delightful place to play golf there are very few people who have been able to find it.

It was here that Bobby Jones played his famous 'perfect round' of 66 in the qualifying rounds in the Open Championship of 1926. He had 33 strokes for each half and 33 each of shots and putts.

This wonderful example of heathland golf lies only a few miles from the centre of London and to play there is one of golf's great experiences. Jones certainly felt that to be the case for, after scoring 68 in the second qualifying round in which the only blemish was a single five, he declared that he would 'like to take the course home'.

When golf moved inland away from its original linksland environment to bring more players into the fold, it was soon obvious that rough heathland with its firm turf and well-drained soil was perfect for golf and shared many of the characteristics of seaside golf. But the land that Willie Park Jnr, son of the first Open Champion and twice winner of the title, was given to build the Old Course was very different in 1900, when he set about the task, than it is now.

When the course was opened for play the following year there were no trees to obscure the views across the heath. Since then thousands of trees have been planted and, today, virtually every hole runs through great stands of pine and birch creating a wonderful atmosphere of tranquillity and solitude.

Sunningdale Golf Club

Ridgemount Road, Sunningdale, Ascot, Berkshire, SL5 9RW

◆

Location: Quarter of a mile from Sunningdale railway station

Tel: 0344-21681

Courses: Old – 18 holes, 6586yds, par 72. New – 18 holes, 6676yds, par 70

Visitors: The club welcomes visitors but by prior arrangement only. A letter of introduction and handicap certificate are necessary

Green fees: £84 per day

Take your choice. To the left and right, birch and pine; in the foregound heather; and then good old sand – and lots of it.

Golf course architect Harry Colt, who was secretary at Sunningdale for 17 years, made some improvements to compensate for the increased distances players were able to accomplish with the arrival of the Haskell ball.

In 1922 he built the New Course which is very different in character, being more demanding but enjoying less of the subtlety of its older companion.

The Course

Despite being almost 500 yards in length, the 1st on the Old Course at Sunningdale can be comfortably reached in two shots when the course is running in the summer months. It is downhill all the way with the only trouble on the right, where the out-of-bounds follows the line of splendid houses that marks the border of the course. There is a deep bunker on the left of the green but it presents very little threat to the great majority of players.

The 7th is the third hole in a run of superb par 4s after the first short hole. The drive is over a mound in front of the tee while the approach to the green, marginally over 400 yards away, is along a fairway

which gently doglegs to the right. It requires a careful shot which must not be allowed to slip right where it will find the rough off a protecting mound.

From start to finish: an aerial view of the 1st tee and the 18th green and, of course, the famous Sunningdale clubhouse.

In common with all great courses Sunningdale has a marvellous finishing hole. A long drive uphill is required and it must avoid a deep bunker to the left and heavy rough on the right to leave any chance of getting home in two.

The second shot should be aimed at the big oak tree which stands sentinel between clubhouse and green, and the shot must carry a string of cross bunkers to avoid disaster. A German bomb which left a huge crater in 1940 provided the opportunity to put in the additional bunker protection that the 18th now enjoys.

It is within easy reach of London's West End for those in search of the city lights, while to the west the A4 threads its way through the Berkshire Downs.

One of the great sights in golf: you've birdied the 18th (or not) and refreshment awaits you in one of the best clubhouses in England.

FACILITIES

The marvellous old clubhouse at Sunningdale is one of the great post-game watering holes anywhere in the golf world. A comfortable bar and a first-class dining room await those fortunate enough to play there, but make sure to avoid a Monday when there is no catering. Arrangements to hire golf clubs can be made and caddies are available. The club also has practice facilities.

THE REGION

Sunningdale lies only a stone's throw from Wentworth and from that great centre of English horse racing, Ascot. Windsor Castle is just 20 minutes' drive from the course.

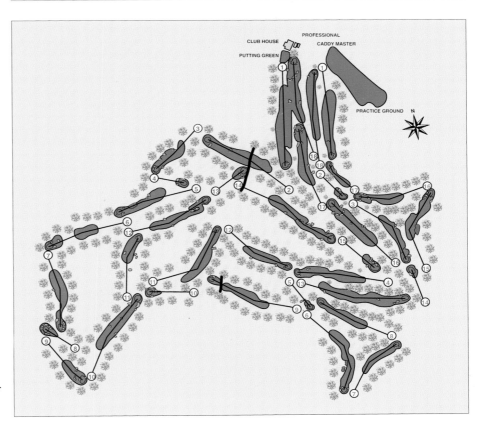

Sunningdale: the Old (red) and New (blue) courses.

The road runs through the bottom of the Kennet Valley where there is much of interest for the traveller. There are reminders of the days when the A4 was the main coach road to Bristol from London. Handsome market towns such as Marlborough and Hungerford still retain their marvellous old coaching inns and provide pleasant diversions from the pressures of the golf course.

To the north-west the Vale of the White Horse, named after the ancient hill carving at Uffington, attracts many visitors. For those interested in the Sport of Kings, the area around Lambourn is famous for its racehorse training areas.

ACCOMMODATION
The Berystede Hotel near Ascot is difficult to find for the uninitiated but the effort is worthwhile for those wishing to stay close to the Sunningdale course. This is a splendid hotel which enjoys a fine reputation for its restaurant and its excellent cellar.

Alternatively the Pennyhill Park Hotel in Bagshot offers outstanding facilities to its guests and is also very close to Sunningdale and, of course, Wentworth next door.

One to go: the 17th green looks straightforward enough but beware the bunker to its left which has spoilt the cards of countless players.

The Wentworth Club

FOUNDED 1924

ALONG THE BURMA ROAD

The West Course at Wentworth, home of the World Match Play Championship, is one of the most famous of England's inland courses. Christened the 'Burma Road', it has a reputation for being one of the longest and toughest courses in Britain.

Over the years of that great championship first played in 1964, however, there has been some remarkable scoring prompting some Wentworth watchers to wonder if modern equipment and softer greens have perhaps pulled some of the teeth from this great course.

Wentworth was one of the first developments in Britain to be based on the American country club philosophy to provide not only facilities for golf, but also swimming, tennis and even a ballroom. The development rights and planning permissions were granted in 1923 and the Wentworth project was to include within its 1750 acres provision for large houses, each on at least an acre of ground and close to the fairways.

Two 18-hole courses and a short nine-hole layout were planned and built under the direction of golf course architect Harry S. Colt. Lying in that marvellous stretch of sandy heathland to the south-west of London, the ground with which Colt was given to work was a prize indeed. What he created has stood the test of time exceptionally well. The East course was completed first and the longer West course was opened in 1924.

They were built in a marvellous setting amid woodland of fir and silver birch and today masses of rhododendrons add to the peaceful beauty of the estate. It has been described as 'millionaire's golf' – which perhaps it is – but this does not detract from the quality of the golf on either of the courses. A third 18-hole course was built to a design by Gary Player, John Jacobs and Wentworth's resident professional Bernard Gallacher, and is a worthy addition.

Henry Cotton described the clubhouse, part of which was once the home of the Duke of Wellington's sister, as 'one of the most beautiful in England'. Later, Wentworth House and its estate were acquired by an exiled Spanish count, Ramon Cabrera.

After he died his widow, the Countess de Morella, purchased most of the adjoining land to create the estate as it exists today.

In 1993 refurbishment work on the clubhouse was completed and virtually doubled its size. The cost was a staggering £10 million but the Wentworth Club

---

Wentworth Club Limited

Wentworth Drive, Virginia Water, Surrey GU25 4LS

◆

Location: 21 miles south-west of London, Tel. 0344 842201

Courses: West Course – 18 holes, 6945yds, par 72.

East Course – 18 holes, 6176yds, par 68.

Edinburgh Course – 18 holes, 6979yds, par 72

Visitors: Welcome on weekdays by prior arrangement. Play with a member only at weekends

Green fees: On application

The 13th is typical of Wentworth – a rich green carpet set in the heart of the Surrey countryside.

now boasts one of the most magnificent clubhouses anywhere in the world.

THE COURSES

There have been many great and memorable events held over the years at Wentworth. In 1926 an informal match was played between the professionals of Great Britain and America which the British won comfortably. Although it was not the first match between the countries it was, in effect, the forerunner of the Ryder Cup which was inaugurated the following year.

Ben Hogan made his only appearance in England over the Burma Road in 1956 when he played in the World Cup (then the Canada Cup), partnered by Sam Snead. The Ryder Cup was played at Wentworth three years earlier when the Americans scraped home by a single point.

In more recent times the famous Burma Road has witnessed some marvellous matches in the World Match Play Championship, including five victories by Gary Player, two by Arnold Palmer, and four wins in

five years by Seve Ballesteros.

The long par 4 3rd on the West Course is one of Wentworth's toughest holes. It is uphill all the way and the drive must not only be long but needs to avoid a dangerous bunker on the right as well. Recent alterations to the fearsome two-tier green, where three and often four putts were common, have been widely welcomed by all who play here.

The 7th is perhaps the best of the holes played out on the heath itself. It is not overly long at just a yard under 400 yards in length but the second shot is uphill all the way to another double-tiered green where two putts and a par can, with justification, be

At just under 400 yards the 7th is not the most testing at Wentworth. The two-tiered green, however, demands a rare delicacy of touch with the putter.

considered a major accomplishment.

The 17th hole on the Burma Road has become, by virtue of the television coverage of the World Match Play, one of the most famous in golf. The drive is downhill to the corner of a dogleg turning left at around the 300 yard mark. The fairway runs away to the right and the drive must be held up close to the out-of-bounds fence on the left to leave any chance of getting home in two. The gardens of lavish Wentworth houses sweep down to the very edge of the fairway all the way to the green on this fearsome par 5. It is here that the climax of many of the great matches in the World Match Play have been fought out.

FACILITIES

With three championship standard golf courses, a nine-hole executive course, a driving range and putting green, Wentworth lacks for nothing in golf facilities. In addition it has 14 outdoor tennis courts on the three grand slam surfaces, French clay, Greenset Supreme and grass, as well as all-weather.

The club has a heated outdoor swimming pool set in rhododendron gardens and a clubhouse which would be the envy of any club anywhere.

A new health and fitness centre with an indoor swimming pool will soon be completed.

THE REGION

Wentworth is situated within a stone's throw of Sunningdale and shares similar benefits of easy access to London and to the open countryside of Berkshire to the west. Windsor Great Park is virtually next door as is the M25 with its access to the routes to the south coast.

ACCOMMODATION

The Berystede Hotel near Ascot and the Pennyhill Park Hotel in Bagshot are ideal for access to the Wentworth Club.

In 1993 the refurbishments to the clubhouse cost an estimated £10 million. For those lucky enough to play here, it looks like money well spent.

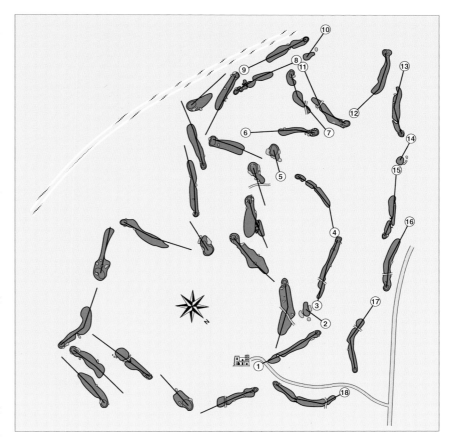

The West Course at Wentworth (numbered).

Royal North Devon Golf Club

FOUNDED 1864

HISTORIC AND UNSPOILED

The links of the Royal North Devon Golf Club at Westward Ho! are the oldest in England and, in years gone by, were ranked second in historic importance only to Hoylake.

Ponies and sheep still wander the course preserving the flavour of earlier times. Pot bunkers and sea rushes, a fearsome vegetation which can impale a golf ball let alone a player, are features of this classic seaside links.

A primitive form of golf was played here from as far back as 1853 organized by the family of the vicar of Northam, the Rev. I.H. Gosset.

Old Tom Morris was brought down from Prestwick in 1860 to advise on future development. Four years later the North Devon and West of England Golf Club was formed with the vicar as the first captain.

Old Tom then made the long journey south again to lay out two courses, one of 17 holes and the other of 22 holes. Several changes were made, but the last major reconstruction work was done by Herbert Fowler in 1908. Little has altered since then.

Westward Ho! is named after the famous novel by Charles Kingsley and is renowned, too, for the many fine players who have been associated with it.

> **Royal North Devon Golf Club**
>
> *Golf Links Road, Westward Ho!,*
> *Bideford, Devon, EX39 1HD*
> ◆
> Location: Two miles north of
> Bideford
> Tel: 0237-473824
> Course: 18 holes, 6662yds,
> par 72
> Visitors: Welcome at any time
> Green fees: On application

J.H. Taylor learned to play at Westward Ho! He became interested in the game when he caddied for the teenage Horace Hutchinson who was later to win the Amateur Championship twice and become an eminent writer on golf.

Taylor was then a houseboy in the Hutchinson household but within a few years he became the first English professional to beat the Scots at their own game, winning the Open Championship five times between 1894 and 1913. In 1957 he was made President of the club.

The course has hosted the Amateur Championship three times. In 1912 John Ball from Hoylake won the last of his eight titles, beating Abe Mitchell at the 38th hole. Robert Harris took the honours in 1925 and Eric Martin Smith was something of a surprise winner when the Amateur was last played there in 1931.

In this fine old clubhouse you will receive a traditional West Country welcome in keeping with the club's standing as the oldest in the country.

THE COURSE

In the first hundred years only four scores under 70 were recorded in the club's medal competition, emphasizing the severity of the test.

In more recent years, the greens have become more mellow in character and some of the fire has gone from them. However, the club is now actively engaged in returning the greens to hard and fair surfaces. When the work is complete, there are many who feel Westward Ho! will be the finest links course in England.

If you like an audience when you're caught in a bunker, then this is the place for you. You can take your time, though – the sheep have seen it all before.

The famous 4th hole, which is only 354 yards long, has one of the most frightening carries in golf facing the tee shot. The 'Cape' bunker with its face of built-up railway sleepers is only 170 yards from the tee but it is 100 yards wide! There is no option but to carry it; between it and the tee lies nothing but sandy waste and rough.

The first of the home holes is the last in a short loop of four holes at the furthest point from the clubhouse. It is also one of the most testing Westward Ho! has to offer although it is only 372 yards long.

FACILITIES

The clubhouse at Westward Ho! reeks of the tradition of this venerable club and is both comfortable and welcoming. There is a bar and a fine dining room and the facilities offered to guests are first-class. Golf clubs are available for hire from the professional's shop.

THE REGION

The West Country is a glorious part of England for the visitor. To the north-east of Westward Ho! is the Exmoor National Park where the landscape is rather gentler than that of Dartmoor and Bodmin.

This is an area of open fields and wooded valleys romanticized by R.D. Blackmore in his classic romantic novel, Lorna Doone. You can almost sense the presence of the evil Carver and John Ridd as they fought to the death. Bideford, only two miles from the course, and Barnstaple are both busy ports. And Minehead is only a short distance away.

Bideford Bay has a wonderful sandy beach and there are many visitors to the showpiece village of Clovelly which it shelters.

ACCOMMODATION

There is no shortage of choice in hotel accommodation around Westward Ho! Culloden House is close to the course and offers a warm welcome to visitors. In Northam the Durrant House Hotel is a perfect base for a protracted stay in the area.

For those who want something a little special, the Penhaven Country House at Parkham near Bideford was once a rectory and now offers splendid facilities to guests – golfers and non-golfers alike.

5

France

The 'Auld Alliance' between the Scots and the French undoubtedly played a major part in the introduction of golf to France perhaps as early as 1767.

However, the game only began to develop seriously in the country about a century later after the first French club was founded at Pau in the French Pyrenees, close to the Spanish border. Scottish regiments were garrisoned there after the Peninsular War, and the Scottish Duke of Hamilton is widely reckoned to have been the prime mover in the formation of the club in 1856.

The recent remarkable growth in the popularity of golf in France has seen an almost frenzied golf course building programme which, over the space of five years from 1987, has seen the number of French courses blossom from around 175 to more than 400. France is therefore rapidly catching up with Scotland, the home of the game, in terms of the number of golfing facilities available to visitors.

The French Tourist Board and the French Golf Federation have been very active and effective in promoting the game in France. The Federation, particularly, has shown great foresight in its endeavours, not only to encourage more and better facilities, but also to keep the cost to the golfer as low as possible.

The grape harvest in the Loire valley. For many visitors, this is the picture of France they cherish most – a summer's day, an exquisite cuisine and the best wine in the world.

Frequent Channel-ferry crossings make the courses of northern France easily and quickly accessible from Britain, and the Channel Tunnel can only help to generate more visitors to the country. There is a vast choice of courses for the visitor, from the renowned links at Le Touquet and Hardelot just across the Channel to the famous courses of Chantilly, St Nom-la-Bretêche, St Cloud and Paris International on the outskirts of the capital.

Brittany has wonderful courses to offer, while further down the west coast the famous playground of the rich and influential, Biarritz, has several more. The south of France continues to expand its choice of courses in addition to the well-established clubs at Monte Carlo, Cannes Mougins and Mandelieu.

In summer the French Alps provide magnificent golf in a thrilling setting. Chamonix and Bossey are only two of many excellent courses in the region providing the visitor with unforgettable golf.

Add to this the gastronomic delights of the country and the fine and relatively inexpensive accommodation and it is little wonder that golfing tourists are flocking to France in gathering numbers from all parts of Europe.

Golf de Chantilly

FOUNDED 1906

FAR FROM THE MADDING CROWD

Chantilly is set in one of the great forests of the Ile de France and is widely regarded as one of the finest courses in the world.

For more than a thousand years a great castle, one of the most magnificent in the country, has stood at Chantilly where much French history has been written. The estate was owned by the Condé family, apart from a short spell when it was annexed by Louis XIII, and the castle was almost destroyed during the French Revolution.

Following the suicide of the last Duke of Bourbon in 1830, Chantilly passed to the Duke of Aumale, a son of the last King of France, Louis Philippe. In 1897 the estate was bequeathed to the Institut de France and later under the presidency of Prince Murat, the Chantilly club was founded.

The club has two courses in a truly beautiful setting 40 kilometres north of Paris. Much of the championship course, Le Vineuil, is very open despite the surrounding woodland and its 6408 metres are among the most testing in continental Europe.

Course designer Tom Simpson was commissioned to lay out 18 new holes at Chantilly in the 1920s, and to redesign the original championship course. It was Simpson's work on the championship layout that has made Chantilly the classic challenge it remains today. Unfortunately, much of his work on the new course was severely damaged during the Second World War and nine of the holes were taken out of play.

However, the modified original course has survived in splendid glory. This is a place of sublime peace and tranquillity in the very heart of one of Europe's greatest horse-racing areas.

The list of French Open Champions is an indication of the quality of the test. George Duncan won the first French Open at Chantilly in 1913. His winning score of 304 was the highest in the history of the event.

Arnaud Massey, Sir Henry Cotton and Argentinean Roberto de Vicenzo – twice a winner – are on that roll of honour, along with England's Nick Faldo and Peter Oosterhuis.

THE COURSES

Although Simpson reduced the number of bunkers on the course, many of those remaining are extremely penal. Typical are the fairway bunkers on the dogleg 7th which menaces the drive down the right side all the way to the green from the landing area. Severe bunkering around the green adds to the threat.

Three uncompromising par 5s and four tough par 3s, three of them almost 200 metres in length,

---

Golf de Chantilly

Vineul-St-Firmin, 60500

Chantilly

◆

Location: 40km north of Paris

Tel: (33) 44 57 0443

Courses: Le Vineuil – 18 holes, 6408m, par 71; Les Longères – 18 holes, 6432m, par 72

Visitors: welcome midweek but by introduction only at weekends. The courses are closed on Thursdays

Green fees: FFr350

The 14th at Chantilly. You'll need to hit straight and true to get your par here.
The trees will gratefully gobble up anything that the bunkers miss.

contribute to the par of 71. Of the remaining par 4s, nine are close to the 400 metre mark.

The forest itself is also a major threat. It is particularly menacing at the first of Chantilly's par 5s, the 8th. In addition to the trees that stand guard along the whole length of the left side, a string of bunkers is positioned across the fairway at a threatening distance from the putting surface.

A good drive is needed to open up the green on the 13th, one of the toughest of the long par 4s. This sharp dogleg calls

There can be few more attractive holes at Chantilly than the 8th but the possibilities for error are almost limitless. The walls of these bunkers present the most daunting challenge. Best to avoid them.

for a demanding second shot over a deep grassy ravine to a green surrounded by trees.

The 15th is the third of a string of three holes, starting at the 13th, which present a stern test and are crucial to any round at Chantilly. The drive needs to be long and straight to give a clear approach to a green well protected by deep bunkers front and left.

The first of this trio of holes, the 13th, is one of the toughest of the course's long par 4s. Again the drive is the key to opening up the green on this sharp dogleg left. The approach shot is a demanding one over a deep hollow to a green surrounded by trees.

Of the short holes, the 6th at 198 metres demands particular respect. The hole is completely screened by trees with the green set diagonally to the shot while bunkers front right and left make it a very difficult green to hold. Club selection is crucial

and only an accurate stroke will find any success here.

The final hole is a fitting climax to this great course. It is a long par 5 of 545 metres with a string of bunkers running diagonally across the fairway to put pressure on the drive. It was here in the French Open of 1974 that Peter Oosterhuis, needing a par to win, produced marvellously controlled golf to take the title. With the wind helping, he carried the bunkers with a one-iron from the tee and then found the green with a towering spoon shot. Two putts produced a finishing birdie to beat Peter Townsend by two strokes.

FACILITIES

There is no shortage of first-class restaurants. Among those particularly recommended close to the golf course are the Relais Condé in Chantilly and the Relais

The 15th green. What this picture doesn't tell you is the quality of the challenge you will have had to face to get this far. The excellent clubhouse has an almost cricket pavilion look about it

There is a peace and tranquillity in Chantilly reflected in both its architecture and the surrounding countryside. It's hard to believe you are so close to the hustle and bustle of Paris. The beautiful château is well worth visiting.

du Coq Chantant on the Route de Creil.

For those who prefer the city lights, all the delights of the French capital are less than an hour's drive away, while the beaches of Normandy are within easy reach to the north west.

The Region

Chantilly lies in the prosperous region of Picardie to the north of Paris and has much to offer visitors apart from excellent golf. This is beautiful countryside with an air of quiet dignity and opulence.

It is essentially an agricultural region but it is also thoroughbred race horse country and a Mecca for followers of the Sport of Kings. As lovers of the sport will know, many of the great blood lines of French racing can be traced to the region.

Accommodation

There is a wide choice of excellent accommodation close to the golf course. Recommended hotels nearby are the Campanile, Chantilly and the Château de la Tour, Gouvieux.

Paris hotels can burn a hole in your pocket very quickly. For those seeking sensible accommodation in Paris itself, the Résidence Lord Byron on the Rue de Chateaubriand is worth considering. This smallish hotel is located close to the Arc de Triomphe and the Champs Elysées, which makes it the ideal choice if you want to mix some exploring with your golf.

In an area dominated by grand and sometimes impersonal hotels, it has earned an enviable reputation for personal service and reasonable prices, at least by the standards of the area.

Golf de Fontainebleau

FOUNDED 1909

OF THE OLD SCHOOL

The golf club at Fontainebleau is one of the longest established in France and enjoys a well-deserved reputation as one of the best in the country.

Founded in 1909, it was originally a Tom Simpson design, but came in for some extensive alteration and development at the hands of Fred Hawtree some 50 years later.

The course has a wonderful setting running through avenues of majestic oak and pine trees. Beautiful springy turf underfoot brings back recollections of several of Britain's finest courses.

This is a long course from the back tees placing a premium on length and accuracy with the driver.

A welcome sight for any golfer who has come through the Fontainebleau experience. The atmosphere in the clubhouse is friendly and relaxing.

Trees come uncomfortably close to the fairways on some holes, but the rough is not desperately penal. The rolling contours of the greens take a little getting used to and require some careful attention with the putter.

THE COURSE

The course opens with a not too testing par 4 of just over 300 metres. The short 2nd is 169 metres and needs care with club selection to extract a par. The layout then begins to show rather more teeth with the long, slightly dogleg left 5th – a very solid par 5 of 485 metres.

A trio of demanding par 4s follows and there is little respite at the 8th which is 510 metres long and out of reach for all except the very longest hitters.

After the par 3 10th, which is not short at all at 170 metres, another par 5 puts the player's long game to the test. It boasts a dogleg to the left, measures 515 metres from tee to green, and plays all of that. It is followed by another par 5 which also doglegs to the left, but this is a much shorter hole at only 435 metres and presents a realistic birdie opportunity for many players.

The Fontainebleau finish is interesting rather than

> **Golf de Fontainebleau**
>
> *Route d'Orléans, 77300*
> *Fontainebleau*
>
> ◆
>
> Location: Off N51 south west of Fontainebleau
>
> Tel: (33) 64 22 2295
>
> Course: 18 holes, 6074m, par 72
>
> Visitors: Welcome at any time.
>
> Course closed on Tuesdays
>
> Green fees: FFr350-640

There can be few French greens that are better protected than this, the 14th at Fontainebleau. Those bunkers have spoilt the card of many a vistor as he or she approached the closing holes.

long. The 17th, for instance, is well under 300 metres and, while the 15th and 16th are longer, they normally only require a solid drive and a middle iron to get home.

The sting comes in the tail at the 18th – a tight dogleg to the right. A good drive is needed to open up the green for the second shot. It'll need to be a long one as well if the drive has not found the right part of the fairway.

It is a fitting finishing hole for one of France's most enjoyable courses.

FACILITIES

A friendly bar in which to enjoy a post-round drink and an excellent dining room are very much part of

the Golf de Fontainebleau style. There is a good practice ground and the club has its own tennis facility.

THE REGION

Like Saint-Nom-la-Bretêche, Fontainebleau is within easy reach of the centre of Paris. It is also ideally placed as a starting point to wine and dine though the 'gastronomique' areas of France.

There are few who would need much persuasion that a journey down the Rhine Valley through Champagne and Burgundy would be the ideal complement to a few rounds at Fontainebleau or others of the fine courses of Paris. The cuisine of Burgundy is considered to be the finest in all of France and the wines are both plentiful and delicious.

The 3rd hole sits in a perfect setting, marred only by the presence of the inevitable bunker. The springy turf recalls some of Britain's finest courses.

While most of the châteaux are private residences, it is still possible to visit many of them. Look out for the 'degustation' sign, which means wine tasting. Where this is posted, the visitor is sure to find a warm welcome.

Spend some time in the fields picking ripe grapes and learn how the wine is made. It's the perfect antidote to problems of the swing!

ACCOMMODATION

Close to the golf course, the Novotel d'Ury will satisfy requirements very well indeed but, for those heading for Champagne and Burgundy, a highly recommended stop would be at Fare en Tardenois, north-east of Paris.

Tucked away beside the ruins of a castle the Hostellerie du Château is only 80 kilometres from Charles de Gaulle airport. Accommodation is in 23 individually decorated bedrooms with elegant decor. One of the rooms has been built in the tower and dates back to 1527. The location is quiet and exceptionally tranquil and there are beautiful views of the Champagne countryside.

The château offers an excellent menu in its restaurant with such delicacies as 'turbot au Champagne', and, of course, has a splendid wine list.

There are tennis courts available to guests and the chateau has built a nine-hole course ideal for a little practice to ensure you are ready for the next stage of the golfing gourmet trail.

Golf d' Hardelot

F O U N D E D 1 9 0 5

A TOUCH OF FRENCH POLISH

Tom Simpson designed the first 18-hole course at Hardelot in 1931. It has many of the characteristics of the fine heathland courses of southern England which, as the crow flies, are not too distant from this northernmost part of France.

Golf d' Hardelot

Ave du Golf, 62152

Neufchatel-Hardelot

◆

Location: 14km. south of

Boulogne-sur-Mer

Tel: (33) 21 83 7310

Courses: Les Pins – 18 holes,

5870m, par 72; Les Dunes –

18 holes, 6014m, par 73

Visitors: Welcome with

handicap certificates

Green fees: FFr270 weekdays,

320 weekends

THE COURSE

The course curves through the pine forest with splendid grace offering an uncompromising challenge similar in many ways to Woburn or The Berkshire, the latter which Simpson also designed.

Les Pins is unusual in that 10 of the holes are equally divided in number between par 3s and par 5s. Par 4s are therefore something of a rarity and the visitor doesn't get to tackle one until the 3rd.

Following two tough opening par 5s, the relative lack of difficulty of this modest 346 metre dogleg left is welcome even as early as this stage of the round. It's back to alternate threes and fives until some respite eventually comes at the 8th where only a short iron approach is needed.

Enjoy the breather because the next is the toughest of the eight par 4s on the course. A low swinging hook from the tee is the ideal shot on this daunting 380-metre hole. However, even when perfectly executed there's still a lot to do. The approach shot needs a high fade to hold a well-guarded green. There are some who prefer the direct route across the trees, but it is a long carry and only rarely successful.

The back nine follows much the same pattern as the front with only the 13th and the 16th holes offering any relief from the great stands of impenetrable pines which border the fairways. The clatter of ball hitting wood at Hardelot is the only sound that regularly disturbs the peace and tranquillity of this marvellous old course.

The new Les Dunes layout has been built in similar vein but is longer than its older sister by slightly over 140 metres from the medal tees.

The 2nd is widely regarded as the best of the

The 16th at Hardelot is the first hole on the back nine to offer a reasonably trouble-free fairway. Enjoy it, for it is the last respite you will get.

outward nine holes. A drive going left will almost certainly be gathered into the trees by the slope and, even from the refuge of the fairway, the approach to the green is difficult enough. It has to be played from a hanging lie with a long iron and with a careful eye on a deep, penal bunker in the front right of the green.

The 9th brings the player back to the clubhouse to face a 150-metre carry over water to the green. It is not, however, the toughest of the par 3 holes on the Dunes. That honour is held by the 16th which is played uphill and needs a full carry of well over 150 metres.

The challenge is on at the 17th for there is a clear sight of the pin. But beware: the most widely heard noise at Hardelot is the clunk of ball on pine.

Only the perfect tee shot will do here. Anything which a player mishits will almost certainly find its way to the bottom of a sheer drop of 15 metres to the front right of the green.

The Dunes course is much more hilly than the Pines and some critics complain about the fact that on twelve of the holes the pin cannot be seen from the tee.

But it is unjustified carping. This is a fine layout and once it has matured it will be one of the outstanding courses in this part of France.

Hardelot is fortunate in having former Ryder Cup and English World Cup player Peter Dawson as the Director of Golf. Peter was coach to the Danish Golf Union until 1992. In 1993 he became coach to the Swiss national team.

FACILITIES

The Hardelot complex offers a wide range of attractions in addition to the excellent golf. The complex has a swimming pool, tennis courts and horse-riding and La Brasserie du Golf at Le Pins is considered the equal of any in Hardelot. The club has floodlit and other undercover practice facilities as well as excellent locker room accommodation.

THE REGION

Hardelot is a rather chic resort enjoying an attractive location with the combined pleasures of wonderful forests and unspoilt beaches. It offers a wide variety of restaurants and bars as well as outstanding sporting facilities.

ACCOMMODATION

The Hotel du Parc near the golf courses at Hardelot is already a firm favourite with visiting golfers and it's not difficult to see why it is so appealing. It has 81 rooms, all with private bathrooms, satellite TV and telephone. There are two restaurants and a piano bar.

For those who would rather be a little further away from the resort to enjoy the Picardy countryside, the Hostellerie des Trois Mousquetaires at Aire-sur-la-Lys has much to offer.

Since the number of rooms at this popular hotel was doubled in 1988 it has been a little easier to obtain a reservation. Prior to the conversion of a pavilion in the grounds to provide the additional rooms, bookings had to be made months in advance.

France

Golf de la Grande Motte

FOUNDED 1987

A CANTER IN THE CAMARGUE

Provence. The very name conjures up images of lazy days caressed by the wonderful climate of the south of France and an endless supply of the best wine the country has to offer. Alas, the popularity of Peter Mayle's best-seller, and the adaptation of it for television, seem to be responsible not only for bringing this glorious part of the world to a wider audience but also for encouraging hordes to head south to catch some of the action.

Golf de la Grande Motte

34280 La Grande Motte
◆
Location: 18km east of
Montpellier
Tel: (33) 67 56 0500
Course: Main course –
18 holes, 6161m, par 72;
Compact course – 18 holes,
3200m, par 58
Visitors: Welcome at any time
Green fees: Main course:
FFr180-220, Compact course:
FFr100-120.

Fortunately, the golfer planning to put club to ball in the accepted fashion and take in some of Provence on the way should not encounter too much trouble.

At Le Golf de la Grande Motte a few kilometres east of Montpellier the visitor can still enjoy the glories of the area and some wonderful golf in relative peace and quiet.

La Grande Motte is on the very western tip of the Petite Camargue, part of that watery wilderness at the mouth of the Rhône.

Romantic visions of herds of white horses galloping across this glorious wasteland are easy to conjure up. The truth is slightly different.

There are certainly beautiful white horses running in herds in the Camargue. The problem is that visitors don't get to see too many of them, unless they make the effort to stay at one of the ranch-like hotels which have a herd of the famous animals for hire.

The course, which was laid out by Robert Trent Jones in 1987, is one of the finest in the whole of the south of France. Quite unashamedly American in its concept and style, it has been built on reclaimed land as part of a marina resort. It would not be at all out of place in any of the sunshine States of America.

THE COURSE

The Trent Jones handprint of jigsaw shape bunkers, water hazards and clever contouring of the greens is

The Camargue. It is little wonder that this wonderful area of southern France – and the legendary white horses that roam free there – hold such a fascination for travellers.

Deep in the heart of Provence La Grande Motte, which was laid out by Robert Trent Jones in 1987, is unashamedly American in both concept and design. The result is a wonderful course offering a unique challenge which will test all golfers – whatever their standard.

there for all to see. You may feel you have played it before, and maybe you have a few thousand kilometres away, but it still doesn't get any easier.

The tree planting has taken the edge off the sameness of the landscape and there is no doubt about the quality of the challenge here.

The European Tour was quick to spot the potential. The Tour Qualifying School has been a regular visitor here for the annual battle for aspiring pro-

six gruelling rounds. It took eight holes starting at the crack of dawn before Peter Lonard, an Australian, won through.

There are plenty of others whose dreams have been left in tatters at La Grande Motte.

FACILITIES

Golf de la Grande Motte caters well for its members and visitors with a relaxing bar and a fine restaurant.

This is the 7th at La Grande Motte and the obstacles speak for themselves. If those two bunkers don't get you, then the water is certainly in with a chance.

fessionals to try to win the all-important card which will give them access to the lucrative PGA European Tour. Because there are now so many hopefuls trying to qualify, the event is shared with Golf de Montpellier-Massane a few kilometres away.

In one memorable event in November 1991, three players were left to fight out the 40th and final place in the school in a sudden death play-off after

Locker room facilities are first-rate and the practice ground is excellent.

There is a compact course and a short course in addition to the championship layout and the club also has its own tennis courts.

THE REGION

La Grande Motte lies in one of the most beautiful

regions of France. Provence is a area of contrasts and colours. Settled by the Romans around 120 BC and covered in olive trees, it is known for its warm climate and rolling hillsides.

This is the region that produces some of the world's most popular wines to complement the excellent regional cuisine.

The mysterious and romantic Camargue has now mostly been drained, and dikes keep the two princi-

Visitors might prefer to make the short journey to Golf de Montpellier-Massane, the PGA European Tour's winter base, where the Golf Hotel offers excellent facilities for visiting players. This three-star hotel has a swimming pool and tennis in addition to first class bar and restaurant facilities.

Massane is one of the leading instruction centres in Europe and is the base for the 'Golfy-Leadbetter' Academy under the direction of David Leadbetter.

The lush green is not the only feature that the 3rd and 14th holes share. It's not that the bunkers are particularly deep, it's just that there is such a vast expanse of sand.

pal arms of the River Rhône from returning it to lake and marshland. The famous Camargue horses and bulls are reared on the plains and there is an abundance of wildlife.

ACCOMMODATION
There is no shortage of hotel and auberge accommodation around Le Golf de La Grand Motte.

The 360 degree practice ground has been set up to re-create every golf shot imaginable.

For those who wish to explore the Camargue, the Mas de la Fousque ranch hotel in Les Stes-Maries-de-la-Mer offers four-star luxury, albeit with matching prices, but the bedrooms are the epitome of comfort and have private terraces built over the lagoon. The hotel also has a herd of the white horses for hire!

Golf Club du Touquet

FOUNDED 1904

PLAYGROUND OF THE RICH AND FAMOUS

There is a very British feeling about the golf club at Le Touquet, which is hardly surprising since it is so close to England and has been the haunt of such eminent golfers as King Edward VII when he was Prince of Wales.

Le Touquet is only a half-hour drive south of Calais – much less than that from Boulogne – which puts it comfortably within a couple of hours of London using the hovercraft. The Channel Tunnel link brings this magnificent French course within even easier reach of British golfers.

British Prime Minister Arthur Balfour officially opened the Forest Course at Le Touquet in 1904, seven years after he had completed his term as Captain of the Royal and Ancient Golf Club of St Andrews. It quickly became established as playground for the wealthy and famous, particularly after the Prince of Wales became a regular visitor in the 1920s. It was one of the places to be seen for the fashionable fraternity of that era and remains to this day a popular watering hole for the well-heeled.

P.G. Wodehouse, whose writings on golf are the wittiest in the history of the game, was another who found the charm of Le Touquet quite irresistible.

He lived opposite Le Manoir Hotel, very close to the first tee, at the time the Germans occupied France during the Second World War. Wodehouse was interned by the Nazis and heavily criticized in Britain at the time over radio broadcasts he made. Latterly, however, the Establishment relented and golf's funniest writer was knighted shortly before his death.

It is not difficult to understand what Wodehouse found so beguiling about the Pas de Calais and the fine courses that have been built there.

Le Touquet offers two first-class, yet completely contrasting, 18-hole layouts. Master architect Harry S. Colt was responsible for both with the sea course (La Mer) one of his great achievements.

Golf Club du Touquet

Av. du Golf, 62520 Le Touquet

◆

Location: On the south side
of Le Touquet

Tel: (33) 21 05 6847

Courses: La Mer – 18 holes,
6082m, par 72; La Fort –
18 holes, 5912m, par 71

Visitors: Welcome at any time.

Handicap limit 24 on La Mer

Green fees: FFr180-320

Le Manoir is one of the best known retreats in French Golf. And it is set right on the golf course here at Le Touquet.

The French Open has been played there on six occasions, the first as far back as 1914 when J. Douglas Edgar from Britain won with a score of 288. Seve Ballesteros was only six strokes better with a score of 282 when he won the last French Open to be played at Le Touquet in 1977.

THE COURSES

La Mer is a classic links golf course laid out among the sand dunes and might as easily be on the east coast of Scotland as on the north coast of France. Three of

However, the course relents a little towards the turn, although the 8th is a big par 4 of 410 metres demanding two very well struck shots to reach the green. The 9th is only a short iron uphill to a tiny target but it has to be accurately struck for there is no margin for error.

The best holes are played around this stage of the round amid tall and dramatic dunes covered in tough brush and gorse. The 10th is a beautiful par 4 of 410 metres which doglegs to the left.

The tee shot is played from an elevated tee with

You'll need to hit straight and true at the 15th for although the green beckons invitingly, treacherous vegetation lurks menacingly on either side of the fairway.

the first four holes are par 5s and help to make up as demanding an opening as it is possible to find.

The first is a tough par 5 of 470 metres and although the second is a relatively short two-shotter it is by no means a give-away par. Two more substantial par 5s then make visitors wonder if they will ever have a fairway wood out of their hands.

wonderful views out to sea. Only a drive which cuts off a fair-sized slice of the dogleg will allow a reasonable opportunity to reach the green with the second. With the prevailing wind normally from the left, it is the supreme test for the longest club in the bag.

Major developments at Le Touquet have meant considerable construction work going on in more recent times. Part of the course and the clubhouse were destroyed by bombing during the war and changes to the original course had to be made. As part of the alterations four of the holes – the first two and the last two – were moved back across the road on to the sea side and it may not be long before Le Touquet returns as a major tournament venue.

The Forest course at Le Touquet is in complete contrast to La Mer. It is shorter and flatter and more

One of the bunkers which stands sentinel at the 9th green. Although this is a shortish par 3, you'll need to be accurate here for the green is not as big as it looks.

parkland in style. The fairways wend their way through avenues of pines and rolling countryside. Nonetheless it presents a good challenge and a pleasant alternative to its much tougher neighbour.

FACILITIES

Visitors will find the restaurant and bar at Le Touquet both friendly and welcoming. Locker room facilities are in keeping with a club of such standing and there are good practice facilities. The new nine-hole short course will be popular with beginners and those who prefer a relaxing version of this great game.

THE REGION

Le Touquet may not be quite the exclusive playground of the well-to-do as it once was but it is still a popular resort with beautiful old-fashioned hotels, smart shops and chic restaurants and bars.

It also boasts the largest equestrian centre in northern France offering top professional tuition and wonderful rides through spectacular forest country or along the miles of sandy beaches.

The Pas de Calais is a region of great natural beauty, charming historic towns with half-timbered houses and wonderful old churches and cathedrals.

The great apple orchards of the region produce a renowned cider, the beef is the best in France and the restaurants serve unrivalled seafood.

ACCOMMODATION

Le Manoir Hotel is one of the best-known golfing retreats in the world and is set right on the golf course. Resident golfers enjoy unlimited golf free of green fees during their stay while non-golfers receive special reductions of up to FFr140 per night from the middle of April until the end of October. The hotel has a highly commended restaurant and bar.

The four-star Westminster Hotel is very much a reminder of the British influence in the area before the Second World War. This is a grand hotel in traditional vein near the centre of Le Touquet and only five minutes from the golf courses. It has an indoor swimming pool, squash court, fitness club, snooker room, sauna and jacuzzi, and satellite television in all 115 rooms.

The Westminster is renowned for the quality of its cuisine and is perfect for either short golfing breaks or longer holidays.

Paris International Golf Club

F OUNDED 1991

A NICKLAUS TESTER

A liberal sprinkling of water hazards and extremely large bunkers very much in the American style are the hallmarks of the first Jack Nicklaus golf course in France. Founded in 1991, the Paris International Golf Club lies only a few kilometres from the centre of the French capital and is built in the magnificent grounds of the Château Empain.

Bearing in mind its pedigree, it is hardly surprising that it is an unashamedly American-style golf course complete with all the fashionable accessories such as an island green and spectacular fountain. Perhaps it would not have been to Old Tom Morris's taste but the members at this rather exclusive club in the Paris suburbs are entirely delighted with the course that Jack built.

This is the 9th where a good drive well to the right will give an open shot to the green. Err in direction, however, and the water awaits you.

THE COURSE

The course spreads through woodland in something of a figure-eight pattern. Nicklaus has emphasized the natural movement of the ground with some judicious shaping of his own to which he has added several lakes and streams.

The water is very much in evidence from the beginning but it is confined to the area to the left of the first tee presenting little in the way of hazard, even to cold swings on the opening hole.

This rather leisurely opener, followed by an interesting but not over-testing short 2nd, is all the early comfort Jack is prepared to concede. At the 3rd, the full force of the Nicklaus philosophy of confronting the player with a problem and making life very difficult for him if he does not solve it comes into play.

This 504 metre par 5 has a long tongue of a bunker running all the way down the right side of the fairway beyond the driving area. Alongside the bunker is a lake, while the left side of the fairway is protected by rough and trees.

The hole then turns slightly to the right and a nest

> **Paris International Golf Club**
>
> *Route du Golf, 95560*
>
> *Baillet-en-France*
>
> ◆
>
> Location: North of Paris near Bouffémont
>
> Tel: (33) 13 46 9 9000
>
> Course: 18 holes, 6319m, par 72
>
> Visitors: Welcome on weekdays but pre-booking essential. With members only at weekends. Course closed Monday
>
> Green fees: FFr450-700

of bunkers guards the right side in the landing area for the second shot. A large bunker eats into the front right of the green to complete the picture.

Water threatens at the 6th and 8th and again at the very testing 9th where only a good drive well to the right side gives an open shot to the green.

The waterfall cascading in front of the 13th green ensures that this is the most photographed hole on the course. And don't forget the glorious backdrop.

Paris International has almost its own version of 'Amen Corner' from the 12th to the 14th. The 12th, a long par 4, doglegs slightly to the left and demands a long and straight drive between stands of giant trees. A little lake on the right is out of range from the tee for all but the longest players from the back tee, but from the more forward tees it starts to come into play.

The next is the most memorable hole on the course. A formal water hazard, oval in shape and with a waterfall tumbling in front of the green, ensures that the short 13th will be the most photographed hole. It is a 140 metre carry from the back tee to reach the putting surface.

Nicklaus has provided something of a bail-out option to the right in the form of a patch of fairway, but it is not much of a concession. The trio is completed by the very testing 14th which, although not over-long at 301 metres, requires great care.

Water again figures strongly in its defences and Nicklaus has constructed a shallow green protected by a dangerous bunker to the front and right.

An island green at the last, a par 5 of 477 metres, completes a very interesting and rewarding course.

FACILITIES

Paris International has a splendid clubhouse with every modern facility as befits a club of this standing. It has an excellent restaurant, comfortable bar and visitors can enjoy the swimming pool or the tennis courts if they still feel energetic after their round.

THE REGION

The golf club is within half an hour's drive of the centre of Paris and all the delights of Europe's most romantic city.

ACCOMMODATION

Paris has a myriad of hotels from which to choose but many are expensive and some impersonal. The small hotel of distinct character is more often to the golfer's taste and two fine examples are the Hôtel de la Bretonnerie and the Hôtel St-Louis Marais.

The former is a 17th-century town house on the Rue Ste-Croix-de-la-Bretonnerie in the Marais district. The Hôtel St-Louis is also in the Marais district on the Rue de Cardinal Lemoine.

Golf de Saint-Nom-la-Bretêche

F OUNDED 1 9 5 9

HOME OF THE LANCOME

Situated 25 kilometres west of Paris in the pleasant countryside of La Tuilerie is the Saint-Nom-la-Bretêche Golf Club. It is one of many fine and very exclusive golf clubs in the Paris area and is internationally known as the home of the Lancôme Trophy.

The club has two 18-hole courses which were laid out by Fred Hawtree and opened for play in 1959. Both are set in undulating but lightly wooded countryside, with the Red course the higher and slightly longer of the two.

The World Cup was played at Saint-Nom-la-Bretêche as the inaugural event for the championship course in 1963 when Arnold Palmer and Jack Nicklaus won with a score of 482.

The championship layout uses the first hole of the Blue Course and, thereafter, the remaining holes of the Red Course.

The club hosted the French Open in 1965 and again in 1969 before the Lancôme Trophy was established there in 1970. It has been played there since Tony Jacklin was the first winner of this bizarre trophy – a *bas relief* of a male torso with a golf ball in the heart – in the year he won the US Open at Haseltine.

The Lancôme is one of the richest events on the European Tour and one of the most stylish. The Paris smart set invade the wonderful clubhouse to parade their finery in what was once a farm of the Palace of Versailles and later became the headquarters of the invading German army.

Like peacocks displaying their plumage, the splendidly dressed Parisians turn this golf event into an annual fashion parade much to the delight of the sponsors.

Golf de Saint-Nom-la-Bretêche
Hameau de la Tuilerie-Brignon, 78860 Saint Nom la Bretêche
◆
Location: Off N307 south of St Nom-la-Bretêche
Tel: (33) 130 80 0440
Courses: Red Course - 18 holes, 6148m, par 72; Blue Course – 18 holes, 6095m, par 72
Visitors: Welcome at weekdays. Course closed Tuesdays
Green fees: FFr485

All peace and tranquillity but there's a watery grave awaiting any shot that's slightly off-line here at the 7th.

THE COURSES

There is nothing complicated about either of the layouts. On the Red course the short 3rd is played from what is virtually an island tee across water to a well guarded green. It is not a long hole at just over 160 metres, but it presents a demanding shot with a middle iron.

At just under 500 metres, the longest hole is the 12th. It is also one of several holes that do not have a fairway bunker to threaten tee shot or approach.

The most memorable feature of the course is the horseshoe lake that separates the 9th and 18th greens and claims many a victim. A little island in the centre acts as an additional area of fairway.

FACILITIES

Saint-Nom-la-Bretêche has one of the most magnificent clubhouses in the whole of Europe. This 18th-century manor house is beautifully furnished in the style of Louis XIII and has every facility.

A well-appointed bar and a superb restaurant await the visitor after the toil on the course and the club has its own swimming pool for those still feeling energetic after their round.

As befits a golf club of this stature, there are first-class practice facilities and an extremely well-appointed professional's shop as well.

THE REGION

The club is only a short journey to the centre of Paris and the delights of Europe's most romantic city.

Beautiful and sophisticated Paris is almost a collection of small towns or villages rather than a city, with each one offering the visitor something slightly different. These 'arrondissements' all have their own unique character and style and offer almost endless opportunities for exploration.

The problem is deciding where to begin. Whether

With a setting like this, it's little wonder that the Saint-Nom-la-Bretêche is the home of the Lancôme Trophy – one of the richest and most stylish events on the European circuit.

A typically French welcome awaits you at the end of your round here in one of northern Europe's finest clubhouses. It is an 18th-century manor house furnished in the style of Louis XIII.

it be in the area around the Place de la Concorde, with its elegant and expensive shops along the Rue du Faubourg Saint Honoré, or Paris's two islands, Ile St Louis and Ile de la Cité, there is something for all tastes to enjoy.

Notre Dame is located on the larger of the island, Ile de la Cité. From there it is only a short walk to the Latin Quarter or a pleasant stroll to the Louvre.

Ile St Louis is a charming island and perfect for those who nurse a passion for antiques combined with an appetite for good food.

ACCOMMODATION

There is a myriad of hotels available to the traveller to this part of France. From small pension accommodation to grand hotels the choice for the visitor to this enchanted city is almost endless.

But for those who might like to concentrate on their golf and spend a few days in the area of Saint-Nom-la-Bretêche itself, Motel Mercure du Chesnay and the Novotel Le Trianon de Versailles are both within easy reach of the clubhouse. Both offer excellent accommodation.

6

Germany

The origins of golf in Germany can be traced back to the health requirements of the very rich. Their obsession with the health spa resulted in the first courses being built at several of the spa resorts and, as a consequence, golf in Germany has a background of being the preserve of the very rich.

In 1960 there were only 50 courses in the whole of Germany. Membership of these clubs was very exclusive. It was not sufficient just to be wealthy to be able to play up till that time; prospective players had to be super-wealthy.

It is widely believed that it was the successes of Bernhard Langer which set the golf boom rolling in the country. However, this is only part of the story.

Germany had a major boom in the game between 1960 and 1980 before the game started to become so popular in the rest of Europe, and before Langer really began to make his mark. During that period the number of courses being built in Germany more than tripled trying to keep pace with a demand fuelled by a booming West German economy.

This is the beautiful old town of Regensburg deep in the heart of Bavaria which boasts everything, including the River Danube, an old stone bridge and its own Cathedral.

However, the emergence of Langer as one of the great players in world golf gave the game another hefty boost and the demand accelerated even more. Today, golf in Germany is growing faster than anywhere else in Europe. By the turn of the century it is expected that there will be more than a million regular players, with a steady stream of new courses being built to meet the demand. In the period since 1980, the number of courses has doubled yet again to more than 300 and the momentum is showing no signs of slowing down.

Currently between 60 and 70 courses are in either the design or construction stage with new developments being constantly brought before the planners.

There are many truly great golf courses in Germany. One of the finest championship courses in Europe can be found at Club Zur Vahr only a few kilometres north of Bremen. The Frankfurter club, which dates back to 1913, is one of the country's toughest, while the Golfclub Beuerberg, near Munich in the foothills of the Bavarian Alps, was voted the country's top course by Germany's Golf Sport Magazine in 1993. There is a wide choice for the tourist, throughout Germany with Hamburg and Munich ideal bases from which to explore the delights of German golf.

Many of the courses, however, are nine-hole layouts although this does not necessarily detract from their quality. And there is always much of interest to tempt the tourist in addition to some excellent golf.

Golfclub Beuerberg

FOUNDED 1982

IN THE SHADOW OF THE BAVARIAN ALPS

Take the Munich to Garmisch motorway, turn off at the Seehaupt exit and left through Beuerberg. Enjoy the drive through the town and turn right after the Loisach bridge. The signposts are clear; you are close to the magnificent Beuerberg Golf Club in the foothills of the Bavarian Alps.

In the 1993 ranking of its country's golf courses, the German golf magazine, Golf Sport, voted Beuerberg the nation's best course. In a country which is enjoying a massive golf boom with many new courses being built, and which already has many great courses, there could be no higher accolade.

But it is hardly surprising in view of the pedigree of this great course. Designed by master craftsman, Donald Harradine, who has built magnificent golf courses throughout Europe, Beuerberg has all the qualities which make Harradine courses so memorable.

The clever use of the land, the natural feel about the layout, the utilization of the contours; these are all hallmarks of Harradine's work and very obvious at Beuerberg.

Add to these qualities the fact that the course could hardly be in a more spectacular setting, and it is little wonder that the Golf Sport judges rated it number one.

Golfclub Beuerberg
Gut Sterz, 8196 Beuerberg
◆
Location: 45km south-west of Munich north of Penzberg
Tel: (49) 81 79 617
Course: 18 holes, 6518m, par 74
Visitors: Welcome on weekdays, with members only at weekends.
Course closed December to April
Green fees: DM80.

This is Bavaria in all its splendour – a veritable German paradise. It is also the view the player gets from the 14th green.

THE COURSE

Harradine laid out the course in the foothills of the Bavarian Alps and had it ready for play in 1982. It is surrounded by wonderful views of the mountains, which even in summer have a covering of snow.

The course is built on easy hill country with the fairways running through stands of deciduous trees giving it a parkland feel.

Harradine has used water to considerable effect at

Beuerberg. There is hardly a hole on the course which is not threatened by pond or stream. Charming little bridges add a romantic touch to the water hazards together with small wooden houses which decorate the ponds.

His strategic use of bunkers is masterful too and, combined with back tees which can extend the course to well over 6500 metres, this is a mighty challenge indeed.

Par from the back is 74, a measure of just how big Beuerberg really is, although from the men's regular tees the challenge is perhaps a little less daunting.

But like many of Harradine's layouts, length is not the critical factor. Often the course plays a little more easily from the back tees than from the forward ones. Shorten the course and stiffen the penalty for the wayward shot is very much the Donald Harradine philosophy.

The ease of the opening hole, a fairly simple and straightforward par 5 of 490 metres, belies the challenge which stretches out ahead.

The par 3 14th at Beuerberg. It may not be over long, but it makes considerable strategic demands.

The prospect of a birdie as an opener, with another chance of the same at the shortish par 4 2nd, might well lull the unwary into a false sense of security.

This might be reinforced by the 3rd, a modest 332 metres even from the back tee, but from this point on the player knows he is in a serious battle with Donald Harradine.

From the back tee, the par 5 4th is a monumental hole of more than 580 metres and out of range to anything less than a jet airliner. Three good blows are required to reach the sanctuary of a green not disposed to give anything away to the player in terms of its own defences.

The next looks innocuous enough on the card at only 250 metres, but do not be deceived. Harradine has built a classic short par 4 which is pretty to look at but has all the benevolence of a starving piranha.

The tee shot must be carefully placed to open up a short approach to a green with a dangerously narrow entrance. To the left and behind the green there

ing, but reasonably comfortable par 4 of 350 metres.

The opening hole of the back nine is played downhill and requires nothing much more than a short iron approach tacked on to a solid drive. It is memorable not so much for its challenge as for the spectacular views of the mountains.

The snow-covered Alps and clear mountain air add a feeling of well-being and tranquillity to Beuerberg which few courses in Europe can match.

It is a foolish player who allows this feeling of

The 12th is the stuff dreams are made of – a gently undulating fairway, a shady green, with the forest and the mountains in the background.

is water and, inevitably, there are the Harradine bunkers menacing anything slightly off line.

The only one-shot hole on the front nine is the 8th. It is a middle-iron hole of 150 metres to another well protected green. The half closes with an interest-

peace and contentment to gain too strong a hold for there is much work to be done on the back nine, despite the fact that from here on it is marginally shorter than the first.

There are only four par 4s on the inward half. The

10th is the easiest of them with the 13th and 16th tricky rather than demandingly long.

The two par 3s, the 11th and the 14th, again are not over long but, in true Harradine style, are very demanding strategically. And the three par 5s are all severe examinations of shotmaking and nerve.

The final hole is one of the toughest on the course. A lengthy par 4 of 414 metres from the back, it demands a long and accurate drive and a careful approach. A long iron and, often, a wooden club are needed to get home here.

FACILITIES

Beuerberg offers visitors excellent facilities in its picturesque clubhouse with a friendly bar and a first-rate restaurant. Clubs are available for hire and caddies are available if booked in advance. There are no golf carts at Beuerberg. The practice facilities are excellent and the club even has a children's playground.

THE REGION

Beuerberg lies in a particularly beautiful part of Bavaria on the site of an old manor house.

The region has many interesting historical attractions in addition to magnificent countryside perfect for touring.

In Beuerberg itself the 12th-century convent is a popular attraction for visitors, as is the church built in early Bavarian baroque style and dating back to 1630. Its stucco decoration is magnificent.

The charming old town of Bad Tolz, with its impressively decorated houses in Market Street, and the famous eighth-century monastery at Benediktbeuern, are also very popular attractions.

For those who want a break from the rigours of the Beuerberg challenge, there are beautiful walks

The clubhouse at Beuerberg offers first-class facilities to members and visitors alike. There is even a children's playground.

around the lakes at Kochel and Walchensee and the area is a hillwalker's paradise.

ACCOMMODATION

The Gästehaus Gut Fastenberg in Beuerberg is ideally situated for the golf club and as a base from which to tour the region. It offers good facilities and bicycle rental for those seeking a little more energetic stay.

In Berg, the Standhotel Schloss Berg is close to the lake and within easy reach of the course. There are magnificent views from the hotel which is small and comfortable. For those who want a city base, Munich is only 40 minutes' drive away. However, there are many hotels nearer the course.

Club zur Vahr

FOUNDED 1905

FEARSOME IN THE FOREST

In 1971, just a year after it was officially opened, Club zur Vahr hosted the German Open at its new course at Garlstedt near Bremen. The event attracted an all-star line-up from more than 20 countries. More than 6000 people – a record for a German sports event at the time – saw Britain's Neil Coles win with a remarkable score of 279.

After his victory during which he shared the course record of 68 with Peter Thomson – a record still intact to this day – Coles declared that the Bremen course was, in his opinion, one of the best championship courses in Europe.

There are few who would disagree, for this is a superb layout built in thickly forested, undulating countryside which is so naturally difficult that only 24

This is the 18th green. And afterwards, the Club zur Vahr's clubhouse doors open to provide excellent food and drink combined with a delightful welcome.

bunkers needed to be added as additional hazards.

The Gardstedter Heide course is part of the Club zur Vahr sports complex which has a number of sports and social activities attached to it. It was built as the result of a decision by the club to create a golf course capable of hosting major professional events.

There has been a golf course at Bremen since 1895 and the club still has a nine-hole layout to the east of the town. But it is the Gardstedter course for which it is now so well known.

It was the brainchild of August Weyhausen, a former German Junior Champion, who was then the club's president. His vision was for

> **Club zur Vahr**
>
> *Garlstedter Heide GC, Am Golfplatz 10, 2861 Garlstedt*
>
> ◆
>
> Location: Off the B6 12km north of Bremen
>
> Tel: (49) 421 230 041
>
> Course: 18 holes, 6435m, par 74
>
> Visitors: Pre-booking essential on weekdays. Weekends by introduction only
>
> Green fees: DM60-70

a course that would reflect the qualities he had admired when playing the great championship links courses in England and Scotland.

Weyhausen brought in course architect, Dr Bernhard von Limburger, a former German Amateur Champion, to assist him in planning the course. Together they conceived a layout that would be enjoyed by club members but could also be stretched to create a test worthy of championship golf at the highest level.

THE COURSE

There is no doubt that they succeeded in both aims. The course demands sound tactical planning, even from the members' tees, and when it is pushed out to its full championship length of nearly 7000 metres it is a fearsome test indeed.

Trees dominate the course and many of the holes are doglegs calling for long and accurate driving from the tee. It can be a punishing course to play for the wayward player but immensely satisfying for those who can 'find' a way round.

Many holes offer more than one

The 6th hole demands a long and accurate drive. The trees seem to be strategically placed to cause the most trouble.

way to approach the green, but all demand that the fairway is found from the tee. Thick undergrowth between the tall pine trees bordering the fairways has meant there is little need for fairway bunkers. Only the long par 5 15th has a bunker in the fairway – the few others that have been built into the layout are all around or near the greens.

Former Open Champion Peter Thomson, himself a successful and highly respected golf course architect, has rated the par 5s as the outstanding holes with the 2nd and the 6th, both of which have two routes to the green, the pick of the crop.

At the 2nd, only a perfect drive down the left side gives any hope of reaching this 500 metre par 5 in two strokes. A stream crosses the fairway around 280 metres from the tee, with a pond just beyond. A pair of trees guards the centre of the fairway.

The 6th is a long dogleg to the right, again demanding a long and accurate drive. It is out of range for all but the very longest players, but even to play safely with the second shot is difficult because of a lone pine which dominates the fairway on the left.

Of the short holes the 3rd is a testing par 3 at around 200 metres. A solid long iron is needed here

and there is little room for error. Trees are a threat on both sides of a green well guarded by two strategically placed bunkers.

The pattern of dogleg holes is maintained right to the finish where the 18th is a testing two-shotter of 400 metres. The tee shot needs to be both long and accurately struck down the left side of the fairway to open up the green for the approach. A long iron soundly struck is needed to reach the green nestling close to the clubhouse.

A lone bunker on the front left provides the only protection, but a clutch of trees to the left and the thick forest to the right are very intimidating.

The German Open has been played at Club zur Vahr on two occasions since Neil Coles' victory. The event went back there in 1975, and 10 years later Bernhard Langer was the popular winner for the home crowd in an event that was badly hit by torrential rain and had to be reduced to 54 holes.

FACILITIES

The Garlstedter Heide course has a bright, modern clubhouse with a bar and a comfortable and attractive restaurant. It has excellent locker room facilities and, as one would expect from a relatively new club, a very good practice ground.

Club zur Vahr's other course is a nine-hole layout, east of Bremen, which is also well worth playing. It is a par 36 of around 3000 metres where visitors are also welcome, although an introduction is needed at the weekend.

THE REGION

Northern Germany has much to offer the traveller in addition to the excellent golf at Bremen. Bremen is within easy reach of Schleswig Holstein, the country's most northerly province, known as the 'Land Between the Seas'.

This broad strip of land separates the Baltic from the North Sea and has Denmark at its tip. It is splendid and fascinating countryside where dikes protect the farmland from the ravages of the ocean on the North Sea shore.

The landscape is hilly and features long fjords eating their way far inland from the sea. Out on the islands, which can be reached by ferry, there is marvellous scenery of duneland and steep cliffs plunging into the sea.

Quaint little thatched cottages complete the picture. On the Baltic coast there are miles of clean white sand beaches which are very popular throughout the summer months.

Not far away is the industrial and trading city of Hamburg on the River Elbe. Heavily bombed during the war, the city has been painstakingly rebuilt in the old style. The city has a fine arts museum and St Michael's church is a popular tourist attraction.

The city's notorious red-light district, along the Reeperbahn and surrounding streets west of the city centre, has earned the city something of an unfair reputation. It is a very small element of an otherwise refined and dignified city.

ACCOMODATION

There is a vast selection of hotels to suit all tastes in Bremen and Hamburg but, for those interested in exploring further afield, there are many delightful little country hotels set off the beaten track which offer great value.

The Hotel Töpferhaus near the village of Holzbunge on the Bisten lake is typical. It lies on the south shore of the lake just a short drive from the village and has 37 rooms. It enjoys a fine reputation for its restaurant and includes sauna and tennis.

The old part of the hotel has wonderful views of the Bistensee at the bottom of the lawn and the rooms retain their antique furniture and a great feeling of warmth and welcome.

There is a comfortable atmosphere in the town square here at Bremen. It is a place where people meet to talk, drink or just simply to watch the world go by.

Frankfurter Golf Club

FOUNDED 1913

TOUGH AND UNCOMPROMISING

The famous Frankfurter Golf Club has held a consistently high position in any rankings of Germany's golf courses. It is one of the country's toughest and best, and certainly no place for the faint of heart.

Frankfurter Golf Club

Golfstr 41, 60528 Frankfurt/

Main – Niederrad

◆

Location: Five kilometres
from Frankfurt

Tel: (49) 69 666 23 18

Course: 18 holes, 5869m,
par 71

Visitors: Welcome but
pre-booking is essential

Green fees: DM75-95.

The club was founded in 1913 but the present layout owes most to the craftsmanship of master golf course architect Harry Colt in 1928.

Some modernization work was carried out in the 1960s when an additional 50 bunkers were added. This represented a 500 per cent increase on Colt's strategic bunker plan and brought the golf course into line with the advance in equipment which has taken place over nearly four decades.

THE COURSE

Frankfurter is not a long golf course at 5869 metres, but it plays much longer than the bare figures suggest because of the rolling terrain and very little roll in the fairways.

The course is set in the middle of a vast wooded area with fairways running through great avenues of trees. Accuracy and length from the tee are critical and there are few players who come off the course not having used every club in the bag.

It is extremely demanding, both in terms of shot-making and in physical endurance, for there are steep hills to be climbed as well as difficult strategic decisions to be taken.

The strength of Frankfurter lies in its par 4 holes. Eight of them average close to 390 metres and there is little respite from the start.

The first two holes are uncompromising par 4s, both around 370 metres, with tight fairways and well-defended greens. The next is a monster par 4 of 400 metres demanding two very long shots to reach

The Frankfurter clubhouse offers an excellent bar and first-class food – the perfect place to relax after what will certainly have been an arduous round.

---

the green with the first of them having to be carefully threaded down the fairway to avoid the trees.

A pleasant par 3 follows, and then a short but dangerous par 4 where the approach must be truly struck to avoid menacing bunkers.

The 1st at Frankfurter is an uncompromising par 4. You'll need to avoid the bunkers to the front of the green, always assuming you've missed the trees *en route*.

The first of the par 5s, the 5th, is testing enough and a lay-up hole for all but the longest hitters, while the short 8th applies the pressure again with the need for a long tee shot to reach a well defended green 185 metres away.

The front nine winds its way around the outside of the course and finishes back at the clubhouse with one of the toughest of the par 4s. A long and accurate drive is needed here to open up a long approach to a large and difficult green.

The back nine is slightly shorter than the front but is still fraught with danger. The 11th is a typical example. A shortish par 3 of only 153 metres, it is still one of the toughest holes on the course. Trees and bunkers threaten the tee shot which must be perfectly struck to find the safety of the green.

Unlucky for many, the 13th is one of the fiercest of the par 4s, but not over-long at 365 metres.

There is some respite at least at the next, the penultimate of the par 5s, which even players of moderate length should be able to reach in two.

However, what the course gives at the 15th it is very likely to take back at the 16th. This short par 3 of 150 metres looks innocuous enough from the tee, but has claimed enough victims in its time to confirm that looks are often deceptive. Disaster lurks and you'll need to take great care with club selection to avoid the menacing bunkers.

The German Open has been staged at Frankfurter on a number of occasions, and among the illustrious names who have won there are Seve Ballesteros and Tony Jacklin.

FACILITIES

The Frankfurter Club has a welcoming bar and a good restaurant open to visitors. The practice facilities are

The Frankfurter bunkers are among the most treacherous you will find in Germany. The consolation is that it is also one of the prettiest courses in the country.

extremely good and the professional's shop offers a good range of equipment for hire.

Caddies are available as are trolleys, but Frankfurter has no motorized carts.

THE REGION

There is much of interest for the visitor to the historic city of Frankfurt. The Paulskirche, restored after war damage and where the German National Assembly met after the famous 1848 revolution, is now a national monument.

The Palmengarten features exotic plants from all over the world, while the three staggered gothic towers of the Romer, the historic town hall, are very much a landmark.

Many German emperors have been crowned in St Bartholomew's Cathedral, so impressively built in red sandstone. The Senckenberg Natural History Museum attracts many visitors to its excellent and fascinating prehistoric collection.

And for those who work up a thirst after a good round of golf and a journey around so many interesting cultural centres, the locally made apfelwein (cider) of the Sachsenhausen pubs should prove to be an excellent restorative.

ACCOMMODATION

Two excellent hotels ideally placed for visiting both the golf club and the city are the Hotel Gravenbruch Kempinskl Frankfurt and the Steigenberger Frankfurter Hof. Both offer excellent accommodation.

Also, there are many excellent restaurants in the city offering plenty of local specialities as well as international cuisine.

Golf Club Hubbelrath

FOUNDED 1961

IN THE VALLEY OF THE RUHR

Set in open and attractive countryside only 15 kilometres from Düsseldorf's international airport, and less than that from the city centre, Hubbelrath Golf Club is relatively new but has already earned a reputation as one of Germany's top courses.

It is very much a product of the golf boom which has swept through Germany in more recent times, thanks mainly to the success of Bernhard Langer on the international golfing stage.

The area around Hubbelrath was originally open countryside but the judicious planting of many hundreds of trees and bushes has turned it into a splendid woodland setting for a fine and challenging course.

The old town of Düsseldorf features old streets and, seemingly, a never-ending supply of pubs. It is only a short drive from Hubbelrath.

The layout is very much parkland and there are some wonderful views across the countryside over Düsseldorf and Ratingen towards the industrial valley of the Ruhr.

Hubbelrath is not particularly long as championship courses go but the rolling terrain and clever use of the ground makes it a good enough test for anyone – whatever their standard.

The club has hosted the German Open International Championship four times – in 1973, 1977, 1986 and 1992. It also staged the Ladies' German Open in 1988. Some modifications have been made to the layout to stiffen it up for professional championship golf, but they had little effect on Vijay Singh in the 1992 German Open.

The Fijian returned a remarkable score of 26 under par for the four rounds in a record-breaking victory.

Golf Club Hubbelrath
Bergische Landstr 700,
4000 Düsseldorf
◆
Location: Off A1, 12km east
of Düsseldorf
Tel: (49) 21 047 2178
Course: 18 holes, 6042m,
par 72
Visitors: Welcome on
weekdays but only with a
member at weekends
Green fees: DM70-100

THE COURSE

Many of the holes are tight from the tee and put a high premium on accuracy. The greens are also very tricky with some alarming slopes.

The course is very much a conventional layout

with two par 3s and two par 5s in each of the halves. Not one of the par 4s is over 400 metres, which accounts for the modest overall length of the course, but two of the par 5s are more than 500 metres and present quite a challenge.

Toughest of the single shot holes is the 14th which measures 202 metres from the back tee and demands a long and accurate tee shot to find sanctuary in a well-guarded green.

The two opening par 4s do not give the player much opportunity to play himself in quietly. At around 380 metres, both are very demanding before the layout relents slightly with a shortish par 4 before the first of the short holes.

The 4th is a relatively simple par 3 of modest length but it does need care and a sure touch with the putter on a tricky green.

At 505 metres, the next is the longest of the par 5s and only the very biggest of hitters can reach the green comfortably in two shots. There is little help from lush fairways which present excellent lies but permit very little roll.

Hubbelrath has a formidable finish with a tough par 5 17th which, again, only the longest player has any hope of reaching in two shots.

It is followed by a beautiful little finishing hole, not demanding of length at a modest 342 metres, but from which it is extremely difficult to extract a par. It relies for its defence on a wick-

edly sloping green and many have fallen prey to its wiles over the years.

In 1972 the club built a second 18-hole layout known as the West Course, which is an interesting if not over taxing challenge. It measures only 4325 metres but is an ideal beginner's course. It can also be an interesting diversion from its bigger and more illustrious sister.

FACILITIES

Hubbelrath has a modern clubhouse with a bar and restaurant and has first-class locker room facilities. There is a good practice ground enhanced by the short West Course and there is also a swimming pool and tennis courts.

The club also boasts an extremely well-stocked professional's shop.

Caddies are the order of the day at Hubbelrath,

The 7th at Hubbelrath where the twin dangers of bunkers and water combine to ruin all but the most accurate player's cards.

which gives the club a nice traditional and exclusive feel about it.

THE REGION

Hubbelrath is only a short drive from the centre of Düsseldorf with its old town centre and a seemingly endless stream of cosy pubs.

For those who might wish to explore the elegant shops of the city, a promenade along Kinigsallee should fit the bill very nicely. There are fine art collections featuring the work of Paul Klee and oth-

This, Hubbelrath's 10th, is a gorgeous hole. The fairway is reasonably generous and the elevated green is a delight to putt upon.

ers, and the Hetjens Museum is popular with lovers of ceramics and ancient pottery.

The prehistoric museum at Neanderthal, where the famous Neanderthal skull was discovered, is also well worth a visit.

ACCOMMODATION

The Hotel Inter-Continental Düsseldorf is well situated for those visiting Hubbelrath, as too is the Steinberger Parkhotel in the city. The latter offers transfers between the airport, the hotel and the golf course as part of its service.

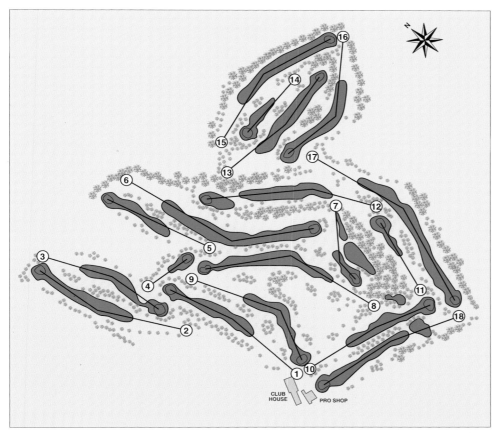

The course at Hubbelrath.

Golfclub St Dionys

FOUNDED 1972

HEATHLAND IN BARDOWICK

In the 1993 Golf Sport rankings of golf courses in Germany, the fine layout of the St Dionys Golf Club south-east of Hamburg took fourth place. It was a fitting tribute to an excellent layout built on heathland near the village of Bardowick.

It is an historic site, the village having been founded by Charles the Great, and was known for the quality of the potatoes grown there until the golf course was built.

The layout dates back to 1972 when an area of agricultural land was turned over to recreational use. The free draining, sandy soil of the heathland proved itself to be ideal for golf course construction.

Deciduous trees, firs and pines, were planted in their thousands to create a woodland through which the fairways could wind their way.

This is wonderful holiday golf with virtually no rough to speak of yet, at more than 6200 metres, the challenge is stiff enough.

Although there is little in the way of conventional rough the thick heathland bushes present their own difficulties for the player who strays from the fairway. The sandy soil drains so well that all-year-round golf is a genuine option at St Dionys, a rare luxury for most golfers in this part of Europe.

THE COURSE

This a relaxing place to play golf rather than a battle against the golf course architect, and visitors will find an air of tranquillity about St Dionys.

None of the par 4s is over 400 metres and most can be reached comfortably in two strokes.

There is little indication of this at the 1st, however, since it is one of the longest holes and requires two well-struck shots to reach the green.

There is a little respite at the next with a not too challenging par 4 of 360 metres although, again, only two well struck shots will yield success.

Golfclub St Dionys
Widukindweg, 2123
St Dionys
◆
Location: 50km south-east of Hamburg
Tel: (49) 41 33 6277
Course: 18 holes, 6225m, par 72
Visitors: Welcome but must have club membership card and handicap certificate. Pre-booking is essential. Some restrictions on weekend play
Green fees: DM60-80

There can be few more attractive sights at the end of the round than the clubhouse here at St Dionys, where a warm welcome is always guaranteed.

At 525 metres, the long par 5 4th is the longest hole on the course and is something of a monster. It is normally out of reach in two strokes for all but the longest hitters but, played sensibly, a par is not too difficult to achieve.

The short 8th is not short at all at 189 metres and needs a very solid blow with a long iron or even a wood to reach the sanctuary of the green.

On the back nine the 11th is a par 5 offering at least some opportunity to claw something back. At a modest 450 metres the longer hitters can get up comfortably in two, and for lesser mortals there is always the chance of a pitch and putt.

St Dionys has a well balanced finish with a testing par 3 at the 16th needing a medium-to-long iron. A shortish par 4 17th of 350 metres comes next followed by a telling two-shotter to finish.

This final hole is an uncompromising par 4 of 390 metres and the longest of the par 4s on the course. Only a long drive and the most solid of approach shots will yield any success here.

The par 3 15th. If the water doesn't get you, the trees at the back of the green are ready and waiting.

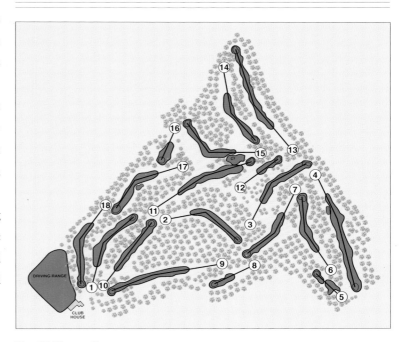

The St Dionys Course.

FACILITIES

The St Dionys Club offers visitors excellent facilities. There is a friendly bar and a good restaurant in the clubhouse which is open from 11am until 9pm every day except Monday. The professional's shop has clubs available for rental but no golf carts.

THE REGION

This northern part of Germany features large inland lakes such as the Plöner See and the Müritz lake which covers an area of 115 square kilometres. More than 1000 lakes of various sizes make up the Mecklenburg 'Lake District' with almost endless possibilities for exploring a fascinating countryside.

The city of Hamburg is only a short drive from St Dionys and is famous for its harbour and the lake in the centre of the city. A trip on one of the many Alster boats offers splendid views of the business centre and the tall church spires overlooking it.

ACCOMMODATION

There are a few hotels in the area around St Dionys but popular with visitors to the club is the Hotel Bergstrom Lüneburg in the town of Lüneburg.

Wittelsbacher GC Rohrenfeld-Neuburg

FOUNDED 1988

SERENE AMONG THE OAKS

Rated number five among all of Germany's golf courses in 1993, the Wittelsbacher Golf Club Rohrenfeld-Neuburg is one of the country's newest and most pleasantly challenging courses. Built in 1988 near the historic town of Neuburg on the Danube, this fine course lies in an estate owned for more than 500 years by the Wittelsbacher family, the former Royal House of Bavaria.

Scattered around the course are more than 200 oaks and linden trees many of which are more than 150 years old. The trees are part of the land surrounding the 16th-century Grünau Castle, which is visible from parts of the course.

Course architect Dr Joan Dudok van Heel left the surroundings virtually untouched when he laid out the course, and relied on clever shaping of the fairways and several water hazards as defences. This is not an overwhelmingly difficult course, despite its robust length, but it does present a stiff enough challenge for the average player.

A particularly interesting aspect of the club, whose president is His Royal Highness Prince Max of

Wittelsbacher GC Rohrenfeld-Neuburg
Gut Rohrenfeld, 86633 Neuburg 2/Donau
◆
Location: Seven kilometres east of Neuburg
Tel: (49) 84 31 44118
Course: 18 holes, 6277m, par 73
Visitors: Welcome with home club membership card and handicap certificate
Green fees: DM70-90

It doesn't look it but, at nearly 550 metres, the monster 18th is one of the most challenging holes at Wittelsbacher.

Another view of the 18th green, but this time taking in the new clubhouse where good food and excellent wine await the weary player.

Bavaria, is the double green shared by the 1st and 15th. These holes are very much in the St Andrews mould where his Royal Highness is a member and a regular visitor.

THE COURSE

The first hole is a double dogleg par 5 although, at 452 metres from the regular men's tee, it is not over testing. Its coun-terpart, the 15th, is of similar length and is the first of four fine finishing holes.

The par of 36 on the front nine is made up of the single par 5 at the 1st, a long par 3 at the 6th and seven par 4s, none of which is more than 390 metres.

The back nine on the other hand has two par 5s and two par 3s but is still shorter than the front.

The 17th and 18th are the outstanding holes of the back nine in terms of difficulty. At 428 metres, the penultimate hole is the longest par 4 on the course, even from the front tee, and requires two very big shots to reach the green in regulation.

The 18th is a monster finishing hole of more than 541 metres.

The Wittelsbacher Golf Club has been host to the German Amateur Championship for both men and women since 1991.

FACILITIES

The club is justifiably proud of its new clubhouse with its first-class facilities for members and visitors.

A friendly bar and comfortable restaurant are open from 9am until 9.30pm and the course can be play-ed all year round. Trolleys are available and the club also has electric golf carts for hire.

The professional's shop can supply golf clubs for rental and if you feel like taking the family pooch with you on your round that's quite in order too.

The club also has excellent practice facilities.

THE REGION

Wittelsbacher lies 70 kilometres north-west of Mu-nich in Bavaria, Germany's largest federal state.

It is a region of infinite variety with spectacular scenery and a deep history of art, urban architecture and folklore. There are many areas where the me-dium-altitude mountains provide excellent facili-ties for hiking enthusiasts.

The dramatic highlight of Bavaria, however, is the Alpine chain, a paradise for hillwalkers and mountaineers as well as those who just want to look.

There are water sports available on the many lakes in the Alpine ravines for those so inclined, while those who prefer the city will find plenty to tempt them in Munich itself.

This is a city of fashionable elegance and exciting beer-gardens. There are magnifi-cent cathedrals and churches throughout the region and old towns with historic castles to explore.

ACCOMMODATION

Finding good accommodation poses no problems for players heading towards Wittelsbacher. There are 26 elegantly furnished rooms available in the club-house itself, and in the charming dormy house which is run by the Club on the premises. Several hotels are also within easy reach.

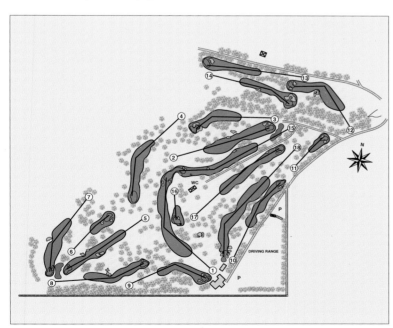

The Wittlesbacher Course.

7

Greece

It is a sad fact of life that Greece, with its wonderful climate and sporting heritage, can lay claim to only four 18-hole golf courses. The Land of the Gods is not, therefore, over-endowed with facilities for the travelling golfer.

However, the courses that it does have are well worth the effort to visit and, in the wonderful Donald Harradine layout on the romantic island of Corfu, Greece can lay claim to one of the finest courses in the whole of Europe.

This beautiful challenge, created like Henry Cotton's famous Penina on the Portuguese Algarve from a former paddy field, remains one of the best kept of golfing secrets. A beautiful clubhouse, a friendly atmosphere and a dedication to please the visitor all combine to make Corfu a club to which everyone who ever goes there immediately wants to return.

Of the other courses in Greece, Glyfada in Athens is the senior club. Opened in 1967, three years before Corfu, it suffers slightly from being on the very threshold of the runway at Athens' busy international airport.

Donald Harradine was again the architect, although Robert Trent Jones was brought in to make alterations in preparation for the World Cup in 1979 when Hale Irwin and John Mahaffey won for the United States.

The course has fairways lined by umbrella pines and features several dogleg holes which make for an interesting and difficult challenge. The redoubtable Scot, Hector Thomson, was the highly respected professional at Glyfada for many years.

The magic of Greece. You can almost hear the bell from the monastery as it rings out across the bay.

Donald Harradine also laid out the Afandu Golf Club course on Rhodes. It differs from Glyfada and Corfu in that it is essentially a links course laid out hard against the sea. It is on the south of the island and its 6080-metre layout is well worth a visit.

The fourth Greek course at Port Carras is less well known and much more remote, situated as it is around 100 kilometres south-east of Thessalonika on the Sithonian peninsula. It is the newest of the four courses, completed in 1979, and has an 18-hole layout of 6086 metres with a par of 72.

There are strong indications that the Greek National Tourist Board is moving towards encouraging the construction of additional courses in the country as the golf boom sweeps into the Aegean.

Corfu Golf and Country Club

FOUNDED 1971

ONE OF GOLF'S BEST KEPT SECRETS

For centuries visitors to the island of Corfu have been captivated by the beauty and romance of this enchanting island in the Ionian Sea.

In Homer's Odyssey, the shipwrecked Odysseus, King of Ithaca, was cast ashore there and given hospitality by King Alcinoos and his daughter Nausicca. With their assistance he returned safely home after 20 years of adventure and wandering.

Legend has it that Odysseus landed in the sheltered bay at Ermones, only two good woods and a long iron from where the clubhouse of the Corfu Golf Club now sits.

Here in the lush Ropa Valley lies one of the true gems of European golf, one of the few remaining secrets left relatively unexplored.

It is hardly surprising, for those who have discovered this wonderful course are, understandably, in no great rush to let go of the secret.

Harradine took what was once a paddy field and turned it into a golfing oasis the equal of which even Odysseus would have had to travel a long way to find. He planted thousands of trees, made marvellous strategic use of irrigation ditches and lakes, and produced a golf course of such enchantment that few can ever resist the temptation to go back once they have set foot upon it.

In terrain and setting Corfu could not be more dissimilar to the Old Course at St Andrews than it is. Poles apart they may be geographically and in style, but in many ways they do seem to share a common bond. To play either successfully the player must first 'find' a way round.

It is this indefinable quality sets Corfu apart from so many other newly-designed courses.

THE COURSE

Towering eucalyptus, poplar and birch line the fairways; richly coloured wild birds patrol the skies above and, in the waters of the lakes, giant frogs cry out their own acclamation of the place.

Harradine built his fairways around and through this miniature nature reserve with a cunning delight. He built greens of Penncross Bent with subtle burrows, and often with steep slopes, which at times can be Augusta-like in their speed and yet, at others, as docile as the clubhouse cat.

He built challenges of carry so tantalizing and seductive of reward, and yet so penal of failure, as to make one wonder if he was architect or sorcerer.

Not for Harradine the accepted wisdom that the longer a course the more difficult it naturally becomes. At Corfu he built what is the ultimate golf-

Corfu Golf and Country Club
PO Box 71, Ropa Valley, Ermones Beach
◆
Location: 2km from Ermones Beach west of Corfu Town
Tel: (30) 661 94 220
Course: 18 holes, 6300m, par 72
Visitors: Welcome at any time. Course closed November to March
Green fees: Gdr10,000

This former paddy field has been transformed into a golfing paradise. Few who have played here can resist the temptation to return.

the green cannot be reached over the trees which then intervene and even a bogey is not a certainty. It is a classic example of the difference 35 metres can make.

Of the other holes on the front nine, the 7th is a classic par 5. It can be reached with two very big shots, but the second must carry an irrigation ditch which runs diagonally across the fairway, making the carry progressively longer towards the green.

Of the holes on the back nine, the 10th was once upon a time one of the toughest par 4s on the course, requiring a long drive threaded tight to the out-of-bounds on the left side. A winter storm changed all that and took away the two giant trees which made this shot a particular necessity.

Today the drive may be slightly less demanding but the hole now still claims as many victims in the water to the right of the green as it ever did before from the trees, largely because the shot to the green is now more accessible. A classic example of 'you win some, you lose some'.

The Corfu finish is a wonderful combination of strategy, shotmaking and finesse. At 205 metres, the short 16th is not short at all, especially as it is played into the prevailing breeze and across water most of the way. It is not unlike the 16th at Augusta, but much longer, and with no escape on the opposite side of the water. At Corfu there is water there too!

Generally, you'll need a wooden club to get up to the pin, and even the same club to lay up short in the hope of a pitch and putt to a well-guarded, and steeply sloping green.

Only a perfect drive at the 17th will avoid the water on the left and the trees on the right to leave the green

ing paradox so that those of modest ability might remain immune to many of the difficulties, while those with pretensions to being able to play remain constantly in the gravest peril. It is a course which becomes relatively easier the further back it is played.

There is not one weak hole here, but there are several great ones. All have their own challenge and each must be tackled with a specific plan and competent execution. The penalties for lack of imagination and judgement are severe indeed.

And yet Corfu is not intrinsically a difficult golf course. There is hardly a single hole which will not readily yield a birdie to good shotmaking and careful, circumspect judgement.

However, the par 4 9th from the championship tee is the exception that proves the rule. From the forward tee a long iron to the corner of the dogleg and a pitch are all that is normally needed, even when the breeze is against you. But the move to the back brings water into play down the left, and further aquatic problems on the right. You have more room there but in any way accessible. And the 18th has broken more hearts than Joan Collins.

FACILITIES

The clubhouse, with its restaurant and professional's shop one floor up and overlooking the large putting green and out to the course beyond, is in an idyllic setting.

The lower level bar is usually thinly populated because the appeal of enjoying a post round drink in the warm sunshine on the lawn in front of the clubhouse is quite irresistible.

The club has a first-class practice ground beside the first tee and caddycarts and clubs are available for hire from the pro shop.

By some standards the facilities might not appear lavish, but it is none the worse for that. One thing is certain: it would be hard to find a warmer and more friendly place to play golf.

The club has its own Corfu Amateur Championship, open to both sexes with official handicaps, and it attracts a large and regular following from all parts of Europe in the middle of May each year.

There are matchplay and strokeplay events on successive weeks with categories for all levels of ability. A follow-up event is held in October.

THE REGION

The island of Corfu has had a varied history. It has been in turn part of the Roman, Byzantine, Venetian, French and British empires. The British brought not only fine architecture, as in the Parliament House, but also apple chutney (eaten during the Christmas season), ginger beer and cricket. To this day, cricket is still played on a Sunday in Corfu Town.

ACCOMMODATION

There is a variety of accommodation available within very easy reach of the golf club. But a popular residence for golfers in Corfu is the Ermones Beach Hotel, less than two kilometres from the course. This hotel is uniquely terraced and overlooks the turquoise waters of Ermones Bay to the hills beyond. It offers excellent accommodation, a large swimming pool, shady lawns and a tranquil bay. A wide range of watersports is available with the sub aqua club particularly popular.

The Ermones restaurant offers international cuisine and local specialities and has its own Greek taverna.

The Hilton Hotel, as owner of the golf club, makes certain its golfing guests are particularly well catered for. Standards are those to be found in Hilton hotels renowned the world over with the Corfu Hilton noted particularly for its international cuisine.

More relaxed eating out in the area is mainly in local tavernas offering traditional Greek fare and some good wine which, although not now as cheap as it once was, is nonetheless still extremely good value for money.

Lunch at Maria's, or one of the other tavernas on the beach at Ermones after a morning round on the course, is almost an institution.

For the non-golfer, as well as the golfer, Corfu offers the perfect opportunity to relax and unwind.

8

Holland

There is a school of thought, and at times it has been a very vociferous one, which emphatically contends that the origins of golf are to be found in Holland. It cites the ancient game of *kolven*, or *kolf*, as the basis of its case but in truth any similarity to golf as we know it today is limited. While very little is known about the misty origins of the royal and ancient game, quite a lot is known about *kolven* which is still played to this day in Friesland and north Holland.

Although the Dutch stick and ball game was occasionally played outdoors on ice it was essentially an indoor activity played on a purpose-built kolf court. The players took aim at fixed marks, such as posts, and there exists much graphical evidence of the game in old Dutch paintings and engravings.

Neither the clubs nor the balls, however, were close to their golf equivalents in design. The ball was about the size of a cricket ball 'made perfectly round and elastic, covered with soft leather and sewed with fine wire' according to an account by the Rev. Walker in 1795.

The image of Holland that the armchair traveller expects and the visitor always treasures – the windmill, a stream and flat terrain.

The clubs had long and very stiff shafts. The heads were brass, perfectly smooth and had no loft, reinforcing the view that *kolf* and golf were separated by more than their initial letters.

But setting aside the argument over the origins of the game, the Dutch have undeniably contributed much to golf as we know it and play it today, although it is only in the last decade or so that the game has seen really major growth.

The golf boom of the 1980s certainly did not pass The Netherlands by and new courses have been built to meet an ever-increasing demand. Many are nine-hole layouts aimed at the newcomer to the game and in many cases have been built as part of, or alongside, a driving range.

This rapid course building programme has almost tripled the number of courses and gone a long way to help satisfy a genuine need for more facilities. However, it is for the more established clubs that The Netherlands is so well renowned. In fact, Holland can claim among its older clubs some of the finest in all of Europe.

The three which follow are a blend of the old and the new and representative of the marvellous traditions that are still so very much part of the game here.

Road communications are excellent in Holland, and in such a small country the itinerant golfer is never very far from a course. Tee times are not difficult to book although at many of the longer established clubs it is always best to call ahead for a reservation and check that the course is available to visitors on the day.

In addition to the courses featured, there is excellent golf to be found at many other courses throughout the country.

Hilversumsche Golf Club

FOUNDED 1910

WOODED BLISS

The Hilversumsche Golf Club, south-east of Amsterdam, is one of Holland's most exclusive clubs. Originally established as a private members' club, it maintains the great traditions it has built up over the years.

The course winds its way through woodland and forest and has many of the characteristics of the fine heathland courses around London. There are shades of Sunningdale here with the sandy subsoil and tree-lined fairways.

The club looks after its members and does not welcome visitors at weekends. They are, however, welcome on weekdays, but it is a good idea to book well in advance.

There are many comfortable hotels around Hilversum, including the Golden Tulip Jan Tabak hotel which has more than 100 rooms.

THE COURSE

Hilversumsche is a very fine test of golf and has been the venue for several Dutch Open Championships over the years. It is not over long by present day standards, but the tight fairways demand accuracy, particularly from the tee. Brain rather than brawn is the order of the day.

There are many fine holes on this layout. After a fairly calm opening par 5, which is ideal to get the player into his stride, the course begins to show its teeth and starts to become rather tougher.

The 2nd is a typical example. At only 310 metres from the back tee, length is not the problem, but the tee shot has to carry rough ground which crosses the fairway. Dense trees threaten on both sides. A good long iron is needed here to gain position for a short approach to a green well guarded by two bunkers in front.

Bigger hitters may be tempted to 'have a go' from the tee, but only the longest as well as the bravest will escape without disaster.

A dangerous bunker eats into the right side of the fairway at the 6th, forcing the tee shot towards trees on the left. The long approach shot here has to

> **Hilversumsche Golf Club**
>
> *Soestdijkerstraatweg 172,*
> *1213 XJ Hilversum*
> ◆
> Location: N201 near junction
> with A27 south–east of
> Hilversum
> Tel: (31) 35 85 70 60
> Course: 18 holes, 5859m,
> par 72
> Visitors: Welcome but must
> book in advance. No visitors
> at weekends
> Green fees: Dfl60-90

There's a symmetry about the bunker layout at the 5th; and what the bunkers miss, the heather will gobble up. Club selection for the approach shot here is vital.

negotiate two bunkers short of the green, and only two perfect shots will find the target.

The 411-metre par 4 15th is another hole out of the same mould. There are no bunkers in the fairway to threaten the drive but the fairway is narrow and hard to hit. Again, a very long iron is required if you are going to get up in two.

FACILITIES

The club has a pleasant bar and a popular restaurant. The locker room facilities are first-class, and very much in line with what visitors would expect from a club of this standing.

There are good practice facilities which are well used by pupils of Martin Morbey, the club's resident English professional.

THE REGION

Hilversumsche Golf Club lies only a short journey from Amsterdam, with its fine art collections and wonderful canals. However, there is plenty to see in the area without travelling far from the golf course.

Hilversum lies in the area known as Het Gooi, or the 'Garden of Amsterdam', one of the most attractive places in Holland. The deep forests are ideal for walking, cycling or horse riding, while there is sailing, wind-surfing and swimming on the nearby lakes of Gooimeer or the lJsselmeer. There is also parachuting and hot-air ballooning for the more intrepid.

And for the less energetic there are many cultural and historic sites in the region which are all worth visiting, including the charming old city of Naarden and the equally famous Muiderslot.

ACCOMODATION

Like most of the rest of Holland, the area around Hilversum has a wide range of accommodation for visitors, from small comfortable pensions right the way up to top rate hotels.

The Golden Tulip Jan Tabak hotel in Bussum, for instance, is close to the course and offers five-star accommodation and service. Less than half an hour from Schipol Airport, the hotel has over 100 rooms and suites, and caters both for the individual guest and for conferences.

The hotel also has an indoor swimming pool and offers a wide range of sporting facilities including some excellent all-weather tennis courts and cycling as well as a solarium and sauna.

And the hotel's elegant Bredius Restaurant offers a large variety of national and international dishes of the very highest standard.

Kennemer Golf & Country Club

F O U N D E D 1 9 1 0

CLASSIC LINKS AMONG THE SAND DUNES

Hanging in the magnificent thatched-roof clubhouse of the famous Kennemer Golf Club just outside Zandvoort is a 17th-century painting of a young golfer and his friend. Unsigned and painted around 1635, it is one of many artefacts in this historic Dutch club which reflect its respect for the early beginnings and the traditions of golf.

Kennemer was founded in 1910 and is the oldest of the major seaside courses in Holland. For the first 18 years of its existence it occupied a small nine-hole course near the village of Santpoort, and used an 18th-century mansion as its clubhouse.

In 1927 the club moved to its present location

The clubhouse at Kennemer reflects the Dutch influence on the game and exudes an opulence that bears comparison with the most exclusive clubs in the world.

outside the busy holiday town of Zandvoort. There, Harry S. Colt was given the task of building a new 18-hole layout amid the massive and spectacular sand dunes which are so much in evidence along this part of the Dutch coast.

Colt was famous for many fine courses in his career, including the Eden course at St Andrews, Moor Park in Leeds, Royal Portrush, St Cloud in northern France and the remarkable Pine Valley course in the United States. The last is generally regarded as one of the world's finest golf courses.

But Colt's layout on such a wonderful site at Kennemer must rank alongside anything he built elsewhere in the world. It is a magnificent natural links reminiscent of the great seaside links of Scotland, with huge dunes, rolling fairways and impenetrable rough of gorse and thicket.

Exposed as it is to the winds of the North Sea, the elements are as great a challenge as the Colt layout itself and Kennemer is one of the toughest courses to be found anywhere in the world. The Club has hosted almost a quarter of the international amateur

---

Kennemer Golf & Country Club

Kennemerweg 78, Postbus 85,
2040 AB Zandvoort
◆
Location: On the outskirts of
Zandvoort off N201
Tel: (31) 25 07 12 836
Courses: 3 of 9 holes
Pennink Course – 2996m, par 36
Van Hengel Course – 2952m, par 36
Colt Course – 3049m, par 36
Visitors: Welcome but should
book in advance
Green fees: Dfl100

---

championships and other international matches in the Netherlands, and has been a regular venue for the Dutch Open as well.

Very few changes have been made since Colt laid out the original course, and those that have been made are the work of another highly respected golf course architect, Frank Pennink. Pennink was given the task of building an additional nine holes which he duly completed very much in keeping with the style of Colt's original.

The Club rotates the three nine-hole layouts for their medal competitions. Each layout is named individually after the three men who left their indelible marks on the club.

The A course is known as the Van Hengel Course after Steven van Hengel, an eminent golf historian, a long-time member of the Kennemer club and leading figure in Dutch golf.

The second nine of the original course, the B, is named the Colt Course after its designer, and the C, or Pennink Course, completes the trio.

Overlooking the course, with its beautiful crisp seaside turf on the fairways and firm, fast links greens, is one of the finest clubhouses in the world.

Designed by famous Dutch architect, A.P. Smits, this magnificent building with its thatched roof sits on the highest point on the course and has a commanding view over the links. Inside you cannot escape the sense of antiquity redolent of the great historic clubs on the east coast of Scotland.

A perfect view to the golfer – a flat green, a single bunker and some width on the fairway. And on the horizon, one of the most attractive clubhouses in Europe.

The magnificent clubhouse with its distinctive thatched roof sits on the highest part of the course. The facilities are first class and it extends a warm welcome to all who play here.

THE COURSES

All three layouts present a tough challenge. The fairways are generous of width but the rough is severe and punishing. With a wind whistling off the sea many of the holes are formidable, and only great accuracy from the tee will find any reward.

There are many fine holes at Kennemer with the 10th on the original course, and the 7th on the Pennink layout, among the most memorable.

The 10th on the Colt Course offers the opportunity for one of the most satisfying drives from a high tee close to the clubhouse, across a valley wilderness to a fairway which turns slightly to the right up to the green. At 330 metres it is not a long hole from the championship tee, but it is a demanding drive as well as a satisfying one. The second shot is played to a narrow green with two deep and treacherous bunkers guarding the front.

The 7th on the Pennink Course is another relatively short par 4 but the drive is blind to a fairway which falls away over the top of a ridge. The second shot is played across a wide fairway bunker to a small green which has no bunkers at all. The wind is the major factor here once the fairway has been successfully reached from the tee.

FACILITIES

As you would expect from one of the leading clubs in Europe, Kennemer has very fine facilities for its members, and for the visitors to whom it extends a warm welcome. The locker rooms are first class and there is a traditional bar and a fine restaurant.

The Club does welcome non-members but they should book well in advance. The exceptions are on Tuesdays (Ladies' Day) or on Fridays (when visiting parties take precedence).

The club has a small but very well-stocked professional's shop run by Jim Buchanan, a Scot who reflects the continuing association between Holland and the Home of Golf.

but there is still a wealth of international motor sport on the circuit throughout the season.

ACCOMMODATION

Because it is such a popular holiday destination there is no shortage of hotel accommodation in the area. For those who like a base with plenty of activity, the Hotel Grandorado can hardly be bettered.

There is a wildness about Kennemer which can surprise the first-time visitor. And although the fairways are quite generous, the heather is merciless.

THE REGION

The area around Zandvoort has much to offer the tourist as well as the golfer. The town itself is a major holiday centre with miles of golden sand and a wide range of beach facilities.

Close to the golf club, and certainly within earshot, is the Zandvoort motor racing circuit which for many years hosted the Dutch Grand Prix. Formula One is no longer seen on this famous circuit,

It is a large hotel which specifically caters for activity holidays. Indoor tennis courts, badminton courts, squash courts, a bowling alley and a fine swimming pool complex are among a wide range of sporting facilities on offer. There is certainly no reason to be idle here.

The hotel has modern rooms with excellent facilities and also offers a range of self-catering accommodation in its own village.

Noordwijkse Golfclub

FOUNDED 1915

THE PERFECT BLEND

There has been golf played near the seaside town of Noordwijk since 1915. Ernst Cremers was the man who brought the Noordwijkse Golf Club into being when a nine-hole layout was built in the sand dunes outside the town.

But the club has had a chequered existence. After the Second World War the course was lost to housing, and in 1972 it was moved to the present site, seven kilometres outside the town.

Frank Pennink, who was much involved at Kennemer not far along the coast, was called in to design the new 18-hole layout, again among the sand dunes. He produced a stern and classic test which

No, these tulips have nothing to do with Amsterdam. They are grown here at Noordwijk.

winds its way between great sandhills and through some beautiful forest areas.

Although it is different in character from Kennemer, it is no less of a challenge and has hosted the Dutch Open no fewer than eight times since the course was opened on its present site.

The clubhouse sits high on a sandhill overlooking a vast stretch of pure links land, which almost demands golf courses to be built upon it. However, the environmental lobby in Holland is currently very strong and, despite the popularity of the game here, there seems little immediate prospect of any more courses being built here.

In fact there are parts of the Noordwijk club which are set aside as areas of special scientific interest. They are roped off and players are given a free drop from within them to preserve the rare flowers and plants.

Noordwijkse Golfclub
Randweg 25, 2204 AL
Noordwijk
◆
Location: Seven kilometres north of Noordwijk
Tel: (31) 25 23 73 761
Course: 18 holes, 5875m, par 72
Visitors: Welcome but must make a reservation. No play between noon and 3 pm. on weekdays. Visitors must play with a member at weekends
Green Fees: Dfl100

THE COURSE

The first tee looks out over a fairway which presents a leisurely opening hole of only 348 metres, usually played downwind. Do not be lulled into a false sense

Pure links golf that bears comparison with any other links course in Europe. This is the 8th, a truly magnificent hole.

of security, though, for it is simply a warming-up hole for the great struggle ahead.

The long, narrow stretch of fairway which snakes its way more than 522 metres from the championship tee is immediate proof of what to expect. A small pool, unusual on such a classic links course, threatens the drive and there is out-of-bounds over the driving range fence for the wild slice.

The next, a modest par 3 of 152 metres, requires a solid middle iron to a green protected front, left and behind by trees. On the right of the green is a bunker. Here, the course starts to make its way through the challenging forest section.

Great stands of mature pines line the fairways in this part of the course, putting the premium on accuracy until the open dune land is reached again at the 8th. The long par 5 9th, which returns close to the clubhouse, is a fearsome challenge – usually into a prevailing wind.

It is pure links golf from here on, over fairways which wend their way between and over massive sand dunes, in much the same style as Royal Aberdeen or St George's.

Noordwijk is one of a triumvirate of great links courses on this stretch of Dutch coastline. Kennemer and The Hague complete the trio.

FACILITIES

The modern clubhouse at Noordwijk has marvellous panoramic views from the bar and restaurant both of which are open to members and visitors seven days a week, except in the winter months when they are closed on Mondays. The restaurant offers fine food in extremely pleasant surroundings.

The club has a first-class practice ground complete with four practice holes, and nearby the Noordwijk Golf Centre has an excellent driving range with a nine-hole par 3 course and a fine restaurant.

THE REGION

There is no shortage of interest for non-golfers in the area around Noordwijk. The town boasts Europe's first major, permanent space exhibition, Noordwijk Space Expo, which is also the Visitors' Centre for ESTEC, which in turn is the heart of the European Space Agency, ESA.

Visitors can spend an hour or a full day at the exhibition and see samples of moon rock, rocket engines and even a space station. Launches of European satellites in the Ariane programme can be seen live in the auditorium.

Noordwijk is an ideal starting point to explore the region. It is close to the lake-land area and the university town of Leiden is just 10 kilometres away. Also close by is Rijnsburg, home of the flower auction centre where millions of fresh flowers are bought, sold and distributed. In August, the annual Rijnsburg Flower Parade visits several towns in the area, including Noordwijk and presents a marvellous collection of flower-covered floats. Noordwijk also has an international jazz festival in September.

Amsterdam with its circling canals and its great art treasures is a 40-minute drive away.

ACCOMODATION

When it comes to accommodation, Noordwijk can claim a wide choice from comfortable small pensions to one of the grand hotels of continental Europe.

The Grand Hotel Huis ter Duin has been setting the tone in hospitality and comfort for over a hundred years. This marvellous hotel was built in 1887 by Heinrich Tappenbeck on a superb beach setting and offers a level of service and hospitality of which it is justifiably proud and for which it is renowned all over the world.

Major renovations were made to the hotel in the 1980s in the run-up to the hotel's centenary celebrations in 1987, but the hotel was severely damaged in a fire in 1990. It was a fire which tragically claimed the lives of three fire-fighters. Miraculously, the hotel was rebuilt in a record time of 11 months.

The hotel is a gourmet's paradise with a restaurant for every mood. The Latour Restaurant which dates back to the very early days of the hotel now provides its guests with a breathtaking view out to sea and a spectacular menu and cellar.

Today this five-star hotel has 18 public and conference rooms including the magnificent Royal Lounge in the original part of the Grand Hotel which, mercifully, was saved from the fire.

The dining room at the Grand Hotel Huis ter Duin. Although there was a fire here in 1990, the hotel quickly recovered its former opulence and grandeur.

9

Ireland

Spectacular scenery and fantastic golf courses await the visiting golfer to Ireland. And when to that combination is added the wonderful warmth of the welcome of the Irish, it is not hard to understand why it is one of the greatest countries in the world to enjoy the game.

The country is festooned with wonderful golf courses, most of which are quiet and positively idyllic for the visitor. There are close to 300 from which to choose, from great championship links beside the sea to hidden little gems in the country. Everywhere there is the Irish sense of humour and fun and amazing hospitality. When it comes to analysing the drama of the golfing day, there is nowhere on earth quite like the 19th hole of an Irish golf club in the company of friends and a glass or two of Irish stout.

The oldest club in Ireland, but only by a whisker, is Royal Belfast which was founded in 1881. Royal Dublin came along only a few years later as the game spread from across the water in Scotland.

There are other courses of great antiquity, too. Portmarnock, one of the greatest golf courses in the world, dates back to 1894. In the days just after the club was founded by W.C. Pickeman and George Ross, the only way to Portmarnock was by rowing a boat across the estuary from Sutton. Today it is accessible from Dublin by road but it remains a remote spot.

The magic of Ireland – green grass, menacing mountains and mysterious waters.

There are many other remote spots across the country harbouring magnificent golf courses set among the most glorious scenery.

In the north there are more than 80 courses in beautiful settings from seaside links to delightful inland layouts as well as the renowned championship links of Royal Portrush and Royal County Down.

On the sunshine circuit of the south-east of Ireland there is a wealth of great challenges, from the marvellous seaside links at Rosslare, to the new and quite outstanding Mount Juliet course in Kilkenny designed by Jack Nicklaus.

In the south-west the great courses of Lahinch and Ballybunion beckon along with Killarney and Waterville.

The list is almost endless, and everywhere the visiting golfer goes in this mystical land he will find the same warm welcome, quiet courses, and green fees that would bring a smile to the face of a bankrupt Aberdonian.

With good roads throughout Ireland, it is easier to explore the country's golfing gems than ever before, and it is an experience that should not be missed.

Ballybunion Golf Club

FOUNDED 1893

MAJESTIC AND UNFORGETTABLE

It requires some effort to get to Ballybunion but the rewards for persistence are well worth it. For here, tucked away in the deep south-west of Ireland in County Kerry, lies one of the truly great links golf courses of the world.

Set among the giant sand dunes, scattered along a shoreline of outstanding beauty and splendour, is the golf course which five times Open Champion, Tom Watson, rates so highly that he makes regular private visits to enjoy the very best of links golf.

The club itself dates back to 1896, but two years after it was founded, it ran into a severe financial crisis and a final entry was recorded in the minute book of 1898. However, thanks to the intervention of a retired Indian Army officer, Colonel Bartholomew, the fortunes of the club were revived.

Together with a small group of associates he formed the club as it exists today and brought in Lionel Hewson, former editor of Irish Golf, to lay out nine holes. It was another 21 years before the course was extended to 18 holes but, by 1937, Ballybunion was thought of highly enough to be chosen to host the Men's Irish Close Championship.

In the late 1970s the course was under severe threat from coastal erosion and a campaign was launched to save it. 'Friends of Ballybunion', under the leadership of Jackie Hourigan, raised more than £100,000 for the appeal and the erosion was halted.

THE COURSE

Before the 1937 Irish Men's Close Championship the club brought in the architect Tom Simpson to suggest some changes. But he found little that needed to be done and confined his labours to the re-siting of three greens and the addition of a fairway bunker at what is now the first hole.

In 1971 the order of the holes was changed when a new clubhouse was built. The course now begins at the original 14th hole, but the controversial bunker left over from the 1937 changes is still known as 'Mrs Simpson' – presumably in honour of the great man's wife.

Ballybunion's 11th hole, which runs along the top of the cliff, is one of the most dramatic in the game of golf. Often exposed to the fierce wind from the sea, it presents a daunting challenge, with a huge dune on the left of the fairway and a green guarded by two enormous sandhills.

The 16th is not the longest of the five par 3s but, at 216 yards, it is the toughest. The green presents a tiny target, with a huge sandhill threatening on the left and a punitive bunker on the other side.

Ballybunion Golf Club

Ballybunion, Co. Kerry

◆

Location: One mile outside Ballybunion on the L106

Tel: (353) 6827 146

Courses: Old – 18 holes, 6542yds, par 72; Cashen – 18 holes, 6477yds, par 72

Visitors: Welcome at any time. Pre-booking at weekends recommended

Green fees: Old £30; Cashen £20; joint £45

The 6th green on the Old Course. It's not difficult to see why five times Open Champion, Tom Watson, rates Ballybunion as one of the finest links courses in the world.

Although it is played downhill it is brutally demanding, particularly into the teeth of the wind which blasts in from the Atlantic.

A wasteland of rough sand known as the 'Sahara' has to be crossed at the 18th just as the hole takes a sharp turn to the left after the tee shot. This wasteland represents a very interesting feature to the finish of this famous links. The second shot is blind to the green adding even more mystery to a fine finishing hole.

The great American golf writer, Herb Warren Wind, assessed the

The Ballybunion clubhouse opens its doors to all who brave her course in true welcoming Irish fashion.

Old Course at Ballybunion as the finest seaside course he had ever seen. Tom Watson, one of the course's most famous regular visitors, is on record as sharing his view. It is hard to put up a case against it.

In the early 1980s, American course architect Robert Trent Jones was asked to design a second course at Ballybunion. He was so impressed by the piece of ground he was given to work on that he declared it was 'the finest piece of linksland I have ever seen'.

The natural – if demanding – terrain at the 10th, also on the Old Course, ensures that it is a hole that has everything.

There are some who feel the Cashen Course is even more dramatic than the original. Certainly the dunes are bigger and some of the carries are as demanding as anywhere else in the world of golf.

The course finishes with two par 5s, one of which is 612 yards long. At this point, most intrepid players will be ready to relax. They will not be disappointed.

FACILITIES

The members love golf and they love to share it with visitors. Ballybunion, in true Irish tradition, boasts a wonderful clubhouse in which to reflect on the day's dramas on the course.

The 19th hole is ideally placed between the two courses and it would be hard to find a friendlier, more blissful place to be.

A convivial bar and a good dining room are there to be enjoyed by all, and the locker room and other facilities are first-class.

THE REGION

County Kerry is Ireland's most popular tourist area. Internationally known places like Killarney, Cabirciveen, Derrynane and the Iveragh and Dingle Peninsulas come immediately to mind.

It is an area of outstanding scenic variety from majestic mountains to glorious beaches, sparkling lakes and cascading waterfalls.

Taking a break from the golf to drive round the 'Ring of Kerry' is an experience not to be missed. This 100-mile round trip on the spectacular Iveragh Peninsula offers a panorama of breathtaking seascapes, mature woodland and Ireland's finest mountains.

There is almost a Continental air about the charming villages of Sneem and Waterville where palm trees and fuchsia take the first-time visitor by surprise.

The stately Muckross House should be on every itinerary and an end-of-the-day tour in a jaunting car is still everyone's favourite.

ACCOMMODATION

Killarney boasts many fine hotels including the Great Southern, the Castlerosse and Cahernane. But for those wishing to stay in Ballybunion itself, the Golf Hotel and Cliff House Hotel are both very well appointed. The Marine Hotel is more intimate and has a fine seafood restaurant.

Take your choice and enjoy the experience.

Killarney Golf Club

FOUNDED 1893

A BREATH OF PARADISE

Killarney is Ireland's most famous beauty spot and the perfect spot to relax and let the cares of the world slip by. It is the perfect golfing run-in to the great links courses of County Kerry. This is parkland golf rather than heathland or links and a wonderful pipe-opener for either Lahinch or Ballybunion.

Much has been done in recent years to attract tourists to a remote area. As a result there is much for the non-golfer to enjoy and which might also encourage the player to tarry a while longer before pressing on to the greater challenges ahead.

There has been golf played in these parts for a hundred years, but the first course was a modest affair built in a deer park owned by the Earl of Kenmare. In 1936 the Earl's heir, Lord Castlerosse, brought in Sir Guy Campbell to lay out a course that would do greater justice to the natural beauty of the area. The 18-hole layout was officially opened in 1939.

Lord Castlerosse, far from being merely the developer of the project, became actively involved in the actual design work and continued to suggest a number of improvements right up until his death in 1943.

Another 18 holes were built in the 1970s and the two present courses, Mahoney's Point and Killeen, are a combination of the original course and the new holes. Together they form part of the Killarney Golf and Fishing Club.

There is no more beautiful setting than the shores of Lough Leane with the splendour of Macgillicuddy's Reeks and Carrantuohill, the highest mountain in Ireland, as backdrops. Kerry County Airport is currently extending its runway to allow jets to land there. At only eight miles from Killarney, access to the course will be much easier.

THE COURSES

Of the many great courses to be found in this rather special corner of Ireland, Killarney is the most accessible. Only eight kilometres from Cork, the club sits at the starting point of the hundred-mile Ring of Kerry Road with some of the most beautiful scenery in the world.

The spectacular finishing holes of Mahoney's Point have contributed their part to earning the course international renown.

The Killeen Course, apart from being longer, shares all the same charm and challenge of its more illustrious neighbour and it hosted the Irish Open in both 1991 and 1992.

There are great holes on both courses with the 1st,

Killarney Golf and Fishing Club

Mahoney's Point, Killarney,

County Kerry

◆

Location: Three miles west
of the town off Killorglin Road

Tel: (353) 64 31034

Courses: Mahoney's Point –
18 holes, 6500yds, par 72;

Killeen – 18 holes, 7000yds,
par 72

Visitors: Welcome at any time.
Some weekend restrictions

Green fees: £26

The 18th on Mahoney's Point (top) has been described as the best short hole in the world. But whether you play this course or its sister, Killeen, there can be no more beautiful setting (above).

A par 3 of 210 yards, it demands a tee shot across the edge of the lake to a green surrounded by rhododendron bushes and trees, not to mention some sinister bunkers.

It was this hole which prompted the late Henry Longhurst to comment that it was in his opinion 'the best short hole in the world'.

FACILITIES

A new £1,000,000 clubhouse provides members and visitors with everything they could wish for. There is a warm and friendly bar and a first-class dining room; in fact the Killarney clubhouse is everything that the modern clubhouse should be with a little bit still in hand.

The club will be hosting the Curtis Cup in 1996.

THE REGION

Killarney is the place of which it was once said: 'See what the Almighty can do when He's in a good mood.' The millions of visitors who have made the journey there over the years are testament to that.

The beauty of Killarney is remarkable. The lake by the side of the golf course is overshadowed only by the mountains and the remarkable Macgillicuddy's Reeks.

ACCOMMODATION

Killarney has plenty of good hotels and other accommodation. Among the best are the Great Southern Hotel, the Castlerosse Hotel and the attractive Kathleen's Country House less than two miles from the town centre.

the 3rd and the 13th the pick on the Killeen, while Mahoney's Point saves the best for last.

The famous Killarney finish begins at the 16th as the course swings back towards Lough Leane. It is a tough par 5 of 500 yards, immediately followed by another beautiful and testing par 4 of 410 yards.

However, it is the last hole at Mahoney's Point which everyone who plays there remembers for a long time after they have left.

Lahinch Golf Club

FOUNDED 1893

THE ST ANDREWS OF IRELAND

On Good Friday in 1892 the Lahinch Golf Club was founded on the rugged coastline of County Clare, two miles from the spectacular Cliffs of Moher.

Lahinch Golf Club

Lahinch, County Clare.

◆

Location: 30 miles north-west of Ennis on T69

Tel: (353) 658 1003

Courses: Old Course – 18 holes, 6699yds, par 72.

Castle Course – 18 holes, 5265yds, par 67

Visitors: Welcome at any time

Green fees: Old £25, Castle £15

Old Tom Morris had come over from St Andrews to lay out the golf course but, other than setting out the greens and the tees, he felt there was little else he needed to do. He declared: 'I consider the links is as fine a natural course as it has ever been my privilege to play over.'

The qualities which Old Tom recognized more than a century ago have stood the test of time and, as any visitor will tell you, are as relevant today as they were then.

This is a magnificent links course. It isn't perhaps as difficult as Portmarnock or Ballybunion, but it is a supreme test of shotmaking just the same.

In 1928, shortly before he built Augusta National with Bobby Jones, the great golf course architect Dr Alister Mackenzie reworked the original layout. Since then the course has changed very little, although it was lengthened slightly in order to accommodate the Home Internationals in 1987.

When Mackenzie completed his work he com-

mented: 'Lahinch will make the finest and most popular course that I, or I believe anyone else, has ever constructed.'

Those who have had the good fortune to play this wonderful course will have no reason at all to disagree with the good doctor.

The course lies some 40 miles north-west of Limerick and overlooks Liscannor Bay. It is not the easiest place in the world to get to but the effort is certainly worthwhile.

The club is only 30 miles from Shannon International Airport, and this is a popular access point for many visiting the area.

You'll need to be on line at the 4th to find the green which is jealously guarded by three treacherous bunkers.

THE COURSES

Lahinch is not as long as some of its famous sisters in the Emerald Isle, but what it lacks in length in makes up for in the premium on accurate shotmaking from tee to green.

Anything straying from the line will find trouble in the sand dunes. As with most Alister Mackenzie courses, many of the greens sit on plateaux and can be very difficult to hit and hold.

But even Mackenzie was not allowed to touch the 5th and 6th, the two

The ruins of Lahinch castle sit casually beside the 7th green, blending into this wonderful course with perfect harmony.

best-known holes at Lahinch. The 5th, known as Klondyke, is a par 5 of a little under 500 yards with a blind second shot over a huge sandhill.

The next, known as Dell, is a short hole of only 156 yards, but the green is blind from the tee and the only indication of line for the player is a white marker stone set into the fronting hill.

There are shades of the 5th at Prestwick here, and since Old Tom was for many years Keeper of the Green at that famous Ayrshire course where the first ever Open Championship was played, it is perhaps hardly surprising.

The second course at Lahinch is much shorter and played on flatter terrain. It lies just across the road from the Old Course and offers an interesting and enjoyable alternative to its more illustrious sister.

The fairways make their way around the remains of O'Brien's Castle and there is challenge here enough for all but the most ardent golfing masochist.

FACILITIES

The Lahinch clubhouse is small but warm and friendly. Hospitality in these parts is legendary, with no shortage of good wholesome Irish fare and the odd drop of stout always available.

At one time, goats used to graze on the dunes and were considered the best of all the weather forecasters. If the going was about to get tough they would make their way towards the clubhouse.

Sadly, the Lahinch goats are no longer to be seen, victims of some so far unexplained malady.

THE REGION

Lahinch lies in one of the most beautiful parts of all Ireland. The Shannon Region offers a wealth of attractions, sporting activities and entertainment.

The beauty of the River Shannon, the majesty of the Cliffs of Moher and the Burren National Park attract many thousands of visitors each year.

There are medieval castle banquets, traditional Irish pub music and some wonderful Irish theatre in addition to many other major visitor attractions.

Away from the pressures of the course, and set on the rugged coastline of County Clare, the coastal village of Lahinch is a tourist's delight.

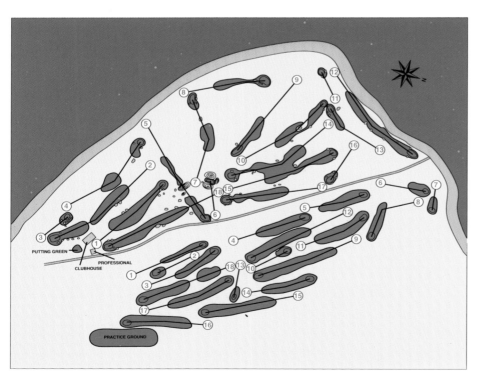

Lahinch: the Old (red) and Castle (blue) courses.

There is also great game and course fishing as well as sea-angling and other water activities on Lough Derg, Ireland's 32,000 acre pleasure lake.

And if you are still looking for more golf, there are 21 great courses in the area in addition to Lahinch!

ACCOMMODATION

There is no shortage of choice when it comes to finding a hotel in the Shannon region.

The Aberdeen Arms Hotel is always popular with visitors to Lahinch, while in the north of the County the Gregans Castle Hotel in Ballyvaughan enjoys a well-deserved reputation.

For those who want something a little special Adare Manor, only a 20-minute drive from Limerick, will not disappoint. Formerly the home of the Earls of Dunraven, Adare Manor is a Grade A listed hotel and sits grandly in the grounds of its own 840 acre estate.

There is excellent salmon fishing and horse-riding nearby and the hotel is shortly to have its own 18-hole golf course in play.

The hotel offers the very best in both French and Irish cuisine and – as you'd expect – has an extensive wine cellar.

Portmarnock Golf Club

FOUNDED 1894

NATURAL AND MAGNIFICENT

Played from the very back tees at more than 7000 yards, it is not difficult to understand why the great South African player and four-times winner of the Open Championship, Bobby Locke, rated the magnificent links of Portmarnock in County Dublin among the very finest and most testing anywhere to be found in Europe.

However, from the normal tees and with a bit of firmness in the ground and roll on the ball, it is less fearsome and perhaps more enjoyable for the 'average' golfer than many other courses.

Water surrounds the course on three sides, and in its earliest days it was only reachable by boat.

Like many another of its calibre there is little documentation of its beginnings, but it seems that in 1893 two men, J.W. Pikeman and George Ross, rowed across the estuary to the peninsula on which Portmarnock now stands. What they found was a wilderness of sand dune and bracken inhabited only by a community of farmers and fishermen.

It was a remote spot, despite the fact that it was only 10 miles from Dublin, but somehow Pikeman and Ross felt it was the ideal place for a golf course. There already had been a course of sorts there owned by the Irish whiskey family, Jameson, close to where the short 15th now stands.

The present course has two loops of nine holes which return to the clubhouse and the original nine holes were laid out in much the same area as the front nine today. Four years after the first nine were built, the course was extended to 18 holes and basic clubhouse accommodation was provided by a humble shed.

Today the clubhouse which shines white in the sun is a much more elegant affair than the shack which burn-ed down in 1904. But the welcome inside is just as warm now as it undoubtedly was then,

> **Portmarnock Golf Club**
>
> *Portmarnock, County Dublin*
> ◆
> Location: Eight miles
> north-east of Dublin.
> Tel: (353) 1846 2968
> Course: (Championship)
> 18 holes, 7147yds, par 72
> Visitors: Welcome at any time
> but pre-booking is advisable
> Green fees: £40-50

The clubhouse at Portmarnock offers its own unique blend of refreshment and hospitality. It's not usually as busy as this – the picture was taken during the Irish Open of 1986.

The 14th. On a calm, sunny day; there's not much to threaten par here, apart from the heather. But when the wind blows, it is a different matter altogether.

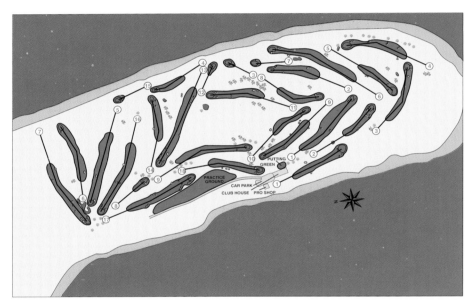

The Portmarnock courses: the Championship (red) and the 9 holes (blue).

discovery. There are many strange stories attached to the passage across the estuary from Sutton but none stranger, and perhaps more apocryphal, than that concerning the club ferryman who had a disagreement with a clergyman on the crossing. The ferryman was not renowned for his tolerance and it is said that the unfortunate cleric, who was not apparently of the same faith as his captain, did not make it across the water to Portmarnock.

THE COURSE

Those who travel there today will find an examination of the most testing nature. Like many of its contemporaries, Portmarnock is a place of moods governed by wind and weather. On a sunny and calm day looking across the estuary to Ireland, there is a magic about the place; yet it can transform almost in an instant to put on a fierce and forbidding face.

making its contribution to that great, indefinable quality which makes golf in Ireland so very special.

Like all the great links courses, Portmarnock owes more to nature than to the hand of man. However, Fred G. Hawtree made some changes to the original layout and his son Fred W. laid out a third nine holes in the early 1960s.

Today you get to the course by road, but many years ago it could only be reached by the ferry which Pikeman and Ross used on their original voyage of

There are no hidden problems at Portmarnock. It is an honest course with inherent difficulty, and the terrain is quite sufficient to provide a wonderful challenge without recourse to modern trickeries.

Portmarnock has hosted many fine tournaments over the years including the Dunlop Masters, The Canada Cup (now the World Cup), the Irish Open and the 1991 Walker Cup.

In 1949 Portmarnock hosted the only Amateur Championship to be played outside the boundaries of the United Kingdom.

When the course was extended originally to 18 holes it measured just over 5800 yards. However, the improvements in equipment, and particularly in the golf ball, have meant that the length was extended to more than 7100 yards for top professional events.

Of the par 4s, seven are more than 400 yards in length and two of the three par 5s measure more than 560 yards.

Despite the length and challenge of this great links, when the wind does not blow and it has been softened by some rain, not even Portmarnock can offer much defence against the great players. When Bernhard Langer won his second Carroll's Irish Open in 1987, his worst round was 68 and his winning total of 269 was no fewer than 19 strokes under the card of the composite course.

FACILITIES

Like many of its contemporaries in Ireland and Scotland the Portmarnock clubhouse is designed strictly with golfers in mind. There are no prissy frills here, just a wonderful old club where the hospitality is traditionally Irish and the welcome always friendly.

Inevitably the bar is the centre of attraction but the club dining room is excellent and always ready to accommodate the healthiest appetite.

Caddies are available by arrangement and a good investment on first acquaintance with this great course. There are, however, no practice facilities.

THE REGION

Portmarnock is only a short drive from the centre of Dublin where there is much to see and do away from the golf course.

This is the city of wide Georgian squares and avenues, landmarks and public buildings, and brick-fronted townhouses, each with its own unique, colourfully painted door.

Among the places of interest that should be on any Dublin itinerary are St Patrick's Cathedral, where Jonathan Swift was once Dean, and 400-year-old Trinity College.

There are castles to visit, traditional Irish dinners to be eaten, with as often as not rousing Irish music to accompany them, and there is always the humour and warmth of this friendliest of cities. Malahide Castle is also well worth a visit and the golfer needing a little time to relax could do worse than take a trip on the Dublin Rail Transit system, known to Dubliners as the 'Dart'. The scenery on the Dublin Bay Rail trip is quite breathtaking.

ACCOMMODATION

There is a vast choice of hotels and other accommodations in the Dublin area and close to Portmarnock.

In Malahide, the Grand Hotel is an excellent base from which to enjoy the delights of both Portmarnock and of Dublin itself. Less expensive than the major hotels of the city centre, it offers first-class facilities and the usual warm Irish welcome.

You'll need to be on target here, otherwise the shrubbery or even the beach beckons. The greens are magnificent.

Royal County Down Golf Club

FOUNDED 1889

IN THE SHADOW OF THE MOUNTAINS OF MOURNE
In a glorious setting in the shadow of the Mountains of Mourne, where the peak of Slieve Donard reaches 2800 feet into the sky, lies the magnificent links of the Royal County Down Golf Club.

Rated by many as one of the most difficult golf courses in the world, it is nonetheless a serenely beautiful place. The views are as spectacular as the golf, and on a clear day if you look west out to sea, you can see the Isle of Man some 40 miles away. And if you look east, the hills of Ballynahinch complete a picture of staggering beauty and splendour.

Some say that, next to Pine Valley in the United States, Royal County Down is the most challenging golf course in the world. The great Welshman, the late Dai Rees, captain of the last successful British Ryder Cup team before assistance arrived from the Continent, felt this to be the case.

There is everything a player could wish for on this marvellous links with splendid individual holes running through narrow valleys of rich, crisp turf, flanked by great swathes of gorse which splash their golden colour across the course in early summer. Wild roses and uncompromising sand dunes add to the severity of the test and help concentrate the mind, but whatever sort of round you are experiencing it is difficult to resist the stunning views all around.

According to the minutes of the club which was formed in March 1889, Old Tom Morris laid out the original course for the princely sum of £4. Since Old Tom was in the habit of charging £1 a day for his labour (plus expenses), we have a good idea of how long he spent on his layout.

Whether the warm-hearted hospitality of the Irish was responsible for his protracted stay (the great man

This is one of the great settings for a clubhouse. You'll find no multi-gyms or tennis courts here – just a unique ambience that the Club jealously and rightly guards.

would often require only a single day to lay out a course), or whether it was a particular devotion to the project, history does not record.

> **Royal County Down Golf Club**
>
> *Newcastle, County Down,*
> *BT33 0AN*
> ◆
> Location: 30 miles south of Belfast
> Tel: 03967-23314
> Course: 18 holes, 6968 yards, par 72
> Visitors: Welcome with the exception of Saturdays
> Green fees: £40-55

We do know, however, that he played the nine holes already existing, over the space of two days when he first came here.

When he departed, he left behind a plan for a full 18 holes which were quickly built, and within a short period the club had gained a reputation as having one of the finest golf courses in all of Ireland.

The course later underwent reconstruction much influenced by George Combe, a founder member of the club and Captain in 1895-96. As chairman of the green committee for many years, Combe had a strong influence in the development of the course and was largely responsible for the evolution of the layout to take the form of two loops of nine holes, each returning to the clubhouse.

At that time, the vast majority of courses were nine holes out and nine back, and the establishment of a returning nine was revolutionary. Shortly after the turn of the century, more changes were made on the recommendation of the then club professional, Seymour Dunn, and four years later by Harry Vardon.

The dogleg 9th which calls for a blind shot from the tee. It is not an easy hole by any means but the magnificent views tend to compensate.

In 1926 the highly respected architect Harry Colt recommended some additional changes which were carried out.

The Course

Over the years the course has changed little. Although there are five holes which call for blind shots from the tee – the 2nd, 5th, 6th, 9th and 15th – and others which demand blind shots to the green, the course loses nothing of its charm because of them.

At 200 yards or more in length, three of the short holes are very demanding, while only the 9th among the long holes is under 500 yards. Stretched to championship length, Royal County Down is only a few feet short of 7000 yards with a par of 72. This, allied to narrow fairways and tight greens, creates the most searching of golfing challenges for even the very best players.

The extent of that challenge is obvious from the very first tee. The drive to a narrow fairway in a valley

This is as good a view of the 3rd and the 4th at County Down as you'll ever see with the Mountains of Mourne sweeping down to the sea.

with sandhills on either side demands a long and straight opening shot. And even the extraordinary view down to the first green contributes to the strain.

All the par 3 holes at Royal County Down are magnificent. The 4th is no exception, although it is not the toughest of them, but it still requires a carry of more than 200 yards over gorse to a long green protected by no fewer than 10 bunkers, the majority of them placed to catch a sliced or short tee shot.

The 5th is one of the great holes at Royal County Down. A dogleg to the right from the tee, it invites the player to cut off as much as he dare with a blind drive across an area of heathery scrub. If he negotiates that element successfully, he is faced with a longish second shot to a green protected by menacing bunkers and backed by sand dunes.

A good drive is a must at the 445-yard 13th, another hole which turns to the right all the way along its length. It requires two demanding shots, with the second of them blind and over a hill.

The weaker the drive the further over the rough of clinging heather must the second be struck to reach the green. A single bunker protects the left approach. Gorse and wild flowers abound in the duneland around the curve of Dundrum Bay making this one of the most idyllic places on earth to play golf.

The club has hosted many important events including the Irish Amateur which is a regular visitor. But the Amateur Championship has also been played there when Michael Bonallack completed a memorable hat-trick of victories in 1970.

FACILITIES

The Royal County Down Golf Club is, first and foremost, a golf club and offers its visitors all the necessary facilities you would expect. However, those looking for saunas and multi-gyms had best look elsewhere. They are not at the top of the list of priorities in this part of County Down.

Practice facilities are also restricted to a short area and there are some catering restrictions at the weekends which may disappoint some.

The Royal County Down ethos is about the golf course and the great traditions of the game which it jealously protects.

And it is all the better for that.

THE REGION

Newcastle County Down lies 30 miles to the south of Belfast, where 'the Mountains of Mourne sweep down to the sea'. It is hard for the golfer to tear himself away from this magical spot but perhaps the lure of Royal Portrush to the north will tempt him onward.

On the drive up the Antrim coast to the north from Belfast, the main Northern Ireland port of Larne – known as the gateway to the Nine Glens of Antrim – is only 21 miles away.

For 25 miles to the north of Larne, the A2 coast road runs along the water's edge on one side and under steep cliffs on the other. The road passes through the villages of the Glens on a truly memorable journey to Cushendall.

The road to the coastal village of Cushendum takes a steady nerve to navigate, but the rewards are worthwhile. A narrow road of steep gradients and sharp bends winds its way around the north-east coast from where there are unforgettable views of the Antrim coast. On a clear day you can even see across to Scotland.

This is wonderful touring country with many interesting and historical places to encourage a regular stop before the journey reaches Portrush. This is Northern Ireland's premier seaside resort and home of the only golf club off the mainland which has yet hosted the Open Championship.

The 5th is one of the great holes at County Down. The green is guarded by some menacing bunkers and is backed by sand dunes. A par here is a job well done.

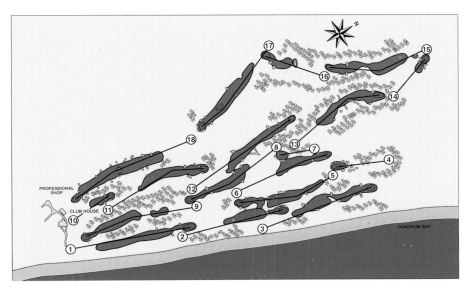

The Royal County Down Course.

ACCOMMODATION

The Slieve Donard Hotel is almost on the golf course for those who wish to spend some time at Royal County Down. Alternatively, the Burrendale Hotel is highly recommended. It is only a few minutes from the club and is renowned for its fine seafood restaurant.

Waterville Have and Golf Links

FOUNDED 1973

A LITTLE BIT OF HEAVEN

For those who make the pilgrimage to Waterville deep in County Kerry – and pilgrimage it is for even by Irish standards it is remote – the reward is not only to find one of the best new courses built anywhere in recent times but also to experience a little bit of heaven thrown in to the mix as well.

The present course was built by John A. Mulcahy, an Irish American who made enough money in the construction business to fund his dream of building his personal golf course in this beautiful corner of Ireland. But golf had been played at Waterville long before Mulcahy's dream became a reality.

In reality Waterville is one of the oldest courses in Ireland. However, new technology did away with the need for employees of Transatlantic Cables, who had been the mainstay of

> **Waterville Golf Club**
>
> *Ring of Kerry, Waterville*
>
> ◆
>
> Location: Two miles north of Waterville on the Ring of Kerry
>
> Tel: (353) 6674 545
>
> Course: 18 holes, 7184yds, par 72
>
> Visitors: Welcome at any time
>
> Green fees: £30

the club's membership, and by the late 1960s the links lay dormant. But the arrival of John H. Mulcahy changed all that and together with architect Eddie Hackett he created today's magnificent links.

The course was quickly acclaimed as one of the finest in Europe, with an elegantly luxurious hotel situated between the Atlantic Ocean and a lake that is a trout fishing paradise.

It is more than a golf course and club; it is also a resort of international standing. It lies only a short drive outside Waterville, which is itself a fishing and resort village still relatively quiet and peaceful and certainly unspoiled.

The remoteness of the place, almost six hours by car from Dublin, three hours from Cork, and two

The 12th at Waterville is a breathtaking hole, where the right club selection and steady nerves are the order of the day.

hours from Killarney, is the main reason why there have not been more important events played there.

The Kerrygold Classic was played there, however, not long after the course was officially opened. Former British and US Open champion, Tony Jacklin, caused something of a controversy when he was leading the event after three rounds, and then persuaded the sponsors and the organisers to put him out first instead of last on the final day. Jacklin was due in the United States the day after the tournament to try to qualify for the US Open and had to catch a plane from Shannon at a time when he should have been going out last as the tournament leader.

Jacklin posted a score of 290 in the morning which was not beaten, and he learned of his victory 35,000 feet above the Atlantic. Runner-up, Irishman Eddie Polland was not amused.

THE COURSE

It would be foolish for most players to tackle the Waterville course from the back tees which make it one of the longest anywhere in the British Isles. Far better to swallow pride and play from more sensible tee positions which will allow you to enjoy this marvellous place to the full. It is a spectacular meeting of land and water with the last three holes which border the ocean as beautiful as any in the world.

The view from the 17th is breathtaking. The hole, called Mulcahy's Peak after the founder, is played from the highest point on the course. From the tee the entire links is visible with the Kerry Mountains on one side and the Atlantic on the other three.

In 1987 Waterville was sold to a group of Irish Americans from New York. They brought with them a great love of the game and determination to maintain the tradition of Waterville. They also brought new equipment and maintenance programmes in addition to renovating the clubhouse and proshops.

FACILITIES

The Waterville Golf Links boasts a fine clubhouse with proshop, good practice facilities and both caddies and electric carts available to visitors. The clubhouse restaurant and bar are both excellent.

THE REGION

County Kerry is Ireland's most popular tourist area and is renowned both for its beauty and remoteness. Lofty mountains descend to gentle, hills that give way to miles of unspoilt beaches. The Ring of Kerry runs along the coast for a hundred miles, with timeless villages like Sneem and Cahersiveen along the way.

ACCOMMODATION

Waterville House is the perfect complement to the Golf Links. The 18th-century manor house offers splendid facilities: sauna, steam room, outdoor heated swimming pool, snooker and billiards. It also has its own private practice range and two beaches.

Swallow your pride and avoid the championship tees at the 16th and, whatever else you do, keep to the fairway.

Italy

10

Golf is still very much a minority sport in Italy with fewer than 30,000 regular players in the entire country. Nonetheless, the country has many fine courses dating back to the early part of this century.

The majority of these earlier courses were built during the 1920s when the game became fashionable in Italy and, as in Germany, was the preserve of the wealthy.

To some extent it remains that way today and the great golf boom that has swept across Europe has largely passed Italy by. There are many reasons for this, not least of which is the problem of planning consent for new developments.

The Italian authorities are much more sensitive to the effects of golf course development than other near neighbours have been in recent years and, on the whole, the golf resort is not a common element in Italian golf.

One notable example, however, is the beautiful new course at Castelfalfi high in the hills of Tuscany. A medieval village is being turned into a luxurious holiday complex with the ancient buildings, preserved and renovated, central to the whole theme. It is a fine example of what can be achieved by sensitive planning, and the golf course is an absolute delight.

Glorious Florence – with the mountains behind and its magnificent cathederal. For golfer and non-golfer, the joy of Italy is unconfined.

Of the longer established clubs, Milano, Roma, Ugolino and the fine course at Villa d'Este still rank among the very best in Europe.

Of the more recent designs, Pevero in Sardinia is an outstanding example. Designed by Robert Trent Jones, the layout was blasted through the rock and scrubland on the rocky coastline of the Costa Smeralda for the Aga Khan. Wonderful views and dramatic backdrops have been worked into what many people who have played there believe to be Trent Jones's masterpiece.

There are other fine courses of quite recent vintage, including Biella and Ogliata in Rome, while a visit to the relatively new layout at Modena will also provide the opportunity for car enthusiasts to take in the famous Ferrari museum nearby.

There are other elements to be taken into consideration. Wonderful Italian food, Chianti Classico, the burble of flame red Ferraris and the zest the Italians have for life, all make Italy a splendid destination for a golfing holiday with quiet courses and excellent facilities. It may not be the golfing capital of Europe but it's a gloriously self-indulgent place to play.

Golfclub Albarella

F O U N D E D   1 9 7 2

GOLF ON THE GULF OF VENICE

A few kilometres south of Venice on the Po delta, there is a vast natural park with a network of lagoons, rivers and canals which are home to thousands of wild birds and other wildlife. The island is Albarella, cool and luxuriant on the edge of the Adriatic.

This is a private island which has been transformed into a holiday paradise where the car takes a back seat and the bicycle reigns supreme. No fewer than 5000 of them are available for hire to visitors to this almost tropical island, and it seems that most of them are in use at any given time.

On the edge of this island playground is a little known, but outstanding, golf course. Built in 1975 by Commander Harris, this fine layout is set behind the sand dunes along the east coast of the island.

Although several of the holes are only a few metres from the Adriatic, the sea is not visible from the course and it does not come into play. But its influence is never far away. The stiff breeze can make the course play considerably longer than the card suggests, and the long wispy bent grasses in the rough are testament to its maritime setting.

Albarella is almost the perfect course for holiday golf. It is challenging without being overpowering and, most importantly, it is enjoyable to walk even at the hottest time of the year, thanks to the breeze and the flat layout.

At the height of summer, it is very much a traditional links course with firm fairways and fast greens

and, because of its seaside setting, the course can be played all year round.

THE COURSE

There are many fine holes on Commander Harris's layout, beginning right at the start.

The 1st needs two very stout blows with a driver and long iron to reach the green into the prevailing wind, while the 2nd, although not quite so long, is just as testing.

It requires a well placed tee shot to the right side of the fairway to open up the green. The hole doglegs quite sharply to the left and the right side is protected by a fierce bunker.

Perhaps the best hole on the course, however, is the long 4th. This excellent par 5 is 500 metres from the back tee and doglegs gently to the right. With out-of-bounds on the left, and a lake running down the entire length of the fairway on the right, the premium is on accuracy as well as length off the tee. A deep bunker on the left side of the fairway in the landing area adds to the problem.

The landing area for the second shot is just as tight. Under most circumstances, the green is out of range into the prevailing wind for all but the longest hitters, and with the fairway running towards the lake on the

> **Golfclub Albarella**
>
> *Isola di Albarella, 45010*
> *Rosolina, Rovigo*
> ◆
> Location: 40km south of
> Venice off the S443
> Tel: (39) 426 33 0124
> Course: 18 holes, 6040m,
> par 72
> Visitors: Welcome
> Green fees: IL50,000

right, the lay-up shot is as difficult as the drive. This is one of the great holes in Italian golf and a par won here is a trophy to be prized.

The par 4 13th is another hole in the same vein. Again, it is a dogleg to the right with a lake running the entire length of the hole and with deep rough on the right. The green is protected by a cluster of bunkers and the water eats into the right front edge of the green. The tendency is to favour the left side but it is very difficult to get up and down from off the green on this side.

Albarella has hosted an impressive number of important championships over the years. These include the Italian Open, won by David Feherty in 1986, and the Italian Ladies' Open in 1990 won by Florence Descampe from Belgium.

FACILITIES

The course is laid out in two loops of nine holes with a very large practice ground set in between. There is an excellent practice putting green with bunker and chipping practice facilities.

The clubhouse has been built as part of the Golf Hotel and overlooks the course. It offers the very best of amenities including a bar, a fine restaurant and a marvellous terrace on which to enjoy a cool glass of dry white wine after the rigours of the round.

With such fine facilities on offer, it is hardly surprising that Albarella is such a popular course. Clientele is mostly German and, of course, Italian during Italy's holiday month of August. Play can be slow at times, but it is a small price to pay for the enjoyment of such a fine course.

THE REGION

The island offers much more than mere golf, however. Albarella has more than 20 sports to offer its visitors with 12 highly specialised sports schools.

The Tennis Centre, for instance, boasts 24 courts in red clay and synthetic grass, and the excellent Italian and Swiss tennis schools.

The riding centre has a hurdle course and organizes treks through the forest and around the lagoons. There is jogging, archery, ski-rolling (on wheels), and a swimming school as well.

The Albarella greens are fast and firm and a joy to putt on. And the clubhouse offers a comfortable setting in which to reflect on what might have been.

The Island of Albarella – the course is clearly visible to the left of the picture. The breezes from the Adriatic ensure an almost tropical climate and the course is playable all year round.

For those who like big game fishing, some of the best of it can be found at the Albarella Angler's Club, which regularly hunts big tuna. The island has a large marina and associated sailing activities including a top-class water skiing school.

And if there is nothing on that list to take your fancy, the island also offers judo, body-building, football, bowling and volleyball as well as an aerobic gym for those who want to be really energetic.

The cultural side is not overlooked either. Theatre, ballet, operetta and chamber music are regularly performed in the Teatro Tenda, the island's theatre, which can accommodate 1500 people.

ACCOMMODATION

Albarella is not short of first-class accommodation. The island has two hotels, the four-star Golf Hotel located on the course, and the Capo Nord Hotel on the beach front. The Golf Hotel offers an excellent standard of service, has an indoor swimming pool and health/fitness centre while the Capo Nord is a typical seaside resort hotel.

There are also villas and apartments available with hotel service if required.

The island also boasts 10 different restaurants offering a range of international, regional and Mediterranean cuisines.

Castelfalfi Golf & Country Club

FOUNDED 1991

THE HIDDEN GEM OF TUSCANY

High in the hills of Tuscany, where in the warmth of summer the world seems to come to a shimmering halt, there is a very special golf course. Few have heard of it and only a handful play there.

At the centre of a triangle joining Florence, Pisa and Siena lies an ancient village, its castle towering majestically over a verdant valley where plump grapes ripen on the vine and await their calling as the Chianti they call Classico.

The castle, old and mysterious, gives its name to the village and, in turn, to a golf course which is one of Europe's hidden gems.

Castelfalfi near Montaione in the region of Florence was built in 1991 as the initial project in what was to become a major leisure development.

Tenuta Castelfalfi bought over the entire village with its ancient and picturesque buildings and hundreds of acres of rolling countryside. In the valleys that wind their way through and around the steep sloping hills of the estate, a golf course of truly outstanding quality has been created.

It is a layout with breathtaking views of mountain and valley, with the ancient castle dominating the scene from above and visible from virtually every hole on the course. There are few more beautiful places in the world to play golf than here.

But, alas, like so many other courses that have been built as the vehicle to sell real estate and timeshare, there has been an under-investment in the course since it was opened. Plans for a luxurious clubhouse lie buried in the unfinished foundations behind the 18th green and visitors use slightly less pretentious, but undoubtedly just as functional, facilities nearby.

The little wooden clubhouse with its porch and bar and stunning views down the course is compel-

Castelfalfi Golf & Country Club

loc. Castelfalfi, 50050

Montaione, Firenze

◆

Location: 20km from San Gimignano, 7km from Montaione

Tel: (39) 571 69 78 46

Course: 18 holes, 6345m, par 72

Visitors: Welcome

Green fees: IL60,000

This is Tuscan golf at its very best, which everyone who loves this game deserves to experience at least once. There can be few more perfect settings for a golf course.

The fairways are neat and the greens are a joy to putt on although the bunkers which protect them will pose problems. Whatever your score, though, you are guaranteed a memorable round at Castelfalfi.

ling in its charm, and reminiscent of days when all clubhouses were like that. Indeed, some would say that this great game was all the better for it.

Even if the odd tee is a little threadbare and the sand in the bunkers is a little too hard in places, this in no way detracts from the quality of a wonderful layout. The greens are a joy to putt on – fast and firm with most on more than one level. The fairways are as neat and well kept as the limited resources permit.

But it is the sheer scale of the beauty, the peace of the place and the joy of playing a course where only a handful of players are ever found that makes Castelfalfi such a special course to play on.

THE COURSE

The short 5th is a glorious par 3 with water front and left and no option to bail out on the right because of a great stand of pine trees. It needs a good blow with a middle iron to make sure of the carry from a tee set high enough to give a clear view of all the problems.

And the long 7th, with its sweeping uphill fairway which turns just enough to the left to make it interesting, will also get your attention.

However, it is the back nine of the Blue course (a Red Course is planned but not yet started) that live in the memory long after you have made the winding climb back to the main Montaione road.

Two holes in particular stand out – the dogleg 13th, with its marvellous views of the old castle, and the challenging par 5 16th, with its island green almost in the style of Pete Dye.

It's a brave and strong player who takes on the challenge of getting home in two here. Swallow pride, lay up and enjoy the view is the best advice.

FACILITIES

Up the hill from the golf course, the development of the leisure complex continues with the medieval village being slowly renovated to provide apartments with spectacular views and modern facilities. Most are for timeshare.

Ancient buildings, long since derelict and dotted throughout the property, are being rebuilt to create luxurious villas. There are three swimming pools,

The Hotel Vecchio Mulino: there are few more pleasant places to relax with a well-deserved glass of Chianti.

tennis courts and an equestrian centre. And there are further plans for a hotel.

The course is set well away from the other facilities. The little clubhouse has basic amenities where visitors can enjoy a snack in a friendly atmosphere, and those who feel in need of a little practice will find a superb driving range.

The club also has a small fleet of golf carts, and anyone planning a visit should seriously consider using one, particularly in the hot summer months. There are one or two steep climbs and some tees are quite a distance from the previous greens.

THE REGION

Not even the Romans could put down the soul of the Etruscans who lived in Tuscany from time immemorial. That spirit lives on today in one of the biggest and most varied regions in the whole of Italy.

From one of the most unspoilt coasts of the entire Mediterranean to the snows of the Abetone, Tuscany offers a feast of natural beauty and peaceful delight and some of the finest buildings and works of art the world has ever seen.

Florence, Siena, Pisa and the island of Elba – where Napoleon was incarcerated – all lie within the region. There are the enchanting peaks of Mount Amiata, where Michelangelo went to choose the marble for the statues commissioned by Pope Julius II. And always there are the fabulous Tuscan hills where the grapes are grown for the Chianti that is Classico.

ACCOMMODATION

There is no shortage of first-class accommodation in the area to suit every pocket. There are small and intimate hotels and pensions set amidst the spectacular scenery. These contrast with, yet complement, the august hotels of the city, splendid in their grandeur and redolent of the region's historic past.

In Montaione, only a few kilometres from Castelfalfi, the Hotel Vecchio Mulino is typical of many small but excellent hotels which offer very reasonably priced bed and breakfast accommodation.

Further afield, the Hotel Villa San Lucchese, set in the hills above Poggibonsi, is well worth a visit to enjoy its fine amenities and excellent restaurant.

It also happens to be perfectly located for a visit to the magnificent city of the beautiful towers, San Gimignano.

Modena Golf and Country Club

FOUNDED 1987

IN THE SHADOW OF ENZO FERRARI

Greg Turner won the 1993 Italian Open at the Modena Golf and Country Club only a stone's throw from the birthplace of some of the great names in Italian high performance motor cars – Ferrari, Lamborghini and Maserati.

But even he must have found it hard to concentrate on the royal and ancient game in these parts because to the car enthusiast this is *the* place. Modena is to the car what St Andrews is to golfers.

However, there is nothing second-rate about the club – far from it. At the Modena Golf Club, you will find a highly exclusive facility which is at one with itself and also rests very comfortably with the general feeling of the area.

There are a number of holes at Modena where the golfer seems to be surrounded by water. You'll need to grit your teeth, ensure your club selection is perfect, and take aim.

THE COURSE

It is not that visitors are unwelcome, but the Modena Club protects its facility as carefully as Senor Ferrari does his down the road. Therefore, the casual visitor needs some command of the language, or a little bit of luck with the automatic barriers at the end of the long driveway, to gain access to the clubhouse.

This very fine course was laid out in 1987 by Bernhard Langer. At around 6200 metres it is not one of the longest of championship courses, but it has clearly (and rightly) been built with the members in mind

Modena Golf and Country Club
via Castelnuovo R.4, 41050
Colombaro di Formigine (MO)
◆
Location: 10km south of
Modena
Tel: (39) 59 55 34 82
Course: 18 holes, 6157m,
par 72
Visitors: Welcome
Green fees: IL80,000

rather than the stars of the European Tour who will make only an occasional and fleeting visit.

Although shortish in length, there is plenty to tax and challenge the handicap golfer here. The dry heat of the Modena summer takes away any fear from the rough, but around the greens where it is regularly watered it can be very difficult indeed.

Virtually every hole is severely protected by bunkers in the landing areas from the tee. They are not too severe, however, and progress can be made from them, but only the better players will have a chance to escape without penalty.

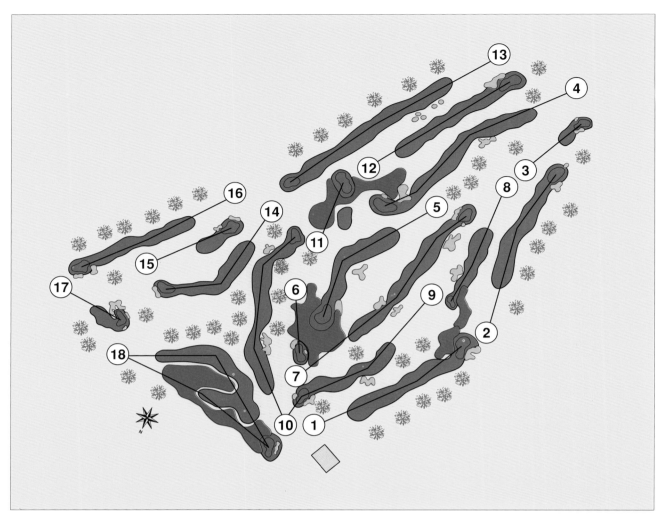

The Modena Golf and Country Club Course.

Modena has wonderful rolling greens where pin placements can be on a different level on virtually every hole. They are firm and true and a pleasure to putt on – once you have reached them.

There are several holes where this is particularly difficult, not the least of them the short 11th. At its very longest it measures a modest 144 metres, but there is trouble everywhere. There are shades of the 12th at Augusta here with water in front and – unlike Augusta – behind the green as well.

A long thin bunker guards the front of the very narrow green and club selection is absolutely critical. Too little club means a watery grave for any tee shot while too much comes up with exactly the same result, unless it is far enough left to avoid disaster. So

choose the club that you use with extreme care.

The short par 4 5th presents a similar problem, as does the short 6th in a little aquatic corner of the course which could prove costly to any card.

The long par 5 13th, with out-of-bounds on the right and a spattering of bunkers down the left guarding the tee shot, is another outstanding hole.

But the final hole at Modena is probably the most memorable. A long par 5 dogleg right, with water down the right and out-of-bounds down the left, demands a perfect tee shot and a very long approach over water if it is to be reached in two.

So don't be tempted to try anything too fancy. Just relax, lay up and take your par. The delights of the clubhouse will shortly await you.

The fairways – and the greens – at Modena are well-nigh perfect. However, there is plenty to tax the golfer here, from the bunkers guarding each green to the strategically placed water hazards.

Red is the colour. A few kilometres down the road from Modena lies the beautiful city of Bologna – a must for any visitor to the area.

The oldest Italian statue, the Venus of Savignano, said to be 30,000 years old, was discovered in a gravel bed in the Panaro River in the region and is now preserved in the Pigorini Museum in Rome.

The list of cultural and artistic achievement is almost endless but, rather ironically, the region is best known for its contribution in a totally different world – that of high-performance motor cars.

Modena is the home of the Ferrari, one of the world's most exclusive cars. In the little town of Marinello, only a few kilometres from Modena itself, is the Ferrari factory which

FACILITIES

The club offers the standard of facilities one would expect from a country club. It has a good restaurant and bar, swimming pool and two grass tennis courts which clearly demand considerable looking after, particularly in the hot months of summer.

Everything at Modena is immaculately presented and the clubhouse locker room facilities are nothing short of luxurious.

THE REGION

Modena is the only region in Italy to be named after a road, the Roman Via Aemelia. It has the tallest medieval tower in the country (95 metres) and claims the sources of both the Arno and Tiber rivers.

The Museum of Ceramics at Faenza is renowned world-wide for the quality of its exhibits, and the region is the birthplace of Italian tenor Luciano Pavarotti as well as the great Italian film directors Fellini, Antonioni and Bertolucci.

produces the mystical marque at the rate of around 10 cars a day on one side of the road, and on the other builds racing cars which have won more than a hundred Grand Prix Formula 1 races since Enzo Ferrari started the company in 1947.

The Galleria Ferrari in Maranello, which houses a collection of vintage and modern Ferraris and traces the history of the company from its early beginnings, is a must for any visitor.

ACCOMMODATION

There is no shortage of excellent accommodation in the Modena area from five-star hotels to simple pensions. The Hotel Daunia on the Via del Pozzo, for example, offers first-class bed and breakfast accommodation, which is considerably better than its three-star rating suggests.

There are plenty of fine restaurants in the region offering a rich and varied choice of cuisines to suit the most discerning of palates.

Monticello Golf Club

F O U N D E D 1 9 7 5

TWO COURSES AND A SPECTACULAR SETTING

With more than 1300 members, a very large percentage of whom want to leave the rigours of business life in nearby Milan behind at the weekends to play golf, it is not surprising that the Golf Club Monticello has need of two 18-hole courses. For this is golf very much on the American style with a lavish clubhouse and wonderful amenities.

The low rise, sprawling clubhouse could as easily be in North Carolina as North Italy, but the difference is that the Italians bring a style to country club golf to which their counterparts in the United States could never aspire.

Even the inevitable buggies are kept from general view as much as possible with strict instructions that they must not be left abandoned around the 10th tee

A tantalizing view of the 7th green, even if the footbridge doesn't look any too stable. For the more affluent Milan residents, this is the perfect antidote to city life.

when players stop for refreshment between nines. An ingenious tunnel system shepherds buggy drivers underneath the clubhouse from the caddie shed to and from the 1st and 10th tees. And members have to drive them in the rough – close to the trees – during play.

Rampaging hordes of buggies are far from the order of the day at Monticello. Members are encouraged to walk. This is a high-key establishment operating on a very low-key level. And it's proved to be a perfect combination.

Members at Monticello are required to own a property at the club to become a member in the first place. Many have made their permanent homes alongside the fairways, while others use them as weekend retreats to play golf and enjoy the area around this beautiful region.

Golf Club Monticello
via Volta 4, 22070 Cassina Rizzardi, Como
◆
Location: 11km south-west of Como. 45km from Milan
Tel: (39) 31 92 80 55
Courses: Red Course – 18 holes, 6376m, par 72; Blue Course – 18 holes, 5981m, par 72
Visitors: Welcome Tuesday to Friday. (Members only at weekends; course closed on Mondays)
Green fees: IL80,000

THE COURSES

The courses are first-class – the club has hosted the Italian Open on many occasions. Sandy Lyle won there in 1992 and other past winners include such luminaries as Greg Norman and Billy Casper.

The Red Course is the championship layout and a wonderful challenge to any golfer, set as it is in such spectacular scenery. Tree-lined fairways and lakes make for an idyllic setting with the high mountains running down to Lake Como offering a wonderfully spectacular backdrop.

The best hole is the 16th, a 393-metre par 4 dogleg left round a lake. A perfect drive is needed here, tight to the corner of the dogleg and avoiding a dangerous

The final hole at the Red course. For sheer quality – look at that fairway and inviting green – Monticello is difficult to beat.

bunker. This should help to set up a long second to a well protected green. A par is a major victory.

The Blue course is a pleasant, if rather less demanding, alternative to the championship layout.

THE REGION

Monticello lies in a truly spectacular region of Italy close to Lake Como and the Swiss border. The Lake itself, viewed from the twisting road which runs around its shores, is quite majestic, and there is a host of small restaurants and cafés which offer refreshment and wonderful views.

Car ferries ply their way between towns across the lake. They are inexpensive and a good way to avoid the inevitable queues of traffic which congregate around this popular tourist spot.

Less than an hour's drive from Monticello, the ancient city of Milan is one of the world's great cultural centres. La Scala Milan, finished in 1778, was badly damaged during the Second World War but was restored to its former glory and re-opened to the public in 1946.

The Vittorio Emanuele gallery is a distinguished shopping-centre with brightly illuminated shops, restaurants and bars. Its coffee-houses have been the meeting places of artists, scholars and politicians for centuries. And the magnificent cathedral set in the heart of the town is a must for any visitor.

ACCOMMODATION

Being in the centre of a tourist area, there is a wide choice of accommodation around Monticello. Small hotels and pensions are plentiful, providing comfortable accommodation at reasonable prices.

If you want the ultimate in comfort and you don't mind paying, Milan has many grand hotels with tariffs to match. But there is plenty of middle-of-the-road accommodation available too.

Typical is the Hotel Sigma in Cantu, close to the course and not far from Lake Como with its breathtaking views. It offers bed-and-breakfast in comfortable air-conditioned rooms and has an excellent restaurant and American bar.

Circolo Golf dell'Ugolino

FOUNDED 1943

HISTORY IN THE GRAND SETTING

The Ugolino Golf Club is set in the heart of the Tuscan hills at the back of Strada in Chianti. Yet it is just a few kilometres from the city of Florence. It is one of the oldest clubs in Italy and has been influential in the development of the game in the country.

Golf was first played in Florence in 1889 as a result of the strong British influence in the city at that time. The first Florentine course was built at San Donato just beyond the Ponte alle Mosse on ground belonging to Prince Demidoff. In 1909 it was rebuilt under the guidance of its then president, J.W. Spalding. The club hosted the first Italian Open in 1905 and again in 1908, 1910 and 1912.

The club at Donato was greatly influenced by the British membership at that time and, as the game became more popular, many old Florentine families joined up and took to the links.

The top names in society ensured the continued development of the club but eventually the course was absorbed by the expanding city around 1920.

The Ugolino Club was built in 1933 by English architects, Blandford and Gannon, and is set out in majestic countryside on steeply rolling land featuring a colourful variety of trees including pine, cypress, oak and olive. The club hosted the Italian Open in 1983, the year of its 50th anniversary, and is perhaps more widely known as the home club of Baldavino Dassu.

Pure Tuscany at Ugolino's 16th. By now, the player will have worked out that this is a thinking golfer's course which responds more to brain than brawn.

Circolo Golf dell'Ugolino

via Chiantigiana 3, 50015

Grassina, Florence

◆

Location: 9km south of Florence

Tel: (39) 55-2301009

Course: 18 Holes, 5741m, par 72

Visitors: Welcome

Green fees: IL75,000

THE COURSE

The course is divided by the Chiantigiana Road. Twelve of the holes have out-of-bounds as a prominent feature and, except in the height of summer when the heat takes its toll, the rough tends to be very long and harsh.

At a little over 5741 metres, Ugolino is not a long course by present day standards but what it lacks in length it more than makes up for in subtlety of design and clever use of the ground.

The greens are small and fast and it is a demanding course to walk, particularly at the height of summer. However, the club has a small fleet of carts and they are well worth considering for anyone planning a visit in mid-summer.

After a short and pleasant opening hole which falls away downhill and doglegs quietly to the left to offer a simple and reassuring par, the test becomes a little more demanding.

The first short hole, the 4th at around 200 metres, is a beautiful hole and an indication of some of the problems the course has to offer. Played from an elevated tee across a valley and up to a slightly elevated green, it requires a solid blow with, perhaps, a five iron. You need to be careful to avoid the umbrella pines which flank the left side.

There are few prettier sights in European golf than the 10th hole here. The mountains form the perfect backdrop, and the wonderful old clubhouse overlooks the fairway.

The 9th is an outstanding hole. At 461 metres and uphill all the way, it is a tough hole by any standards. Add to that a drive which has be threaded through an avenue of poplars and pines to a landing area dominated by a single tall pine tree in the centre of the fairway, and the difficulty appears in more acute perspective.

By now the intelligent golfer will have learned that Ugolino responds to careful thought rather than brute strength.

FACILITIES

Ugolino boasts a very fine old clubhouse which, apart from some modernisation, has changed little since it was built in 1933. The architect was Gherardo Bosio who created a classic circular column gallery at the entrance with long balconies running on the two sides.

It is a peaceful place to take a cool drink after the travails of the course. The restaurant offers good food and friendly service.

Visitors are made very welcome here, but this is a busy club with more than 800 members. The exception is in August when, like the rest of Italy, the members head for the coast.

With Ugolino only nine kilometres away, the Hotel Excelsior, in the heart of Florence, offers superb accommodation.

The club also has a luxury swimming pool and excellent tennis facilities.

THE REGION

The Ugolino Club lies a few kilometres outside the ancient city of Florence.

It is in Florence that the genius of Michelangelo can best be seen. The Sacrestia Nuovo is situated in the heart of Florence close to the Duomo and the railway station and represents one of the artist's finest achievements.

Together with the Sacriestia Nuovo, the Medici Chapel is a must for any visitor to the area although the region has almost an embarrassment of riches in fine art and wonderful architecture. Indeed, to truly appreciate the area would take a lifetime.

ACCOMMODATION

There is a vast range of hotels to choose from in and around Florence – from small pensions to luxury hotels. The Hotel Excelsior is a magnificent hotel from which to explore the surroundings. However, Florence attracts visitors all year round so you must be sure to book well ahead.

Portugal

The development of golf in Portugal can be laid at the door of the British who brought the game to Oporto towards the end of the last century. In 1890, a group of wine shippers laid out nine holes for their amusement and in the process created not only the oldest club in Portugal but the second oldest golf club in Europe. Ten years later the course was moved to its present site and the club has flourished ever since.

However, it was not until the delights of winter sunshine golf began to be fully appreciated that golf really began to flourish in Portugal. There are long-established courses in Estoril and Lisbon but it was the opening up of the Algarve as a winter golfing destination which really set the ball rolling.

The late Sir Henry Cotton was brought in to design a course at the western end of the Algarve near the fishing town of Portimao in the mid-1960s. It was part of a golf hotel complex known as Penina and it was to become the three-times Open Champion's masterpiece.

Penina was opened for play in 1966 after Sir Henry had planted several hundred thousand trees in a former rice paddy and created a course with huge tees which he could stretch to 7000 metres if the mood took him. Penina was the catalyst for a steady stream of golf course developments mostly allied to property sales and holiday resorts.

Dreams of Portugal recall whitewashed walls and exquisite pottery and then the complete experience floods back – with unbridled pleasure.

Three years after Penina was opened for play, the beautiful Vilamoura course, a few kilometres to the west of the international airport at Faro, was completed. Frank Pennink was the architect and his design through the rolling Algarve countryside with its fearsome umbrella pines quickly became a winter rendezvous for thousands of British golfers escaping from the winter chill at home.

More courses were built including the beautiful layout at Palmares, with its stretch of pure seaside links holes, at the very western end of the Algarve. It was opened for play in 1975.

Unfortunately Portugal did not learn from the mistakes of neighbouring Spain which hiked the cost of golf on its courses much faster even than the raging demand for them. Portugal followed suit with the result that it is now a very expensive country in which to play golf, unless the visitor is there as part of a package arrangement or has some other form of discounted green fees.

Palmares Golf Club

FOUNDED 1975

CLASSIC CONTRAST IN THE ALMOND GROVE

Along Portugal's Algarve coast road, west of Portimao heading for Cape St Vincent and the most westerly coast of Europe, the busy little town of Lagos clings defiantly to its fishing traditions and resists the burgeoning tourist traffic spreading remorselessly from the east. Just outside the town – and you have to be quick to spot it – stands a modest signpost which proclaims the road to Palmares.

Only those with an intimate knowledge of the world's golf courses will know that it leads to one of golf's rare hidden gems.

The Palmares Golf Club was founded in 1975 when course architect, Frank Pennink, was given the task of designing an 18-hole layout on a wonderful piece of ground straddling the main Portimao railway line near Meia Praia.

What Pennink created is a course that is unquestionably one of the most enjoyable places to play golf anywhere in Europe. It ranks among that small group of courses which has an indefinable something that brings golfers from all over the world back time and time again.

It is not a lavish club. But to enjoy a cool drink sitting on the veranda at Palmares with its glorious view across the Lagos bay

Palmares Golf Club
Meia Praia, 8600 Lagos,
Algarve
◆
Location: North-east of Lagos
beyond Meia Praia station
Tel: (351) 82 76 2953
Course: 18 holes, 5961m,
par 71
Visitors: Welcome at all times
but pre-booking essential
Green fees: Esc7000

after a round is to experience something special in the world of golf. There are many who would be happy just to sit on the veranda and soak in that glorious view without venturing on to the golf course at all, but they would miss a truly great experience.

THE COURSE

Palmares is unique in this part of the world in that it manages to combine the best of all possible worlds. The demanding first hole doglegs right and drops from a tee set high up on the hill to a well-guarded green. Here par feels like an eagle and to complete the hole with the same ball you teed off with almost

Lavish it may not be, but the palms in the foreground merely confirm this as one of the most relaxing places to play golf – anywhere.

The pleasant sea breezes from the Atlantic ensure that golf at Palmares is invariably played in the best of conditions. No wonder golfers return here again and again.

borders on a miracle of the first order.

The course crosses the railway line. From there Palmares has a stretch of five holes set beside the sea that are pure links and would not be out of place on the east coast of Scotland. To miss the fairway on any of them is to drop a certain stroke, for the rough could best be described as one giant bunker – rather in the manner of Pine Valley.

Both the 2nd and the 3rd are short par 4s that will yield par with some ease provided you find the fairway from the tee. The next is a delightful short hole of only 142 metres, but it demands a solid blow with a middle iron, usually against a prevailing wind, to reach the sanctuary of the green.

However, it is the next hole which strikes fear into even the stoutest heart.

The 5th at Palmares ranks as one of the great par 5 holes anywhere in Europe. Over 550 metres from

the back tee, and often played into a stiff sea breeze, it turns to the right twice on its journey along the edge of the ocean. Into the breeze it is difficult to bite off anything at all from the first dogleg and it is vital to hit the fairway.

Anything off line will usually require a sand iron to return it to safety. A long second shot has be threaded between the twin avenues of brush and sand to the corner of the second dogleg ready for the approach to the green. A thicket of trees guards the right side, threatening bunkers to the left, and the green itself slopes steeply back to front.

This is no place for the faint of heart. The last of the links holes is a 364 metre par 4 which tracks 90 degrees round the edge of a marsh. The green can be driven but it is a bold shot. Many who hit their Sunday best and are on the very point of celebration have the chalice dashed from their grasp when the ball lands on the green only to bounce through and out of bounds on to the railway.

Those who have learned to overcome their bravado take a more conservative route. After the glories of the classic links, the course winds its way back up the hill to the clubhouse amid almond and pine.

This is beautiful, undulating parkland, not overly long, but with some wonderfully testing holes. The short 10th, played from an elevated tee across a valley to an elevated green, is superb. The 418-metre 16th, played uphill with a dogleg to the left, is the toughest par 4 on the course while the view from the tee at the 17th is quite breathtaking.

Despite its great beauty and majestic charm, Palmares has plenty of teeth as well. Two deadly bunkers guard this two-tier green.

FACILITIES

The Palmares clubhouse is small and friendly with a busy bar and an informal eating area. A Palmares sandwich taken on the veranda with a cool bottle of local wine is one of golf's memorable moments.

The club has a practice ground that is functional rather than lavish and there is a small fleet of buggies for those who prefer their golf on wheels.

THE REGION

Palmares is far from the madding tourist crowd. It lies in a largely unspoiled part of the Algarve coast where the beaches are magnificent and the local restaurants still serve traditional fare. It is not far to the hills of Monchique where the late Sir Henry Cotton once loved to drive to take lunch in a traditional Portuguese restaurant and savour the wonderful views back towards the sea and his beloved Penina.

ACCOMMODATION

The town of Lagos has several small hotels which give relatively easy access to Palmares. However, favourite with the majority of golfers here is the Lagos Hotel which has been catering for golfing groups since the course was opened. It boasts a large swimming pool at the hotel with sauna and Turkish baths and an excellent beach club three kilometres away on the road to the golf course. A shuttle bus runs guests to the beach club and the golf course.

A variety of restaurants serving a wide range of food can be found in the town. However, for those who want something a little different, the Mandarin Restaurant on the outskirts is renowned among the golfing cognoscenti.

Specializing in Cantonese food it is unusual in that it is built in the house of its owners, Denis and Julie Garvey, and since Denis is also the no-nonsense secretary of the Palmares Golf Club, he can get away with only opening when he feels like it. But it's worth being around when he does!

Penina Golf Club

FOUNDED 1966

HENRY COTTON'S MASTERPIECE

The late Sir Henry Cotton, three times winner of the Open, loved the golf course he built in a flooded rice paddy in 1966. For him it was the culmination of a great career and the place where he would find peace and contentment in his retirement years.

However, what he created at the eastern end of Portugal's Algarve was more than that. It was the first golf course to be built on this beautiful stretch of Portuguese coastline and, in effect, started the Algarve golf boom.

Cotton was presented with a very unpromising piece of land when he was asked to design the layout. It was perfectly flat and flooded when he first saw it, but he fell in love with the area and had a vision of creating the golf course which would be his own masterpiece.

He wanted a course that would be both a pleasure to play for the guests at the five-star Penina Hotel which was being built, and yet a severe test for the best professional players. He also wanted a course that would be covered in trees to attract the local wildlife and which would turn the flat, uninteresting land into a beautiful woodland which, in turn, would complement the magnificent hotel.

That he succeeded there is no doubt. He planted 350,000 trees which grew quickly. The paddy field dried out and Cotton soon saw the fruits of his labours. The result was that Penina became one of the great golf resorts of Europe.

Big names from the world of golf, entertainers and statesmen made their way to this wonderful course to sit at the court of the man they called 'The Maestro' and play his course. And Cotton welcomed them all with open arms.

Penina is a stunningly beautiful and peaceful place just over an hour's drive from Faro international

The fishing port of Lagos is only a short drive from Penina. Here, you can explore the shops and markets before relaxing in one of many delightful bars.

Penina Golf Club

PO Box 146, Penina, Portimao

◆

Location: Off N125 between Portimao and Lagos

Tel: (351) 82 415 415

Courses: Championship – 18 holes, 6439m, par 73; Monchique – 9 holes, 2842m, par 35; Quinta – 9 holes, 1851m, par 31

Visitors: Welcome but must book in advance. Hotel guests have unlimited free golf

Green fees: Championship – Esc 9500; Monchique – Esc 6000; Quinta – Esc5000

It's easy to see why Henry Cotton loved his course so much. The fairways are not ungenerous but the wayward shot will rarely go unpunished. It is the perfect golfing test.

airport. There is a dignified air about the place, very much in keeping with the Cotton image.

Sadly 'The Maestro' is no longer there, but his presence can still be felt along the fairways and particularly on the practice ground where he imparted so much of his golfing wisdom to champions and golfing rabbits alike.

The latest generation of the famous Henry Cotton tyre with which he used to teach his own unique 'method' remains on the practice ground as a reminder of one of the game's greatest players and most innovative teachers.

THE COURSE

The Championship course at Penina is a magnificent test of golf by any standards. Cotton built long tees, some of them nearly 50 metres in length, so that the course could be set up to a suitable length for friendly holiday golf, or for the rather fiercer competiton of the Portuguese Open Championship which has been held there many times.

He also believed in large, fast and firm greens and hazards that would penalize the wayward stroke. Dozens of drainage ditches are testament to that and very much part of the Cotton legacy.

He was a master at extricating the ball from these fiendish hazards, although it was very seldom that the great man was ever in one in regular play. He would take great delight in throwing a ball into one of the hazards and demonstrating his uncanny ability to play it out when it seemed all but impossible for a lesser mortal to hit the ball at all.

For these lesser mortals, the challenge of Penina is obvious from the very first tee, a long hole which doglegs slightly left. The drive needs to be struck long and straight to avoid the eucalyptus trees on both sides of the fairway. Two bunkers guard the approach which should be with a long iron.

Although the 3rd is a modest par 4 of only 301 metres, it is one of the trickiest holes on the front nine. Large bunkers guard the front of a very narrow green with a long bunker immediately behind. When the greens are firm it is a very difficult shot to hold the green, and often the drive must be laid up short to allow a full shot to the green.

The long 5th is probably the best of the front nine holes. At 463 metres, it is possible to get home in two, but the fairway swings sharply to the left, almost through 90 degrees, and a water hazard runs diagonally across the fairway from the corner of the dogleg to the front of the green.

The water makes the 7th a tricky hole also, although at under 300 metres it is a short par 4.

The back nine starts with consecutive par 5s, both of which are dogleg holes and very demanding. The second shot at the 11th is crucial since it has to negotiate a tall tree and two bunkers in the centre of the fairway at the corner of the dogleg.

The 13th is the best-known hole at Penina and was Cotton's own favourite. It is a par 3 of 208 metres with water all the way down the right side. The tee is set on the diagonal and the further back the hole is played, ever more water must be carried. It is a majestic short hole and one where Cotton took great delight in playing manufactured shots with his driver to demonstrate several ways of playing the hole.

There is another good par 3 at the 16th, which also has water to carry. This is followed by the great Penina finish of two 450 metre par 5s.

The first is relatively straightforward although the tee shot must be struck well to carry the stream that runs across the fairway. The last hole, however, is much more demanding. A drive needs to be played short of the water. Thereafter, the hole is uphill to a plateau green and the second shot must avoid a nest of bunkers just short. Only the longest hitters have any chance of reaching the green in two shots.

A few alterations were made to the course shortly before Sir Henry's death, although he was not involved in them.

'The Maestro' left Penina shortly afterwards and was never to return, but the course stands as a wonderful memorial to a great man.

FACILITIES

Being part of the hotel, the Penina Golf Club enjoys all the first-class facilities associated with five-star

The five-star Penina Hotel which provides such a fitting backdrop to the course is – for those lucky enough to stay here – one of the most comfortable hotels in Europe.

Those searching for antiques and mementoes of their stay in Penina will rarely be disappointed. The backstreets of Lagos and Portimao usually yield a treasure or two.

accommodation. The Olympic-size swimming pool is only metres from the first tee and there are several restaurants and bars to choose from.

Robin Liddle and José Lourençu are the club professionals and both enjoy the recent improvements to the practice area.

The club has tennis courts, a short pitch and putt course inside the championship course and a fine extra nine holes known as the Monchique course across the main road from the hotel. Henry Cotton also designed this course which has an orange grove running down the right hand side of the first fairway.

He is said to have ensured that the first row of orange trees were bitter to ensure that players who felt like a free orange after their tee shot were thwarted. After the first bitter orange no-one ever tried the second row!

The Region

The Algarve has long been a winter haven for travellers with its soft and mild climate. When Portuguese golf began to mushroom after the opening of Penina and the construction of other fine courses such as Vilamoura and Quinta do Lago, the charter flights to the region became more and more laden with golf clubs.

However, there is a lot more on offer in the Algarve than mere golf. Wonderful beaches, water sports and spectacular scenery allied to marvellous traditional Portuguese food make for an entertaining holiday away from the golf course.

The busy fishing ports of Portimao and Lagos are close to Penina with their fine shops and markets. Lunch of fresh sardines grilled in a restaurant on the very waterfront where they were landed, and washed down with a cool glass of the local wine is very hard to beat. There is nightlife for those who want to find it and Penina has its own casino.

Accommodation

Now owned and operated by Forte Hotels, the Penina Hotel is one of the most renowned in the whole of Europe. It enjoys a five-star rating and offers a wide variety of restaurants from the elegance of its Grill Room to the poolside barbecue.

Traditional Portuguese, International or Italian cuisine are featured in most of the restaurants. The hotel has its own private beach only a few minutes on the shuttle bus from the hotel. Windsurfing, jet skiing and sailing are available to residents and a snack restaurant is open all day long.

Residents at Penina enjoy unlimited free golf on the hotel courses and there is a reciprocal agreement with Forte's Donna Filipa Hotel and the relatively new course at San Lorenzo situated at the other end of the Algarve.

The San Lorenzo course was opened in 1988 but it is difficult to book because hotel guests have priority. However, residents at either hotel have access to both courses.

Penha Longa Golf Club

FOUNDED 1992

MODERN CLUB IN HISTORIC SETTING

Less then a year after the Robert Trent Jones Jnr course at Penha Longa was opened, it was announced that the 1994 Portuguese Open would be played there, bringing instant recognition to this new layout on the Estoril coast.

The announcement ended a six-year run of the Portuguese Open on the Algarve and re-established Estoril as a premier golfing destination. The Penha Longa club is at the heart of a new resort development at Quinta da Penha Longa, which includes a five-star hotel with plans for five villages featuring luxurious villas and town-houses.

The course is the first built by Robert Trent Jones Jnr in Portugal and he has set an interesting and challenging layout amid some spectacular scenery in the heart of a region with more than 600 years of history.

The course lies in the foothills of the town of Sintra and is only 17 kilometres from Lisbon airport. There are stunning views of the Sintra Mountains, as well as the sweeping panorama of the Atlantic Ocean, with the towns of Estoril and Cascais in the foreground.

Penha Longa Golf Club

Quinta da Penha Longa,

Lagoa Azul, Linho

◆

Location: Outside Estoril on EN 7 towards Sintra

Tel: (351) 19 24 9022

Course: 18 holes, 6260m, par 72

Visitors: Hotel guests and by introduction by club members only. Current handicap certificate required

Green fees: Esc8000-12,000

This is a well-guarded green. What the bunkers miss at the 16th, the trees waiting behind the pin will gratefully receive.

The ground is undulating and Robert Trent Jones Jnr has built an American-style course making the best use of the movement in the land. Although concrete cart paths snake their way around and over the undulations it is still a design perfectly in tune with its surroundings as well as a fine test for all players – whatever their handicap.

Four sets of tees have been built to ensure that Penha Longa can not only set a stiff challenge for the top professional players but also make it enjoyable for those less gifted who prefer to play their golf in a less rarefied atmosphere.

THE COURSE

From the very back tees the course is only just over 6200 metres, but clever design and strategic use of water on several holes has taken the emphasis away from length and put a much higher premium on strategic play and accurate shotmaking.

Penha Longa is unusual in modern design in that it does not have returning loops of nine holes. Like many of the links courses of Scotland, the turn for home is at the furthest part of the course.

The first three holes are played along a narrow strip of land which is shared with the final three holes before the course opens out into an undulating plain. The course has a 'loop' from the 6th to the 9th before heading for the furthest corner of the course at the 10th green, and then turning for home.

A refreshment halt at the 9th green has been included in the design to ease any suffering which may have set in by that point so far away from the clubhouse.

The loop has two of the most challenging holes in the layout. At 455 metres from the back tee, the 6th is not a long par 5 but it is demanding nonetheless. Almost a double dogleg, it requires a well-placed drive down the left before a decision is reached on whether to attack the green with the second shot.

Water guards the left approach to the green and eats into the putting surface itself. A lay-up second shot down the right to take the water out of play for a short approach is usually the best option.

At the next hole, water is a major factor again. The tee shot at this 182 metres par 3 has to flirt with the lake which runs down the entire length of the hole on the right. Anything short or drifting to the right will not survive.

Jones used a similar tactic to defend the next short hole, the 15th, although this time the water is on the left. And he completes a testing finish with a demanding par 5 of more than 500 metres back up the valley between pines and granite rocks.

The 7th at Penha Longa, where the old blends so well with the new. The water on the right will test any propensity to slice.

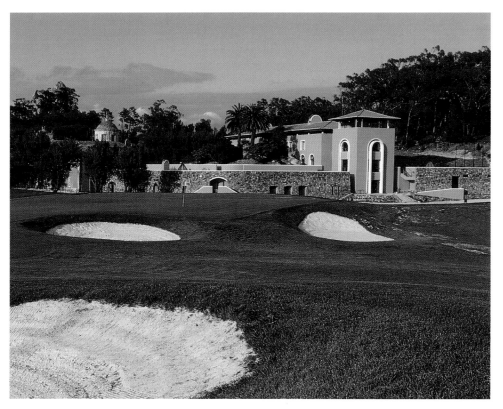

There can be few more welcome sights than the 18th green at Penha Longa with its delightful clubhouse waiting in the background.

The clubhouse which has been built around the old royal stables has a good restaurant and a friendly bar and blends very well into its 14th-century setting.

There is an extensive practice ground with 20 bays in the driving range split between two tees. There are two large practice putting greens with an approach and chipping green.

THE REGION

Penha Longa lies only a short distance from the Portuguese capital and the neighbouring seaside resorts. It is therefore at the heart of many cultural and sporting activities and contains many historical places of interest.

There are several music festivals in the course of the year and the Portuguese Grand Prix attracts thousands of visitors to Estoril.

For those who prefer their entertainment indoors there are many nightclubs and discotheques in the area and the bright lights of the Estoril Casino are always popular.

There are many reminders of the history of this beautiful area in the form of 15th-century monuments much in evidence close to several of the fairways. The greens have been sown with Penncross Bent and are fast and firm.

More than 2500 oak, cork and pine trees have already been planted on the course with a further 2000 to follow. There are also plans for an additional nine holes to be added to the complex.

FACILITIES

Visitors to the new Penha Longa complex will want for nothing in the way of facilities. An elegant clubhouse has been built with the express intention of providing one of the most refined golf clubs in the whole of Europe.

An excellent pro shop offers carts, buggies, trolleys, clubs and even golf shoes for hire. Locker room facilities are first-class and have a sauna and jacuzzi.

ACCOMMODATION

Visitors to Penha Longa might well choose to stay in The Caesar Park, the Quinta Penha Longa resort's five-star hotel. Indeed if they wish to play the course they will have to do so unless they are acquainted with a member who will introduce them. Run by Westin International, the hotel has 177 superb rooms in glorious surroundings.

Quinta do Lago Golf Club

FOUNDED 1974

PEACE AMONG THE UMBRELLA PINES

Originally conceived by André Jordan as a super-luxury and low-density development in the early 1970s, Quinta do Lago suffered badly from lack of investment after the revolution and took a little time to find its feet.

Now, however, this wonderful estate is regarded as one of the most upmarket golf resorts in Europe and its four loops of nine holes are high on any rating list of international golf courses.

Very close to the international airport at Faro, it is quick and easy to get to and after it was opened in 1974 it became very popular.

Today there are four loops of nine holes offering a wide range of 18-hole options. American golf course architect William Mitchell built the original 27 holes at Quinta do Lago. The fourth loop of nine designed

The signs outside say it all, except they don't mention the fourth course. The clubhouse is an excellent place to relax between loops

by Joe Lee became operational in 1990. Lee was also responsible for the magnificent Sao Lourenco course which is also on the Quinta do Lago estate.

THE COURSES

This marvellous golfing country set in rolling countryside strewn with umbrella pines and water hazards has always been rather special. Beautiful fairways with perfect lies and fast greens of Penn-cross bent are its hallmarks. With four loops of nine holes there is an infinite flexibility of play.

Mitchell brought advanced green and bunker construction to the original 27-hole layout and used the contours of the land with great ingenuity and sympathy to produce a marvellous golfing test.

Wide landing areas from the forward tees make the course a joy to play for the handicap player. It is difficult enough though with water hazards and a constant threat from the umbrella pines.

From the back tees the championship layout is considerably tougher as the players in several Portuguese Opens have already found out.

Quinta do Lago Golf Club

Almansil, 8100 Loule

◆

Location: In the Quinta do Lago Estate south of Almansil

Tel: (351) 89 396 0023

Course: Four loops of nine holes. A9 – 3137m, par 36;

B9 – 3225m, par 36;

C9 – 3263m, par 36;

D9 – 3068m, par 36

Visitors: Welcome but pre-booking is essential

Green fees: Esc10,000

FACILITIES

A new clubhouse with a terrace and very refined interior has improved facilities at the course. There is also a swimming pool, sauna and gymnasium for those with energy to spare after the golf. The new clubhouse has a friendly bar and a good restaurant offering ideal after-round menus.

There is a first-class practice facility which is well used and the club has a pool of caddies. Clubs are available for hire, as are golf carts and electric trolleys.

THE REGION

The large Quinta do Lago estate contains just about everything the visitor to this part of Portugal could ask for. It is a sportsman's paradise with a whole range of activities from watersports to tennis and horse-riding.

There are restaurants to suit every taste throughout the estate and just outside in Almancil there are local cafés and bars where the visitor can enjoy the friendly hospitality for which the Portuguese are famous.

Beautiful sculptured fairways are the trademark of Quinta do Logo which is rightly regarded as one of the most refined clubs in Portugal.

The old town of Loulé is a veritable Mecca for shoppers who will enjoy bargain-hunting in the backstreet shops and markets.

ACCOMMODATION

Overlooking a fabulous beach washed by the blue Atlantic and skirting a tidal inlet which offers a haven for protected birds, is the Hotel Quinta do Lago. Set in delightful grounds, this first-class hotel has 141 luxury rooms and nine suites as well as a Presidential

and snooker room, and heated swimming pools indoors and out. The hotel also boasts its own extensive Health Club with massage and gymnasium.

Italian cuisine is the speciality of one of the hotel's restaurants while the Navegador presents a varied

Not only does Quinta do Lago boast wonderful golf, the estate also offers luxury accommodation to let from villas to apartments. And they are all within easy reach of the course.

Suite with its very own private swimming pool.

All rooms are air-conditioned and have balconies and satellite TV. There are tennis courts, a billiards

menu including many traditional Portuguese dishes.

The estate also has a number of luxury villas and apartments to let.

Palheiro Golf

F O U N D E D   1 9 9 3

GOLF IN A SUB-TROPICAL PARADISE

The subtropical island of Madeira off the west coast of Africa has long been a favourite destination for the discerning traveller. There has now been added to its many delights a spectacular new golf course build around Palheiro's formal gardens which are themselves a well-known tourist attraction.

Palheiro Golf
Sao Goncalo, 9000 Funchal,
Madeira
◆
Location: 6km east of
Funchal City centre,
adjacent to Palheiro Gardens
Tel: (351) 91 792 116
Course: 18 holes, 6015m,
par 71
Visitors: Welcome
Green fees: Esc9000

The course is set in a new development only 15 minutes from the centre of Funchal overlooking the bay. The 6015-metre, par 71 course has been designed by Cabell Robinson who has made full use of the hills, ridges and valleys of the Quinta do Palheiro Estate. Almost two thirds of the course lies within pine forest and botanical woodlands which join forces to provide an exceptionally mature golfing environment.

This combination of ingenious landscaping of the course with subtropical shrubs and flowers makes Palheiro one of the most beautiful places to play golf in the world.

The course winds its way through a traditional Madeira quinta founded by the Conde de Carvahal in the early 1800s. The trees and shrubs were imported from all parts of the world and have flourished on this romantic island. Over the treetops are views of Funchal Bay, the sea beyond and the distant and uninhabited Desertas Islands.

In many ways it is the perfect holiday golf course with wonderful scenery, a course which is testing but not overpowering, and a climate which is as good as any in Europe. Sunshine in the winter months and a cooling breeze from the Atlantic in the summer all help to provide perfect conditions for golf.

Clear blue skies and an idyllic view combine with the landscaping of the course to make this one of the most beautiful places in the world to play golf.

THE COURSE

Cabell Robinson has created a layout with generous fairways and a good range of alternative tees to accommodate every standard of player. He has compensated for some lack of length to the course with tight bunkering and made full use of the natural movement in the terrain.

Palheiro does not have returning nine holes. Play is essentially in a figure of eight pattern with the back nine longer than the front.

The most distinctive hole on the front nine is the 3rd. A strong par 4 of 375 metres, it plays shorter than its length suggests by virtue of an elevated tee and a fairway which drops away to a plateau below. The tee is set beside the distinctive Count's Folly, the tower featured on the club's logo. An accurate drive leaves an approach to a terraced green over a lake.

There is only one par 5 on the front nine – the 8th. At 525 metres, it is out of range for all but the very longest hitters and is bracketed by two very good par 3s which demand great care.

The opening two holes on the back nine are both more than 360 metres and very testing while the long par 5 14th is a real monster at 538 metres. There is some respite at the next, a short hole which requires a modest but careful blow with a short iron to find the green. It is, however, the last chance you will find for any relaxation.

Robinson has built a very tough finish into his layout with the 16th and 17th both strong par 4s of around 390 metres and another 500 metre par 5 to finish off.

FACILITIES

The modern Palheiro clubhouse offers first-class facilities to its visitors. There is a bar and restaurant, excellent locker room facilities, and a fully stocked pro shop. Players have the option to walk or use buggies of which the club has a small fleet. There are also caddies available and trolleys for hire.

The club has a chipping green, practice bunkers and a putting green. Video tuition is available from club professional John Blanch.

THE ISLAND

The island of Madeira was discovered by Portuguese explorers in the early 15th century. Along with the neighbouring island of Porto Santo, it basks in subtropical splendour in the Atlantic Ocean 480 kilometres from the coast of West Africa.

The islands are Portuguese and have a population of around 300,000. The capital of Madeira, Funchal, has an important commercial port. The city centre is surrounded by parks and gardens with wonderful views across the sea. The island is temperate and popular with visitors from northern Europe for its winter sunshine. The Atlantic breezes, even during the very height of summer, make the island ideal for active holidays.

The island is easily reached by air. TAP, the Portuguese national airline, operates a regular scheduled service from Lisbon and from London's Heathrow Airport. The British carrier is GB Airways who also fly year-round scheduled services direct to Funchal from Gatwick Airport.

ACCOMMODATION

Palheiro Golf has been developed in conjunction with a small group of principal hotels in Madeira. The founder members are Reid's, Madeira Palacio, Carlton, Eden Mar, Quinta do Sol and the Cliff Bay.

Special discounts and green fees are available to residents staying at these hotels.

The course at Palheiro overlooks the bay at Funchal from a number of holes. Conditions are invariably perfect – whatever the season.

12

Scotland

In an Act of Parliament in 1457, King James II attempted to ban the game of golf and decreed that 'golfe be utterly cryed downe' in the interests of the national defence. His Majesty was concerned that too much practice on the links meant too little practice of archery.

However his subjects, a fiercely independent people, took little notice of him in spite of two further Royal edicts intended to concentrate the minds of subjects on archery, jousting and allied martial activities rather than golf.

The lure of the links proved much stronger than the threat of severe penalties for those who were caught disobeying. With the benefit of hindsight, however, it is not too difficult to understand the monarch's concern. Less than 60 years after that momentous Act of Parliament, the Scots were no match for the English archers at the Battle of Flodden in 1513, when they suffered ignominious defeat and the loss not only of their king but also of the flower of their noble families.

It is known, however, that the game was well established in Scotland more than a century before James II tried to ban it. It was then a rudimentary form of the sport we know today and was probably developed by the fishermen of the east coast of

Beautiful Edinburgh is rightly ranked as one of the great cultural centres of Europe

Scotland who found the rough linksland between the sea and the agricultural land ideal for knocking stones about with sticks as an amusement on their homeward journey from the fishing.

During the 16th century the game became firmly established on the east coast and began to spread further afield. King James VI became a convert before he acceded the English throne as James I in 1603, and his mother, Mary Queen of Scots, was also a notable player. So keen was she, in fact, that she fell foul of the Church for playing golf only a few days after the murder of her husband, Lord Darnley, in 1567.

Today Scotland is accepted as the Home of Golf. The Royal and Ancient Golf Club of St Andrews administers the game worldwide in conjunction with the United States Golf Association, and some of the most famous courses in the world are to be found in Scotland.

Today, Scotland has close to 500 courses and many of them are survivors from the very earliest days of the game. The choice for the visitor is virtually limitless, from the great seaside links courses which host Open championships to the most humble of municipal layouts.

Golf in Scotland remains, as it has always been, the game of the people.

Blairgowrie Golf Club

FOUNDED 1889

A WARM WELCOME AT ROSEMOUNT

The famous Blairgowrie Golf Club, more widely known as Rosemount, has a very genuine claim to be the finest inland course in Scotland. Set in heavily wooded countryside, the two courses offer a decidedly marked contrast.

The Rosemount Course is a serene and demanding layout which underwent some changes in order to accommodate the new Lansdowne Course, a product of the design team of Peter Alliss and Dave Thomas. The latter is a modern layout owing much to the American way of thinking, but is a perfect foil to the Rosemount Course where Greg Norman won his first ever European event in 1977.

Golf was first played at Blairgowrie in 1889 over a nine-hole course close to the Black Loch on land owned by the Dowager Marchioness of Lansdowne.

The 18th green, with the clubhouse overlooking it. Blairgowrie has a fine reputation for food as well its traditional Scottish hospitality.

A move to extend the course to 18 holes in 1906 failed and it was 1927 before the 18-hole Rosemount course was finally opened. Today, the club has a total of 45 holes with the addition of the Lansdowne and the 'Wee' course.

There was some resistance within the club before the new Lansdowne course was built and ready for play in 1975. The Alliss-Thomas design was vastly different to the traditional Rosemount Course and there were some who felt the contrast was too great. But over the years the new course has become fully integrated into the Rosemount scene and it has matured into a first-class layout offering a very stiff test indeed.

The Rosemount course is the one which made Blairgowrie's reputation. That is not in the least surprising for this is one of the classic inland courses.

The fairways wind their way through great stands of fir and pine with silver birch adding splashes of colour along the way. It is not unusual to encounter deer quietly grazing behind the greens. Peace and tranquillity are very much the order of the day here.

Blairgowrie Golf Club
Golf Course Road, Rosemount, Blairgowrie PH10 6LG
◆
Location: 15 miles north of Perth
Tel: 0250-872594
Courses: Rosemount – 18 holes, 6588yds, par 72; Lansdowne – 18 holes, 6895yds, par 72
Visitors: Welcome but some restrictions apply
Green fees: £32 per round, £45 per day, £34 per round at weekends

THE COURSES

The first hole sets the tone for the round. It is a marvellous par 4 which swings to the left before dropping down an incline to a wide green. A single bunker guards the left side.

The course then wends its way through the forest with fairways bordered by deep heather. The only contact with other players is at the crossing points where routes between holes converge.

Rosemount has a classic finish. The 16th is only a yard or two short of a par 5, and the tee shot is played over the corner of the Black Loch and uphill through the trees to a fairway angled to the left. Only a very long and accurate tee shot will leave the green in range for the second shot.

The 17th is a beautiful par 3 with a double-tiered plateau green which is approached over a gully of rough and heather. It is a difficult green to hold with severe penalties for shots that fail.

The last is a tight dogleg right requiring a good drive well to the left to avoid a group of tall trees at the corner. A semicircle of bunkers guards a low-lying green making club selection difficult.

By contrast, the Lansdowne course is much tighter, putting a higher premium on accuracy from the tee, particularly over the opening holes. It is also longer than its older sister by quite a bit, but there is some consolation in that the trees are not so dense and there is usually some opportunity for escape back on to the fairway.

Most of the greens are also open at the front bringing the pitch and run shot more into play than on the Rosemount Course.

The Lansdowne may lack some of the traditional character of the Rosemount Course but it makes up for that in the pure quality of its challenge.

There are many fine holes, with the 17th perhaps the pick of the crop. It is a very long par 5 of 553 yards around a curving fairway which never seems to end, to a green with a single sentinel bunker on the left.

The last is a fine finishing hole demanding a very solid approach shot across a long dip in the ground to a green which is set up on a plateau.

FACILITIES

Blairgowrie not only offers magnificent inland golf but also a warm and friendly reception for visitors. The Rosemount clubhouse is renowned for its catering and the quality of its service.

This is not the place to look for *nouvelle cuisine*, however. The Rosemount menu is for golfers and excellent it is too.

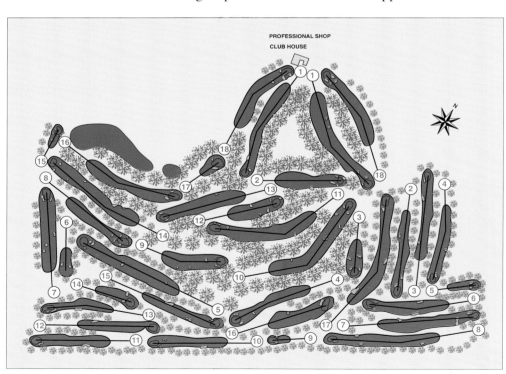

The Blairgowrie courses: Rosemount (red) and Lansdowne (blue).

The 15th and monster 16th holes (top) on the Rosemount course are precursors to a great – if testing – finish. The par 3 17th (above) looks simple enough, but strategically placed bunkers and a two-tier green make it difficult to hold.

many Scottish clubs – and professional Gordon Kinnoch runs one of the best stocked pro shops in the country.

THE REGION

This part of Perthshire is one of the most beautiful in Scotland. From the south the approach road is over the Sidlaw hills and through the fertile plain which looks onward to the Grampian mountains where Highlands and Lowlands meet.

At Dunkeld, only a few miles from Blairgowrie, local salmon are prepared and oak-smoked at Springwells, while at Blair Atholl visitors can see how whisky is made at the famous Blair Atholl Distillery. They can also stay to enjoy a 'dram' while they are there.

To the east at Forfar, which itself has a fine 18-hole course, the visitor can search out and watch the fascinating work of the bagpipe maker.

ACCOMMODATION

Rosemount itself has several hotels ideal both for the visiting golfer, and as a base to visit the local area. The Rosemount Golf Hotel is very close to the course and is popular with golfers because of its location and the excellent welcome guests will receive there.

Only a little further away are the Dalnore Hotel and the Angus Hotel, both of which offer first-class accommodation at very reasonable rates.

The club has separate locker room facilities for visitors and they are also first-class. The spike bar is outside the locker room, but many who play here prefer to change and make use of the main lounge upstairs where the views across the Rosemount Course are quite stunning.

The club has good practice facilities – unusual at

Carnoustie Golf Links

ESTABLISHED C 1500

THE ULTIMATE TEST OF CHARACTER

The great Walter Hagen, winner of 11 of golf's major championships, once described Carnoustie as the 'greatest course in the British Isles'. In 1993, Golf Monthly, one of Europe's most widely-read golf magazines, came to the same assessment and placed this marvellous Angus links at the very top of its list of Britain's Best 50 Courses.

Over the years there has never been any doubt about Carnoustie's credentials as a great course, but after it last hosted the Open Championship in 1975 it went into something of a decline, which resulted in the course being bypassed as an Open venue. However, considerable improvement work has been carried out on the course over the last decade and it has now been returned to something of its former splendour.

Like all of the great British links courses, the challenge of Carnoustie lies in the meteorological whims of the Almighty. Wind is what makes the difference and, when it blows at Carnoustie, not only is the course unrelenting and unforgiving, it can be virtually unplayable. There is no place here for the faint of heart, or the player with anything other than a game under the tightest control.

What gives Carnoustie its very special quality is that it has no apparent weaknesses. It is laid out in such a way that there are never more than two holes running in the same direction and the battle is with the elements as much as the course itself.

Tommy Armour, Henry Cotton, Ben Hogan, Gary Player and Tom Watson are the players who have won the Open at Carnoustie.

Between them, their winning scores average out pretty close to the nominal par of the course. Holes have been changed and par altered on some courses over the years, but the undeniable fact is that 'level fours' on the Championship course at Carnoustie is a standard which only the greatest players have any

Carnoustie Golf Links

Links Parade,
Carnoustie DD7 7JE

◆

Location: 12 miles east of Dundee on the A390

Tel: 0241-853789

Course: 18 holes, 6936yds, par 72

Visitors: Welcome but restrictions apply at weekends. Pre-booking is essential and a current handicap certificate is required

Green fees: £36

The River Tay at Dundee, like Carnoustie, situated in Angus – gateway to the heart of Scotland.

prospect of matching over four rounds of tournament play if there is any wind at all.

But Carnoustie is not only about championship golf. It is also about accessibility for the golfing public and is also a home course for several clubs in the town.

Like the Old Course at St Andrews, the only qualifications required at this golfing shrine are a genuine handicap certificate and the wherewithal to meet the green fee.

As with most of the courses which developed on the east coast of Scotland, there is little in the way of recorded history. It is known that golf was played on the Barry Links next to Carnoustie in the 16th century. Sir Robert Maule, whom history records as being one of the first players, is known to have enjoyed the 'gouff' on the Barry links, and Parish records confirm the game's existence there in 1560.

Allan Robertson, the first of the great early professionals, laid out 10 holes at Carnoustie around the time of the formation of the Carnoustie Club, which is variously accepted as somewhere between 1839 and 1842.

The course was extended to 18 holes by Old Tom Morris in 1857. James Braid was brought in to revamp the course in 1926 and five years later Tommy Armour, a Scot from Edinburgh who had emigrated to America and became one of the game's greatest teachers, won the first Open Championship played at Carnoustie. The course was well and truly on the golfing map.

THE COURSE

In 1937 Henry Cotton took on a field which included the entire United States Ryder Cup team and beat them all in appalling weather conditions. His 71 in the

The 15th (top) is a hole to be played with extreme care; what the bunkers miss, the heather will gobble up. The 18th (above), once a generous par 5, is now played as a par 4. The bunkers left and right of the green have spoilt many a card.

final round, when play was in danger of being abandoned because of the deluge, ranks as one of the great rounds in Open Championship history.

Carnoustie is famous for its 'finish'. The final three holes are among the toughest anywhere in the world and are strewn with the dashed hopes of thousands. The short 16th – in fact it's anything but short at 248 yards – is played to an upturned saucer of a green and is one of the toughest holes in golf.

The 432-yard par four 17th played into the prevailing wind has the Barry Burn twice winding its way tantalisingly through the fairway, much like a serpent waiting to strike.

In 1968 Jack Nicklaus stood on this tee two strokes behind Gary Player and unleashed such a fearsome blow with his driver that he carried the island formed by the burns at its farthest extremity 300 yards distant. It was a miraculous stroke of some 340 yards in length!

The 18th is now played as a long par four when once it was a shortish par five. It demands a long approach over the Barry Burn in front of the green. Few have played it better than Tom Watson in 1975 in his memorable play-off with Jack Newton. With Newton in a greenside bunker, Watson hit a glorious two-iron to the heart of the green for victory.

FACILITIES

Although it boasts one of the greatest courses in the world, Carnoustie lacks somewhat for facilities beside the first tee.

A stark concrete building has locker room accommodation, but it is basic in the extreme and most visitors prefer to use the facilities of one of the local clubs nearby.

The Carnoustie clubs are friendly and allow visitors locker room facilities and the use of their bars and informal restaurants.

Carnoustie is one of the few courses left in Scotland which still has caddies, but their services must be booked in advance when tee times are arranged.

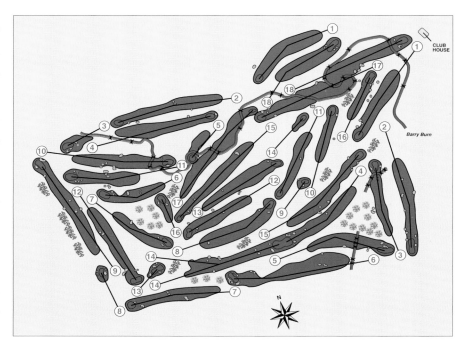

The Carnoustie courses.

THE REGION

Carnoustie lies at the eastern end of the region often described as the 'Heart of Scotland'. It is located in the historic county of Angus only a few miles from the city of Dundee, and it is one of several holiday resorts on the coastline offering a choice of sandy beaches and dramatic, craggy cliffs.

Some of the most historic events in Scotland's history have taken place not far from the great championship links of Carnoustie. The most famous document in Scottish history, the Declaration of Arbroath of 1320, which asserted Scotland's rights of self-government, was written at Arbroath Abbey only a few miles along the coast.

At nearby Scone in Perthshire, the Palace was the crowning place for 42 Scottish kings, and many places are associated with Mary Queen of Scots, golf's first lady player.

Among them are Edzell Castle and the island castle at Loch Leven. There are numerous tourist centres which will provide information from where to find anything from bagpipe-makers to swordsmiths – as well as accommodation.

And of course there is the whisky trail. Carnoustie is only a few miles from the fair city of Perth, gateway to the highlands, where the secrets of the water of life lie waiting to be explored. Guided tours of many distilleries are available as well as tours of traditional Scottish woollen mills and other craft centres.

Then there is simply the splendour of the countryside itself. The Scottish highlands are renowned the world over for their majestic beauty, their glens and their sometimes bloody history.

Peaceful and unspoiled, this is an area easily accessible from Carnoustie and guaranteed to work a special magic on every visitor.

ACCOMMODATION

It is generally accepted that Carnoustie is off the current rota of Open Championship courses because of a lack of hotel accommodation in the town.

This is very misleading. What Carnoustie lacks is a hotel close to the first tee which the championship organizers feel is suitable, and from which they can run what is now a massive operation.

In and around Carnoustie, there is no shortage of first-class accommodation to suit any visitor's taste. From boarding house and friendly bed and breakfast to baronial hall, there is a wealth of choice.

For those who want the atmosphere of an historic Scottish stately home, the Old Mansion House Hotel at Auchterhouse near Dundee is highly recommended. A small luxury hotel, 13 miles from Carnoustie, it was converted by the present owners from a 16th-century baronial home and stands in 10 acres of beautiful gardens and woodlands. It has an acclaimed restaurant serving international as well as traditional Scottish cuisine.

The hotel also boasts a fine wine cellar including some interesting vintages from Russia. There is squash, croquet, tennis and an outdoor pool.

Beauty – and the beasts. The stream may look charming but it rivals the treacherous twin bunkers guarding the green as enemy to a par here at the 10th.

Loch Lomond Golf Club

E S T A B L I S H E D 1 9 9 3

ON THE BONNY, BONNY BANKS

When former Ryder Cup captain, Tony Jacklin, first saw the course at Loch Lomond, he described it as 'the most beautiful new golf course I have ever seen'. And the former Open and US Open champion was so impressed by the layout that he could see it as a possible future venue for the Ryder Cup.

There can hardly be a finer tribute to this Tom Weiskopf design on the west shore of Loch Lomond. The course was finally completed and opened for play in 1993 following uncertainty over its future when the development company went into receivership in 1990.

The course rates as one of world golf's great beauty spots. The 17th green sits, literally, on the bonny, bonny banks of the Loch.

Loch Lomond Golf Club
Rossdhu House, Luss
◆
Location: On the west shore of Loch Lomond off the A82 at Luss
Tel: 0436-860223
Course: 18 holes, 6281yds, par 71
Visitors: Restrictions apply. Pre-booking essential
Green fees: On application

The course has been built on a stunningly beautiful wooded peninsula guarded on three sides by the Loch in the Rossdhu Estate, home of the chiefs of the Clan Colquhoun.

Rossdhu House, the family home of the Colquhouns since 1773, looks out across the enchanted but treacherous waters of the loch.

In the Middle Ages, it was on these waters that the then chief, John Colquhoun 10th of Luss, was savagely murdered by a band of Hebridean marauders led by the chief of clan Maclean.

Weiskopf treated this course with great sympathy for its surroundings, its great traditions and history. He made full use of the rolling landscape and the mature woodland. Azaleas and rhododendrons splash colour around the great house and the castle ruins more liberally even than at Augusta in April. Ben Lomond stands majestic and protective to the north across the bay of Rossdhu and the views to the islands are, quite simply, breathtaking.

THE COURSE

This is a very special place to play golf. A solid drive and middle iron gets the round underway at the opening hole, known as Scots Pine after the tall pine tree which dominates the right hand side of the fairway and threatens the drive. It is a comfortable start; however, there is little comfort to come because this design is a superb examination of course management and shotmaking.

Jay's Corner, the 3rd, is a beautiful, long par 4 of 453 yards which doglegs left and downhill to a green set above the fairway and ringed by trees. Dense undergrowth eats into the fairway to the right and just short of the green, all of which makes the approach one of the most demanding on the course.

The short 5th, played from an elevated tee to a green with a panorama of the loch and its islands as a backdrop, is surely one of the most beautiful holes anywhere the game is played.

The long par 5 6th, known as the 'signature' hole, runs along the very edge of the loch for more than 500 yards with the most stunning views to the east and north. The tee is built up from the shore and the drive must avoid not only the water on the right but also the deep undergrowth on the other side of the fairway. A nest of bunkers in the centre of the fairway forces a choice between a lay-up or a carry with the second. The green is out of range in two for almost everyone, except perhaps its designer; and this is the crucial shot on the hole. Aptly named 'Long Loch Lomond' it is the hole which first time visitors will remember most after their round.

FACILITIES

Uncertainty over the future of the golf club meant that alteration work on the clubhouse at Rossdhu House was not complete when the course opened for play. However, when completed, the clubhouse will have superb facilities including several bars, a first-class restaurant and grill room and several suites of rooms.

THE REGION

Loch Lomond is one of the world's most renowned beauty spots. Only a few miles from Glasgow's international airport, the loch is much more accessible now thanks to the upgrading of the main A82 trunk road. Indeed, much of the infill material used to build the course here came from the construction of the new carriageway.

From the south end of the loch the Highland hills dominate the horizon. For centuries, they stood as the symbols of the unknown for the Lowland folk of Scotland. Beyond them lived the Highlanders with their fierce clans, their distinctive tartan clothes and their Gaelic language.

ACCOMMODATION

There is no shortage of bed and breakfast accommodation within easy reach of the Loch Lomond Golf Club. For those in search of more formal accommodation, however, the Cameron House Hotel is a four-star hotel within a few minutes' drive of the course. In a marvellous setting, it offers extensive facilities, including a Leisure Club, swimming pools, squash courts and a health and beauty suite. It has its own marina, tennis courts and a nine-hole golf course, as well as fishing and shooting.

American cultivated design (by Tom Weiskopf) meets Scottish natural terrain at the 8th. The result – a little piece of golfing heaven.

Nairn Golf Club

FOUNDED 1887

MAJESTIC AND UNDERRATED

The great links course of Nairn Golf Club on the Moray Firth in the north-east corner of Scotland is one of the most majestic in world golf. It is also one of the most underrated.

Set among great stands of whin and heather, there are spectacular views across the Moray Firth to the Black Isle, north to Easter Ross and the mountains to the west. It is a magnificent challenge by any standards with putting greens as firm, fast and true as anywhere else in the world.

Beautiful crisp seaside turf adorns fairways which thread their way through massive gorse bushes and put a high premium on straight driving. Like St Andrews, the wind can be fickle, blowing in the player's face on the way out and promptly changing direction just as he gets to the turn for the long road home.

Andrew Simpson laid out the original course in 1887 for the princely sum of £36. Old Tom Morris was brought north to extend the layout further in 1890 and charged the club £6.10s for his trouble. But the present course owes most to James Braid. The five times Open Champion expanded and refined the course during visits in 1909, 1921 and 1926. Since then it has been lengthened but alterations have been kept to the minimum.

It was the coming of the railway line in the last century which put Nairn firmly on the map and gave the impetus for its development as a holiday resort. 'The Brighton of the North' was how it became known. A combination of perfect terrain, civic ambition and determination by the club founders to create a golf course the equal of anything in the country, all helped Nairn to become the internationally renowned course it is today.

In 1895 the leading players of the day were persuaded north by the inducement of the payment of their rail fares to compete for an exceptional purse for the time of £20.

Influential patronage helped establish Nairn as

Nairn Golf Club
Seabank Road, Nairn
IV12 4HB
♦
Location: Nairn West Shore (A96)
Tel: 0667–452103
Course: 18 holes, 6722yds, par 72
Visitors: Welcome with handicap certificate
Green fees: £26

The old clubhouse has been replaced by an ultra-modern building with top facilities.

a fashionable course, and among those who helped in this regard were Field Marshall Earl Haig, Ramsay Macdonald, HRH the Duke of Windsor when Prince of Wales, Harold MacMillan and Lord Whitelaw, who has had a long association with the club. He is now President.

Lord Whitelaw first played golf at Nairn in the early 1920s and his winning 73 in the junior championship of 1933 was not bettered for more than 50 years.

The club celebrated its centenary in 1987 by hosting the men's and ladies' Scottish Amateur Championships. It was the eighth time that the ladies' event had been played there, reflecting a changing view over the years from the time when it was suggested in the club's book 'that women should be allowed into the clubhouse when the thermometer reached freezing point'.

Now women play a significant role in the modern Nairn club which in recent years has spent more than £800,000 on a new club-

When the wind blows you off course at the 10th, the heather and bushes, as well as the mounds and bunker, lie ready and waiting.

The course at Nairn.

house. It replaced the much-loved old wooden building which could no longer withstand the ravages of time. The party held to mark its sending off on the night before it was demolished was one which many will remember for a long time to come.

THE COURSE

The Nairn layout, like St Andrews, is very much nine out and nine back with a little loop for minor variation. If the wind is against – and that's the prevailing wind – it can be a long battle to the 8th green before

At Nairn, the golfer pits his or her wits – and technique – against nature. The heather, water and weather usually prove to be more than worthy adversaries.

the course reverses on itself for only one hole before stretching westwards again to the 10th

On the way back the 13th, 14th and 15th are played round a little southerly horseshoe off the main loop. And it is at the toe of this horseshoe that the most magnificent views at Nairn are to be had. From the 14th tee, a 206-yard par 3 played steeply downhill, the scene across the Firth is awe-inspiring. To see a well-struck tee shot at this hole hang against the backdrop of a deep blue sky above the forbidding darkness of the Black Isle, is one of the great experiences in golf.

The second shots at the 16th and 17th have to carry water in front of the green – no mean feat when the wind turns around and comes stiffly out of the east as it often does. And even if it is safely negotiated, the work is not done for danger lurks in wait at the final hole as well.

A nest of seven bunkers spreads through a 50-yard stretch of the landing area which makes the drive very difficult, irrespective of wind direction. Two more deep chasms threaten the second shot and the final green is guarded by two more bunkers which are just as dangerous.

FACILITIES

The new clubhouse facilities at Nairn can now compete with any club in the British Isles. A magnificent lower-level locker room has every refinement and the upstairs lounge, dining room and bar are first-class with incredible views over the course and hills to the west.

THE REGION

Nairn has long enjoyed a fine reputation as a holiday destination since the railway made it accessible before the turn of the century. Today, it is as easily reached by road and air. Major improvements to the main A9 trunk road to Inverness from the south have resulted in major savings in journey time, and the airport at Inverness is only a short drive along the coast road which has so much to offer the visitor.

The battlefield at Culloden, where Bonny Prince Charlie's bedraggled followers were slaughtered by the Duke of Cumberland in 1746, has an eerie and sinister compulsion about it. The rows of graves of the defeated clansmen mark a stark chapter in the Jacobean history of Scotland.

To the west lies Loch Ness and the Great Glen where you can experience some of Scotland's most spectacular scenery. Here, 'monsters' are never long out of the conversation.

To the north, the Black Isle is mysterious and beautiful with another fine course at Fortrose and Rosemarkie worth making a stop to visit. From there, the road heads north through wonderful Highland scenery and onwards towards Dornoch.

ACCOMMODATION

Nairn is well served for first-class hotel and bed and breakfast accommodation. The Golf View Hotel, situated beside the course, is highly regarded and quite rightly so by visiting golfers, as are the Clifton Hotel close to the 17th tee and the Newton Hotel.

Royal Dornoch

FOUNDED 1877

A WILD AND GLORIOUS OUTPOST

For wild, natural beauty and formidable golf, the links of Royal Dornoch are unsurpassed anywhere in the world. Even to reach it requires a journey through some of Scotland's most majestic landscape.

But what a joy lies in store for the intrepid traveller when he arrives in the historic old town with its air of peace and remoteness together with the open friendliness of its inhabitants.

Only St Andrews and Leith can claim greater antiquity than Dornoch. Records show that golf has certainly been played here since 1616.

This classic links is strung out around Embo Bay in the mouth of the Dornoch Firth and is completely exposed to the wild moods of the weather in a latitude it shares with northern Russia and Hudson Bay.

It is only when the player reaches the clubhouse with the fine Royal Golf Hotel alongside that the full majesty of the links comes into view. If the time of year is right and the gorse is in bloom the view from the top of the 3rd tee is truly breathtaking. As far as the eye can see, stretching along the magnificent sweep of the bay, is a mass of brilliant yellow running through the humps and hollows that make up this magnificent links.

Organized golf came to Dornoch in the autumn of 1876 when the local Chief Constable, Alex McHardy who was originally from Fife, and Dr Hugh Gunn, a graduate of St Andrews University, organized a meeting to form the Dornoch Golf Club. What was said between the two august gentlemen is not known but the following spring the club was formed and the original layout of nine holes was opened for play.

Old Tom Morris from St Andrews was called in to add another nine some 10 years later and is reported to have been taken by the place immediately, particularly the natural plateaux which made such perfect locations for greens.

Royal Dornoch Golf Club
Golf Road, Dornoch, IV25 3LW
◆
Location: 51 miles north of Inverness on A949 north of Dornoch
Tel: 0862-810219
Courses: Championship – 18 holes, 6581yds, par 70; Struie – 18 holes, 5242yds, par 67
Visitors: Welcome on presentation of handicap certificate
Green fees: £35 per round

A warm tradional Scottish welcome is guaranteed at the Dornoch clubhouse, situated just by the 1st tee.

However, the man who influenced the development of Dornoch most was John Sutherland, one of the most revered names in Scottish golf. He was an estate agent in the town and was appointed secretary of the club in 1883. It was a position he held for more than 50 years and, during his time, he made several revisions to the course in close collaboration with J.H. Taylor, who became a regular summer visitor to Dornoch.

It was the coming of the railway in 1903 which put Dornoch on the golfing map. By that year a sleeping car service could bring visitors overnight from London, and soon the little town became a popular resort.

Among the game's wealthy and famous who made the journey were Roger Wethered and his sister, whom Bobby Jones, never a man known for exaggeration, pithily described as the 'finest golfer, man or woman, I have ever seen'.

THE COURSE

The present course at Dornoch measures a relatively modest 6581 yards and has a par of 70 with four par 3s and only two par 5s on the card. Its very remoteness has mitigated against it hosting many major events.

The Scottish Ladies' Amateur Championship was played there in 1971 and 1984, and the following year the Amateur Championship went to Dornoch. But by and large these famous links have not witnessed much top-flight competition.

That is not to say that they have been deprived of first-class play. Five times Open Champion, Tom Watson, a self-confessed lover of traditional Scottish links golf who plays there whenever he can, rates Dornoch as one of the world's great courses. 'I have played none finer,' he has said. 'It is a natural masterpiece.' There can be no finer accolade.

The inviting 16th green looks out dramatically across Embo bay – a wild and haunting setting in one of Scotland's most beautiful settings.

need to get different art work;
Hugh is sorting this out

The course at Royal Dornoch.

The course follows a natural soft 'S' shape along the curved line of the shore and is a classic 'out and back' configuration.

As with all classic links, the wind is the key factor. When it is in the prevailing west, the first eight holes can lull the player into a false sense of wellbeing. From the 9th tee the battle is on and there is no let-up.

Only the 17th reverses the direction of the homeward journey and it gives little respite. A drive into a hidden valley is fraught with danger if too much liberty is taken with the bunkers and the gorse on the left side. The pitch to the green seldom needs to be of much length but it requires a deft touch over a gaggle of awkward bunkers to a plateau green which is difficult to hold.

The home hole requires two solid blows to make the open green in normal circumstances. When the weather boils up, as it so quickly can in this isolated corner, it often requires three from even the strongest of players, and all of them truly struck well into the bargain.

THE REGION

The Highlands of Scotland are widely regarded as one of the most beautiful areas in the world. Deep lochs, towering mountains, heather and peaceful solitude are the hallmarks. There are ancient castles and historic sites where the often bloody history of Scotland was played out.

With improved road communications, Dornoch is much more easily reached than it once was. Today it is a relatively short drive to Inverness. This city at the head of Loch Ness and the Great Glen is a paradise for visitors who want to savour Scottish history. It was just outside Inverness, at Culloden, that

Bonny Prince Charlie's rebellion was put down brutally by the Duke of Cumberland in 1746.

The visitor centre at the battlefield recounts one of Scotland's darkest hours and visitors never fail to sense the eeriness about the place.

Not too far to the north of Dornoch lies John O'

This is the wild 5th at Dornoch. It's not difficult to see why five times Open champion Tom Watson returns to this course again and again.

Groats, the most northerly point on the British mainland. To the west lie the great mountain ranges of the Highlands with narrow tracks to explore and hardly a soul to be seen for miles. This is scenery on a majestically grand scale.

ACCOMMODATION

Dornoch is well placed to accommodate the traveller to Dornoch. The Royal Golf Hotel is right beside the first tee and is first choice for many.

Also in the town, the Burghfield Hotel enjoys a well-earned reputation among visiting golfers, while the Dornoch Castle is only five minutes' walk from the course and is also very popular.

The Dornoch Castle was formerly the Palace of the Bishops of Caithness and the present building is thought to have been built in the late 15th century.

Royal Troon Golf Club

FOUNDED 1878

A TEST OF STRENGTH AND SKILL

Virtually all the best Scottish west-coast golf courses are strung out like a string of rare pearls along the duneland from Irvine to Prestwick. Royal Troon lies at the southern end of this beautiful stretch of the Ayrshire coastline.

There are stories of golf having been played at Troon long before there was a recognized golf course there. There is evidence in Ian Mackintosh's excellent history of the club of a 'course' of four or five holes as early as 1870 on which the holes were cut with a knife and 'were neither round nor square, but were large enough'.

It was not until 1878 that the club itself came into being and, like so many others around that period, the prospective members met for the first time in a local hostelry, The Portland Arms Hotel. The instigator of this historic meeting was Dr John Highet.

One of Dr Highet's fellow founder members was James Dickie from the town of Paisley on the outskirts of Glasgow. Dickie at that time had a summer house in Troon and was no stranger to the town. It was he who approached the owner of the Estate of Fuller-

Royal Troon Golf Club

Craigend Road, Troon KA10 6EP

◆

Location: South east side of Troon (B749) three miles from Prestwick Airport

Tel: 0292–311555

Courses: Old Course – 18 holes, 7097yds, par 72; Portland – 18 holes, 6274yds, par 70

Visitors: Welcome, but prior booking is essential

Green fees: £72 per day for Old Course plus Portland

ton, the 6th Duke of Portland, to seek permission to build a golf course over the land he owned between Craigend and the Pow Burn.

The present Troon layout has evolved with the help of several notable golf course architects including Willie Fernie, Open Champion in 1883, who was instructed to make alterations when he was the club's professional. James Braid, Dr Alister Mackenzie and Frank Pennink are others who have left their influence on this famous links.

Arthur Havers won the first Open Championship at Troon in 1923 and many illustrious names have joined him on the list of Open Champions who have won there since. Bobby Locke, Arnold Palmer, Tom Weiskopf, Tom Watson and Mark Calcavecchia complete the role of honour.

There is a comfortable atmosphere of affluence at the historic Troon clubhouse – redolent of its illustrious past.

An aerial view of the famous links. The changes of colour read like a relief map and are ample evidence of the great challenges which this great course presents.

THE COURSE

There are several famous holes at Royal Troon, including both the longest and the shortest holes in Open Championship golf. The longest is the 577 yards 6th which demands a long carry, normally into the prevailing wind, to reach a narrow strip of fairway guarded by a triangle of bunkers.

The bunker on the left side of the fairway, 50 yards short of the green, has been a graveyard for many, including the unfortunate Bobby Clampett in the 1982 Open.

The deep cavern of sand on the right-hand side 20 yards further on has also claimed more illustrious victims. The green sits in the lee of a massive dune and is guarded by a wickedly deep bunker which eats into the putting surface on the front left.

The shortest hole is the famous 8th, known the world over as the 'Postage Stamp'. In the 1950 Open,

Herman Tissies, a German amateur player, had only one putt but needed 15 strokes to hole out, including five from a bunker on the left, another five from a bunker on the right and three to escape from the original bunker for a second time!

In 1973, Gene Sarazen, a winner in his time of all four major championships and then in his 70s, was playing in the company of Fred Daly and Max Faulkner. He holed his tee shot with a five-iron in a sentimental return to the Open. Sarazen needed a total of only three strokes to play the famous 8th twice by holing a bunker shot in his second round and, in so doing, did not use his putter on the hole at all.

Sarazen presented the five-iron with which he had holed his tee shot in the first round to the Royal and Ancient Golf Club of St Andrews, where he is an honorary member, and it remains there on display in the clubhouse.

If you find the sanctuary of the green at the 7th, all well and good. Avoid the fortifications if you can.

of Merit winner, Colin Montgomerie.

THE REGION

Royal Troon sits almost at the end of the main runway of Prestwick international airport. But don't let that put you off.

Troon is an ideal base to explore the beautiful coastline of Ayrshire. Trim farmland and rolling moorland pastures run down to beautiful sandy beaches.

There are many connections with Robert Burns and an interesting textile heritage in towns like Kilmarnock and Stewarton.

Royal Troon is one of many fine golf courses in the area. There are a number of country parks and marinas for those who wish to venture further on to the beautiful waters of the Firth of Clyde.

ACCOMMODATION

The traditional Marine Highland Hotel is a Troon landmark and overlooks the 18th fairway of the championship course. The elegant Fairways Restaurant offers only the finest food complemented by an award-winning wine list. It has a wide range of leisure facilities including a swimming pool, saunas, jacuzzi, squash courts, gymnasium and a beauty room.

Close by is the unique and historic Priestland House Hotel built in the last century for Sir Alexander Walker, grandson of Scotch whisky firm founder, Johnny Walker. It has associate hotels at Bridge of Allan and Perth.

FACILITIES

Royal Troon is a very historic Scottish golf club and jealously protects its traditions and values. This is not a club which offers saunas or swimming pools but locker room facilities are modern and functional. The lounges and bars have an air of well-heeled prosperity about them and the restaurant is first-class.

The Secretary at Royal Troon is Mr J.D. Montgomerie – father of the 1993 European Order

The Old Course, St Andrews

ESTABLISHED C.1400

IN THE CRADLE OF THE GAME

The Old Course at St Andrews is the most famous golf course in the world. It is the cradle of the game and its historical and cultural home – the Mecca to which every golfer who has ever played the game wishes to make at least one pilgrimage in his or her golfing life.

Golf is known to have been played on these ancient links for more than 500 years, and some believe for centuries longer than that. During that time the course has simply evolved into what it is today.

Man has had little to do with the design or layout; nature and the hand of God have joined forces to put together this masterpiece. It stands the test of time as a major championship course, defying the development of golf equipment which would seem as strange to Old Tom Morris with his playclub and gutta percha balls of the last century as Concorde would now do to the Wright brothers.

St Andrews is recognized all over the world as the Home of Golf. For it is here that the rules and standards have been set. And it is here that the golfing world still looks for example and guidance.

All the greatest players in the history of the game, with perhaps Ben Hogan the only notable exception, have played over this classic links and crossed the little antique bridge over the Swilcan Burn at the last hole with, before them, the most famous view in golf.

The Royal and Ancient Clubhouse stands sentinel over the widest fairway in the world shared by the 1st and 18th holes. To the seaward side there is the great sweep of St Andrews Bay and the magnificent West Sands, made famous in more recent times as the setting for the opening titles in the Oscar-winning film, *Chariots of Fire*.

St Andrews Links Management Committee

St Andrews, Fife KY16 9JA

◆

Location: In the town of St Andrews by the Bruce Embankment

Tel: 0334-75757

Course: 18 holes, 6566yds, par 72

Visitors: Welcome with a current handicap certificate and prior reservation. A ballot system operates in the summer months.

No play on Sundays

Green fees: £40-50

So many great dramas have started out here – the most famous first hole in golf. The Royal and Ancient Clubhouse sits imperiously behind the tee.

There can be few more varied landscapes than here with the sweep of St Andrews bay and the West Sands dominating the foreground and the town and the opening holes of the Old Course behind.

On the opposite side is the ancient town itself, home not only of the game of golf but of Scotland's most ancient seat of learning, the beautiful University of St Andrews.

THE COURSE

The Old Course is seaside links *par excellence*. There are none of the dramatic sand dunes of Birkdale or Royal Aberdeen, but the fairways are rolling and undulating with enough elevation to make them both fascinating and frustrating.

The course is laid out roughly in the shape of a shepherd's crook. At one time in its history, golfers played all the way out to the Eden estuary and then simply walked all the way back to the local hostelries to analyse their exploits. Quite when it was decided to play back along the holes which had been played on the way out is not quite clear, but ultimately a total of 22 holes played out and back became the accepted round of golf here.

There are only four single greens on the Old Course, the 1st, the 9th, the famous 17th known as the Road Hole, and the green on the final hole known as the Home Hole.

The 1st tee is immediately in front of the big window of the R & A Clubhouse and the shot from there is widely regarded by all who have played here as the most frightening in golf.

The hole itself is quite short but the Swilcan Burn, immediately in front of the green, claims many victims who underclub. Once over the Swilcan Burn, the course sweeps away to the right sharing fairways with the inward holes until it reaches the part of the course known as 'the loop'. It is within this run of five holes from the 7th that the Old Course's only two short holes are found.

The second of them, the wickedly difficult 11th, is known as the High Hole. This is where, on his first encounter with the Old Course, the legendary American amateur Bobby Jones tore up his card and walked off the course. Later, he was to form a deep affection for it and was made a Freeman of the City in 1958.

From the 11th the course makes its way back along the path which has already been trodden, sharing the same fairways used on the outward journey. The double greens are huge with white flags to indicate the holes on the outward journey and red flags to indicate those coming home. The only exception to be found is the flag on the 18th hole which is traditionally white.

The key to playing the Old Course well is to avoid the bunkers, most of them unseen, which lurk everywhere. Many of these treacherous hazards have names, the most infamous of them is Hell Bunker, a vast and deep pit which guards the Long Hole, the 14th.

The strangely named Principal's Nose stands out like a proboscis in the centre of the 16th fairway and must be avoided at all costs. Those who are tempted to carry the drive over it inevitably find their ball nestling deeply in the nasty little pot bunker behind, known as Deacon Sime.

The next is perhaps the most famous hole in golf – the notorious 17th, or the Road Hole. The drive is across the corner of the Old Course Hotel where once old railway sheds stood, although today only an outline remains.

The approach must flirt with the deep Road bunker which eats into the green and is now widely known as 'the sands of Nakajima' after the unfortunate Japanese golfer who was well placed in the

This is the infamous 17th, or Road Hole. The treacherous Road bunker which guards the green has dashed the dreams of many a challenge – Open or otherwise.

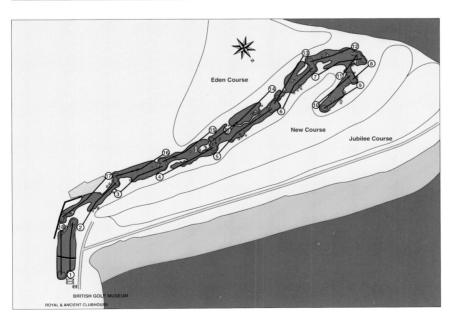

The Old Course at St Andrews.

Beautiful St Andrews has everything, including a castle, university and cathedral. It is also the perfect base from which to explore Scotland.

1978 Open Championship but took four strokes to escape from the sand to end his challenge.

Once past the Road Hole, the Old Course has done its worst in terms of bunkers for there are no more to come. The drive to the final hole is again up the widest fairway in the game to the final green and back into the town itself. No matter what time of day, the critical eyes of spectators are on the players as they complete their round and negotiate the valley of sin in front of the green.

Ripples of applause or deafening silence reflect the level of failure or success on this – the most famous golfing finish in the world.

FACILITIES

Work on a clubhouse at St Andrews starts in 1995 to service the Old, New and Jubilee courses. This will be completed in time for The Open at St Andrews in 1996. Locker room facilities are currently provided in the lower level of the Rusacks Hotel, where there is also a bar and an informal restaurant.

The local golf clubs are not accessible to visitors unless introduced by club members. St Andrews has a new and superb practice facility, although it is some way from the first tee of the Old Course. It is floodlit and has covered bays for inclement weather.

Local professional tuition is available and sections of the practice facility are reserved specifically for that. Caddies are available on the Old Course by arrangement and caddie cars are available for hire from May to September but are permitted only for afternoon play.

THE REGION

St Andrews has played a major part in the historical, educational and religious life of Scotland over the centuries. It is a fascinating town of ancient University buildings and an historic cathedral.

The city lies in the north-east corner of the Ancient Kingdom of Fife. The completion of the road bridges across the Rivers Forth and Tay have made Fife an ideal base for tourists to explore Scotland. The glorious scenery, the lochs, the castles and the mountains are all within easy reach of the Home of Golf.

And in the Auld Grey Toon, as it is known, visitors should not pass up an opportunity to visit the British Golf Museum.

ACCOMMODATION

There are few places in Scotland better served with a wide range of accommodation than St Andrews – from the splendour of the famous Old Course Hotel on the edge of the 17th fairway to inexpensive, but comfortable, bed and breakfast accommodation.

The splendid Rusack's Hotel alongside the 18th fairway has commanding views over the course and facilities for golfers in its own 'locker room' in the basement. The Old Course Hotel has its own professional's shop.

For those seeking something a little less splendid, the Russell Hotel only a long iron from the 1st tee of the Old Course, is typical of many small hotels in the town offering first-class accommodation, an excellent restaurant and a very good cellar.

Southerness Golf Club

F O U N D E D   1 9 4 7

CLASSIC MACKENZIE ROSS

The travelling golfer heading north into the west of Scotland can perhaps be forgiven for bypassing one of the great links courses of Britain in favour of the big names at Turnberry, Prestwick or Troon. It is easily done for the Southerness Golf Club is tucked away in a remote corner of Dumfriesshire.

But for those who take the trouble to delay their arrival further up the coast and play this wonderful Mackenzie Ross layout, there is a great golfing treat in store. This is one of Scotland's hidden gems which, if it were a little more easily accessible, would be as well known as its more illustrious neighbours.

Not that it languishes in the wilderness by any

The 18th, one of the two par 5s of the course, leads directly to the clubhouse where a warm welcome is guaranteed.

means. There are discerning players from far afield who make their way almost religiously to pay homage at this wonderful and traditional links, and put up a grateful prayer for the remoteness that keeps it out of the wider gaze.

The views along the coast of Galloway and inland to the mountain of Criffel are as spectacular as those across the Solway Firth to the mountains of the Lake District. On a clear day there are even views of the Isle of Man. This is a tranquil and beautiful place to play golf on the only truly championship standard seaside links to have been built in Britain since the Second World War.

It has been laid out on a flat stretch of land on sandy soil with heather lining many of the fairways. Mackenzie Ross, a master architect who was also responsible for renovating Turnberry after it had been dug up to make way for an airfield, retained the wild and natural look of the place.

Lovers of the sterile American style of design will not feel comfortable here. This is a course for the traditionalist who likes his golf open to the vagaries of wind and weather and his lies exactly the way God left them.

Southerness Golf Club
Southerness, Kirkbean, Dumfries, DG2 8AZ
◆
Location: 15 miles south of Dumfries
Tel: 0387-88677
Course: 18 holes, 6566yds, par 69
Visitors: Welcome with some restrictions
Green fees: £24 per day. £32 per day at weekends

THE COURSE

There are plenty of natural hollows and dells and Mackenzie Ross made full use of natural plateaux and shelves to build the greens. Tight, crisp turf and firm and fast greens await the visitor as well as a warm Borders welcome from one of the friendliest clubs in the country.

There are many outstanding holes at Southerness. The two short holes in the final four are good

The 16th shows the undulations of the course in a perfect setting with no frills. This is a golf course for the purist.

examples. At 220 yards, the first of them, the 15th, is a test for anyone, while the 17th, at 177 yards, though shorter, is just as demanding.

Only one of the six par 4s on the front nine is under 400 yards and that by only by 10 paces. This gives the clue as to why Southerness has a nominal par of 69 but a standard scratch score of 72.

The only 2 par 5s on the course are the 5th and the 18th, both close to 500 yards, and only two of the par 4s on the back nine are under 400 yards.

The short 7th is another par 3 of well over 200 yards and the 13th hole is a monster par 4, only five yards inside the limit.

Fairway woods and long irons earn their place in the bag in no small measure on this fine layout.

FACILITIES

The Southerness clubhouse is very much in the traditional Scottish mould, with a friendly 19th hole bar and excellent golfers' catering.

The club also has a full-length practice ground.

THE REGION

The Borders area of Scotland enjoys an international reputation for its outstanding beauty and hospitality. On the Solway coast the Gulf Stream's influence has helped create the wonderful Arbigland gardens at Kippford, and not far away is poignant Dundrennan Abbey where Mary Queen of Scots spent her last fateful night in Scotland.

Within a mile of the course at Southerness, the infamous Admiral John Paul Jones was born. Having thrown in his lot with the American revolutionaries in 1775, he harassed British shipping off his homeland coasts as far afield as Lowestoft. Later, he served the forces of Catherine the Great of Russia as Kontradmiral Pavel Ivanovitch Jones before he died in impecunity in France.

He also gave his name to a dance which is still popular in traditional circles. There is evidence of his Southerness upbringing which can still be seen in the town to this day.

ACCOMMODATION

The Baron's Craig Hotel in Rockville and Clonyard House in Colvend are eminently suitable lodgings close to Southerness while, a few miles to the north and west, the Golf Hotel at Powfoot is also popular.

For those seeking something a little special on the gastronomic front, the journey to the Riverside Inn at Canonbie should prove very worthwhile.

Turnberry Golf Course

FOUNDED 1906

SPLENDOUR ON THE GRAND SCALE

There are few more spectacular places to play golf than at the Turnberry Hotel on the west coast of Scotland. Standing on a headland looking out across the Firth of Clyde towards Ireland, this famous hotel looks down on one of the truly great championship golf courses anywhere in the world.

Turnberry lies at the southernmost end of a long stretch of classic linksland along the Ayrshire coast some 50 miles south west of Glasgow. The hotel, with its distinctive white façade and russet red roof, is a commanding landmark on this quiet stretch of Ayrshire countryside.

Behind the hotel stretches the rich agricultural heritage of the land of Robert Burns, while out to sea, across the Firth of Clyde, lies the stark beauty of the Isle of Arran and, beyond, the dark, mysterious Mull of Kintyre.

To the left of this panoramic view from the hotel is the intriguing silhouette of the Ailsa Craig, a great, round island of granite which seems to float upon the water like a piece of giant flotsam and which the locals call Paddy's Milestone.

Only a few can now recall when the stones for one of Scotland's great sporting traditions, curling, were hewn from the granite of Ailsa Craig.

The Ailsa Course – the very name sends shivers down the spine – is one of the great challenges in world golf. It is a course upon which the player can, and often does, experience all four Scottish seasons on one day and where, when the wind rages in from the Atlantic, the game of golf can become a virtual impossibility.

And yet this classic links, which has witnessed some remarkable golfing deeds in its relatively short service as an Open Championship venue, might

Turnberry Hotel, Golf Courses and Spa
Turnberry, Ayrshire KA26 9LT
◆
Location: 15 miles south of Ayr
Tel: 0655-31000
Courses: Ailsa – 18 holes, 6976yds, par 70.
Arran – 18 holes, 6014 yards, par 68
Primarily for hotel residents.
Visitors: By written application only, but should book in advance
Green fees: Ailsa £50, Arran £20 (for hotel residents)

The clubhouse and hotel look forward and across one of the most spectacular golf courses in the world.

An aerial view of the 9th. If you look carefully, you can see the tee on the little finger of land next to the lighthouse. Definitely not for the fainthearted.

well have been lost to golf for ever had it not been for the valiant efforts of Frank Hole, the one-time manager of the Hotel.

Hole fought a persistent post-war campaign to extract from the British Government enough compensation money to attempt to recreate the Turnberry courses, after they had been dug up to build an airfield during the Second World War. He succeeded brilliantly and, with the help of golf course architect Mackenzie Ross, rebuilt the courses, rescuing them from under the runways.

The other Turnberry course, the Arran, is no mean challenge either and, were it not for the presence of its more famous sister, would be a worthy venue for any championship.

The courses are very much part of the hotel operation at Turnberry. The two have always been linked. The 3rd Marquis of Ailsa, after whom the championship course was named, leased the ground to the Glasgow and South Western railway Company in 1899 when he was captain at Prestwick Golf Club further up the coast.

The 1883 Open Champion, Willie Fernie, was brought in to design two 13-hole layouts at Turnberry which were completed in 1905. Shortly afterwards, the Turnberry Hotel was completed and the railway company took over the courses.

THE COURSES

Turnberry went on to the Open Championship rota for the first time in 1977 when the famous battle between Jack Nicklaus and Tom Watson, now known as 'The Duel in the Sun', was dramatically fought out in heatwave conditions.

In 1986 Greg Norman won his first major championship here with a famous victory, and when it was announced that Turnberry would host the 1994 Open Championship, it became firmly established on the championship rota.

There are many great holes on the Ailsa Course. The 5th, for instance, is a tough par 4 of 441 yards which lies in a sweeping valley between the sand dunes. A good drive down the right to avoid two large bunkers in the corner of the dogleg is needed. From there the fairway turns left, following the shore to a green screened by a bunker short and left and other bunkers eating into the playing surface.

The most famous hole at Turnberry is the 9th, out by the lighthouse. There may be more difficult holes in championship golf but there are none with a more spectacular or frightening tee shot.

The tee sits out on a finger of rock high above the crashing surf of the Atlantic Ocean where the player's only protection from certain oblivion if he were to fall off is a fragile looking fence. It is the spot which prompted the eminent Scottish golf writer, Norman Mair, to coin the now classic comment 'for those in peril on the tee'.

The shot must carry across a large chunk of the Atlantic Ocean, but since it is often down a fearsome wind from behind, it is the circumstances of the shot rather than the shot itself which can turn strong men into quivering wrecks. The hole is named Bruce's Castle after the nearby remains of a fortress said to have been used by the Scottish king.

FACILITIES

A magnificent new clubhouse was built at Turnberry in preparation for the return of the Open Championship in 1994. It was built without regard to cost and there is quite simply everything the golfer could wish for in this majestic new building. Coupled with the facilities offered by the hotel, it would be hard to find better anywhere.

The 11th – with the famous lighthouse in the distance – can make or break you. The menacing bunker stands guard – waiting for a misdirected shot.

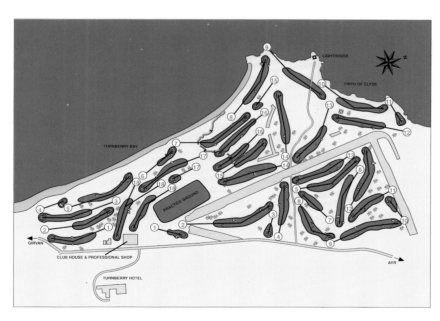

The courses at Turnberry.

The clubhouse has a restaurant and bar as lavish as the hotel itself and the shop of professional Bob Jamieson is widely regarded as one of the finest of any of the world's great golfing resorts.

THE REGION

Ayrshire is one of Scotland's most beautiful and historic counties. It was not far from Turnberry that Robert Burns was born and wrote much of the finest poetry in the Scots language.

The rolling hinterland is beautiful and full of the richness of Scottish history. Culzean Castle, where America's most famous golfing President, Dwight D. Eisenhower, had his own rooms, is set among the most splendid surroundings only a few miles from Turnberry and there are many other equally historic buildings close by.

ACCOMMODATION

The famous Turnberry Hotel is not only one of the great hotels of Europe, but is renowned worldwide. With its stunning panoramic views across the Firth of Clyde to Ireland, and the quality of its accommodation and service, any stay there is memorable.

The opening of its health spa added yet another dimension to this already excellent hotel. A swimming pool together with a complete range of sports, fitness and leisure facilities is included.

The spa also has a first-class restaurant with excellent food and stunning views across the Firth.

13

Spain

There are more than a hundred golf courses in Spain, the majority of which have been built as a direct result of the huge golf boom the country experienced through the 1970s and 1980s.

The winter sunshine of the Costa del Sol to which millions had begun to flock in the decade before was perfect for golf and there was no lack of entrepreneurial spirit to jump on the great holiday bandwagon.

Holiday home developments and timeshare apartments were thrown up everywhere along the south coast and the developers soon realized that there was no better marketing tool than a golf course to help move the merchandise.

Golfers from all over northern Europe flocked to this sun-kissed golfing Valhalla, desperate to escape the winter chills of home. But, alas, the great winter golfing adventure soon turned sour as green fees soared, standards dropped and the five-hour round became all too familiar.

Surly staff, difficulties over tee times and a continued deterioration of the accepted standards and conventions of the game inevitably took their toll and winter golfers began to vote with their feet. In next to no time, the great Spanish golf boom went into sharp decline.

Granada – high up in the heart of southern Spain where the sun always seems to shine, and the sounds, sights and smells of Andalucia are never far away.

However, there remained in its wake many fine golf courses, not only on the Costa del Sol, but also on the Costa Blanca and the Costa Brava where the excesses of the south were perhaps less pronounced.

The origins of Spanish golf lie much further north than Puerto Banus. In Madrid, Barcelona and Bilbao, old clubs with great traditions have preserved their standards and ridden out the storm of golfing commercialism: clubs like the Real Club de la Puerta de Hierro in Madrid, founded in 1904; the Real Club de Golf de Cerdanya high in the hills near Andorra, founded in 1929; and the Real Sociedad de Golf de Neguri outside Bilbao, dating back to 1911; all which were among the pioneers of Spanish golf. Padrena in Santander, which dates back to 1928, is another but is more famous as the course on which Severiano Ballesteros learned to play as a youngster.

There are signs today that Spain has learned some of the lessons of life in recessionary times and that a new order is slowly being established at courses anxious now to lure back the missing golfers. Progress is being made but it is a long haul.

Green fees have certainly tumbled and there is an awareness now that service is important if visitors are to be encouraged to come, and come again.

Spain is clearly fighting back.

Club de Campo Villa de Madrid

F O U N D E D 1 9 3 2

HOME OF THE CADDIE SCHOOL

This beautiful woodland course on the outskirts of Madrid is one of the oldest and finest in the whole of Spain. Designed by the incomparable Javier Arana, it has been the venue of many great championship events in its long history, including the Canada Cup (now the World Cup) and, on many occasions, the Spanish Open.

It has produced many fine champions in that event including Roger Davies, Sam Torrance and the inaugural winner at Club de Campo in 1951, former Open Champion, Max Faulkner.

Perhaps the most memorable victory was that of Eduardo Romero when he defeated Severiano Ballesteros at the 7th hole in an amazing play-off for the Spanish title in 1991.

Club de Campo lies across the valley and in clear view of another of Europe's great championship courses, the Puerta de Hierro Golf Club, which regularly hosts the Madrid Open.

Club de Campo is also the base for Spain's famous caddie school which has produced such great European Tour stars as Manuel Pinero, Antonio Garrido and José Maria Canizares. All learned golf basics there in tandem with their normal schooling.

THE COURSES

The course is laid out in undulating countryside and has many plateau greens. The opening hole is a difficult par 4 of 427 metres featuring a fairway with a sweeping dogleg to the right. The green is difficult to hit, gently sloping and well protected by bunkers.

Four fearsome bunkers protect the double-tier green at the next where only a drive of great length and precision will open up the target for the second shot.

The short 3rd demands a long carry of more than 200 metres over water to a green well defended by trees and sand. There is no respite at the next, which brings water into play again.

Trees line the fairway at the 4th where the best line is down the left side to open up a view of the slightly

Club de Campo Villa de Madrid
Crta Castilla, 28040 Madrid
◆
Location: 4km north-west of Madrid
Tel: (341) 357 2132
Courses: 18 holes, 6118m, par 72; 9 holes, 2900m, par 36
Visitors: Welcome but must reserve tee times in advance
Green fees: Ptas5000-10,000

The par 3 9th at Club de Campo which is protected by this wide, if not over-taxing, bunker. The green is on two tiers.

sloping green. At a modest 377 metres it is not an excessively long hole, but it needs to be treated with the utmost respect.

A tough par 4 uphill follows with a fairway which doglegs to the left and rises to a two-tiered green surrounded by bunkers. A stream close to the driving area makes this 407-metre two-shot hole one of the most difficult on the course.

A tough par 5 of 490 metres, again another dogleg hole, a tricky par 4 of 358 metres, and a short par 3 of 155 metres, where the tee shot has to carry a deep valley to another double-tiered green, complete a fascinating and extremely challenging front nine.

The back nine begins with yet another dogleg, although one slightly less severe. Care must be taken with the tee shot to open up a green cleverly defended with both bunkers and trees.

The next is a tough par 3 of 195 metres where perdition awaits those who come up short, and deep and menacing bunkers await those who miss the green to either left or right.

There are fine views of the city of Madrid at the 12th where two tall trees mark the landing area for the drive and the approach must be very carefully judged.

Severe bunkers and great stands of trees protect the green at the 13th where the drive must again be carefully placed to open up the dogleg on this sweeping par 4 of over 400 metres.

The dogleg theme is maintained at the next – only twofold. A veritable monster of a par 5, this 14th hole is well over 505 metres in length, changes direction twice and

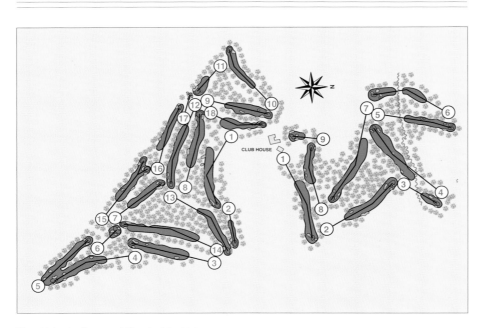
The Club de Campo Villa de Madrid courses.

has a fairway lined by trees.

The course turns back uphill again at the relatively short par 4 15th where the tee shot has to avoid a deep bunker on the right. Care is needed with the approach to a green which is well protected by sand.

At the next, the tee shot has not only to be long but must also be kept to the left to open up the line to the green. Bunkers lurk in that area but no other route will give a clear shot past a lone tree on the right of the fairway to a gently sloping green.

At the 4th – a par 4 of under 400 metres – the tee shot needs to be aimed slightly left to open up a sloping green. The trees on the right await all who carry a slice in their bag.

There are more trees to contend with at the next, a lovely little short hole of 142 metres, and bunkers will trap any but the most precise tee shot.

Club de Campo closes with a comfortable par 4 of 321 metres offering little in the way of menace other than bunkers down the right side which should be easily enough avoided by most players. An invitingly large green beckons.

Facilities

Club de Campo is a large complex with not only golf but tennis, horse-riding and its own swimming pool. There is a comfortable bar and a good restaurant as well as first-class practice facilities.

The Region

The fascinating city of Madrid will be the main focus for most visitors to this part of Spain. It is a city with a long and interesting history from its earliest beginnings as a Moorish fortress.

Madrid came permanently into the hands of the Christians in 1083. In May 1808, during the Napoleonic Wars, the citizens rose against the French and the tragic scenes in the capital inspired several famous works by Goya.

During the Spanish Civil War in the late 1930s, Madrid was subjected to an intense and dramatic siege which lasted for more than two-and-a-half years before the republican forces finally surrendered to the insurgents on 28 March 1939.

The city's museums and art galleries are extremely popular with visitors and there are many fine restaurants to be explored.

Accommodation

Visitors to the area will have little difficulty in finding accommodation to suit their particular needs and budgets. There are many splendid hotels in Madrid itself with the Villa Magna in the city convenient for both Club de Campo and La Puerta de Hierro.

Real Golf El Prat

F O U N D E D 1 9 5 6

ACCURACY AT A PREMIUM

Majestic pines and tropical palms adorn the fairways of this beautiful layout just south of Barcelona and only a few kilometres from the international airport.

Real Golf El Prat

Aptdo 8820, El Prat de Llobregat

◆

Location: 15km south of Barcelona

Tel: (343) 379 0278

Course: 18 holes, 6046m, par 72

Visitors: Welcome at any time

Green fees: Ptas7000-8000

The Real Club de Golf El Prat is another wonderful example of the architectural artistry of Javier Arana. The club was opened in 1954 and two years later, no less a personage than the voice of golf himself, Peter Alliss, won the Spanish Open, the first of many important events to have been staged over this marvellous 6046-metre layout.

Arana made very effective use of a generous supply of irrigation around the course thanks to several wells, and water comes into play on many of the holes. Keen observers arriving by air may well spot the course as their aircraft turns on to the final approach into Barcelona airport close by.

The lush green fairways between the trees and bright splashes of sand are easy to spot and have a very tempting hue about them.

THE COURSE

While the course might look relatively straightforward from the air, when the visitor gets his feet firmly planted on this stretch of Catalonia, it becomes a very different prospect.

The opening hole gives little indication of the severe challenge ahead, however. A modest par 4 of not too daunting length, it requires only a solid drive – avoiding trees on the right and bunkers on the left – to set up a short pitch to a receptive green.

It's much the same story at the next where the green is only 270 metres away and, again, a short pitch should set up a birdie opportunity.

There is water to be carried at the short 3rd where bunkers guard the green right and left, and only a solid tee shot will find the green. The lake on the right at the next catches more than its fair share of wayward drives. For those who manage to steer clear

Comfort is very much in evidence in the splendid clubhouse at El Prat. The atmosphere is friendly and the food and service excellent.

This is a finely sculptured course with lush green fairways and tempting greens. Although just south of Barcelona, the course has a distinctly tropical feel.

of it, however, the approach will be a short one leaving another chance to win one against the head.

A gentle dogleg left follows and is best tackled with a drive down the left side to open up the green, while the 6th is a very demanding short hole with water to the front left and a circle of bunkers to catch anything slightly off line.

After a dogleg par 4 at the 7th, where the approach has to be threaded between bunkers which narrow the entrance to the green, the challenge is back over water again.

The drive at the 8th crosses the water first encountered at the 3rd although this time there is less room for error. The encroaching palm trees provide a splash of glorious colour as the sun strikes the

bright fronds, but they remain temptresses in seductive clothing. Any shot played off line will almost certainly cost at least a stroke.

The front nine closes with a fine par 5 beside the beach featuring a double-tier green.

The journey home begins with a tight tee shot through a chute of trees to a narrow fairway well protected by strategically placed bunkers. A good drive, however, takes the sting out of this par 5 which is then relatively straightforward.

There then follows an interesting par 3 where overclubbing will result in a visit to the lake while anything short will almost certainly find trouble in deep sand. Careful club selection is vital.

The 14th is one of the toughest holes at El Prat.

A tight dogleg right, it features palm trees in threatening profusion and a difficult green with three distinct tiers. Two good shots are required to reach the putting surface but only the surest touch with the putter will leave any chance of a par.

The next is the longest hole on the course at more than 500 metres from the back tee. Again the green itself, with its vast undulations, presents as much difficulty as the remainder of the hole.

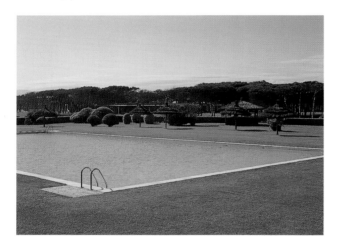

This wonderful club has left nothing to chance. And after your round, you can always relax in perfect surroundings with a dip in the luxury swimming pool.

Surrounded by trees, the par 4 16th and the beautiful short 17th both set up a magnificent finish at El Prat. The final hole is a great par 4 which doglegs to the left around the woods. The drive must avoid a dangerous bunker on the right and the approach must be truly struck to hold a difficult double-tier green.

Among the top names who have won the Catalan Open at El Prat are Seve Ballesteros, Des Smyth, Sam Torrance and José Maria Olazabal – a clear indication of the quality of this course which always seems to bring the cream to the top.

FACILITIES

El Prat has excellent clubhouse facilities to complement its marvellous course. A friendly bar and a fine restaurant, together with a swimming pool and tennis courts, all combine to provide the very best for members and visitors.

There is also a short nine-hole course and a good practice ground.

THE REGION

The eyes of the world were centred on Barcelona and the region of Catalonia when the Olympic Games were held there in 1992. Each year more than 14 million tourists visit the region, making it one of Europe's most popular holiday destinations.

From the mighty snow-clad mountains of the Pyrenees to the beautiful coastline between Cape Creus and the delta of the Ebro river, there is an ever-changing landscape. Long sandy beaches, giant cliffs and calm, sheltered coves are the features of the coastal region which enjoys one of the sunniest climates in the whole of Europe.

There is marshland too, such as the fascinating Ebro Delta, one of the most important migratory bird reserves in the world.

The city of Barcelona, only a short drive from El Prat, is a cosmopolitan city with countless attractions for the millions of visitors to whom it extends a warm welcome every year.

The Catalan people have their own distinct personality. Both European and Mediterranean, their customs, festivals and their delicious food are a faithful reflection of a people proud of their identity.

ACCOMMODATION

Among many hotels well suited to visitors to El Prat are the Neptuno and the Rey Don Jaime in Castelldefels while in Barcelona there is an almost limitless selection to choose from with the Hotel Condes de Barcelona as just one excellent choice.

Those in search of a restaurant offering something special might venture to the Oratavo in Consell de Cent in the city. They will not be disappointed.

Campo de Golf El Saler

FOUNDED 1968

CLASSIC SPANISH LINKS

The Javier Arana designed course at El Saler near Valencia in Spain is one of Europe's outstanding courses. Indeed, there are some, including a panel of eminent figures in European golf, who ranked El Saler at one stage in its relatively short existence as the 'Top Course in Continental Europe'.

There are strong grounds for commending it so highly for it is a demanding test of golf stretching to well over 7000 metres in its championship livery. That most respected of writers, Mr Peter Dobereiner, wrote: 'If it were transplanted to the west coast of Ireland, or to Scotland, exposed to the Atlantic gales, it would be a monster.'

Javier Arana is more widely remembered as a player rather than a course architect; nonetheless, his reputation as a designer is high. He has, however, confined his work to his native Spain and it was not until the spread of European championship golf to that country in the early 1970s that his creations gained more general acclaim.

Club de Campo in Madrid and El Prat in Barcelona are two other highly regarded Arana courses but El Saler rates clearly as his masterpiece.

It is an unusual combination of terrain, ranging from the umbrella pines of the furthest inland part of the course to the spectacular holes built among the sand dunes beside the Mediterranean. All this helps to create a fascinating and richly varied challenge.

El Saler hosted the memorable 1984 Spanish Open when Bernhard Langer overcame a robbery in his hotel bedroom, which relieved him of £3000, was then fined for slow play in the third round, to come back from seven strokes behind going into the final day to win with a remarkable round of 62.

Langer, who won the US Masters the following year, rated the round, which included nine birdies in

Campo de Golf El Saler
Parador Luis Vives, 46012
El Saler
◆
Location: 18km south of Valencia
Tel: (346) 161 1186
Course: 18 holes, 6485m, par 72
Visitors: Welcome at any time
Green fees: Ptas5000

Conveniently situated by the 9th green at El Saler is the club's own extremely comfortable on-site hotel.

11 holes from the 5th, as the best he had ever played in his life. Significantly, too, he also rated El Saler as one of the best courses in Europe.

THE COURSE

The inland aspect of El Saler is most evident at the start of the round. Umbrella pines flourish in a gentle landscape at the furthest point from the sea and the opening hole demands a well-placed drive far enough right to open up the dogleg to the left.

The approach is not too demanding but care must be taken to avoid two greenside bunkers, particularly the one in the front right which poses the greater danger. The steeply sloping green puts pressure on the putter from the very beginning.

Crossing the roadway to the hotel to the short 4th marks a change towards the links aspect of the course. This 175-metre par 3 has a tightly guarded green surrounding by trees.

The 7th and 8th are classic links holes played close by the sea. Both measure 380 metres but run at a 45 degree angle to one another. The 7th is played

If you ignore the skyscapers in the distant background, the 17th, one of the toughest holes at Campo de Golf El Saler, could be on a links course in Scotland.

towards the Gulf of Valencia while the splendid 8th runs parallel with the beach.

Arana used single trees and strategically placed bunkers to great effect on this layout. Typical is the 10th where a tall pine blocks the approach to the green if the tee shot is too far right.

At the next, the combination is a pine tree and a bunker. This par 5, together with the 15th, are the two longest holes on the course at 520 metres. The latter has out-of-bounds to the left putting the premium on accuracy, but the fairway is generous and

only a really wild drive will find trouble in the trees fringing the fairway.

The double-tiered green is protected by three bunkers and needs a delicate touch with the putter.

The demanding short 17th is a perfect example of Javier Arana's feel for the terrain. Surrounded by bunkers, this devilish hole requires a stout blow with a long iron from the tee to a green set on linksland which would do justice to the east coast of Scotland.

Wild sand dunes dominate the tee at the dogleg par 4 finishing hole. From the tee the hole swings

The 7th is played towards the Gulf of Valencia and the lush colour of the green at the 7th contrasts vividly with the approach. The bunkers guarding the green aren't just there for show, either.

The sea breezes which come off the Mediterranean help to make this one of the delightful courses in Europe – any time of year.

to the left with trees creating an added hazard near the green. The hole requires two good shots to get home and presents a daunting finish to a truly spectacular course.

The El Saler greens are firm and fast and an absolute joy to putt on.

The weather in this part of Spain is perfect for winter golf with soft sea breezes making it perfectly playable in the heat of the summer months too.

FACILITIES

El Saler has every facility the visiting golfer could wish for. A friendly bar and comfortable restaurant await at the end of the round. If you have any energy left there is a swimming pool and tennis courts. There is also an excellent practice ground.

THE REGION

The area around El Saler remains one of the finest unspoiled regions of coastal Spain.

The region of Valencia has had a chequered history, having been taken from the Moors by El Cid at the end of the 11th century. It remained a kingdom in name until the 18th century.

The city of Valencia is the third city of Spain with a port at El Grao and sandy beaches on the Mediterranean coast nearby.

The verdant garden-land *(huerto)* around the city is irrigated by canals. This is administered by a court which meets each week (Thursday) at the main door of the cathedral. This magnificent Gothic and Baroque building was begun in 1262, and there are many other fine churches, palaces and museums in the area.

The university dates from 1500 and the 15th-century silk exchange is preserved. The region has textile and boat-building industries and a thriving trade in oranges, rice and silk.

Away from the coastal plain, the hinterland is mountainous and offers the prospect of interesting villages to visit still totally untouched by the advance of Spain's tourist industry. There are few pleasures which can match a drive away from the city in pursuit of the real Spain.

ACCOMMODATION

Although there is a rich choice of accommodation in Valencia, visitors to El Saler need look no further than the golf club itself for accommodation. With an on-site *parador* (state-run hotel) all is well catered for.

Accommodation in the Parador Luis Vives is both comfortable and welcoming. The food is excellent, the wine compulsive, and all this is within a few metres of the first tee.

La Manga Club

F O U N D E D   1 9 7 1

WHERE THE TOUR GOES IN WINTER

The La Manga Club, set in a green valley in the shadow of the Murcian Hills in south-east Spain, is a self-contained sports and leisure resort which has grown into one of the finest in Europe.

It has two 18-hole courses of which the South is the better known, having hosted the Spanish Open on several occasions. The North course is slightly shorter but in many ways is just as stiff a challenge. A third course of nine holes known as the Atamaria Course was added in 1986.

The European Tour Final Qualifying School for young professionals trying to win the elusive playing

Spanish style and opulence are evident in La Manga's Club hotel where luxury is the watchword and the visitor's every whim is catered for.

card that allows them to play the lucrative European Tour has been held for many years now at La Manga, and the European Tour uses the complex as its base during the winter months.

Robert Puttman was the golf course architect given the job of designing two 18-hole layouts for the ambitious La Manga Club project which was opened in 1971.

The previous year, a consortium of American businessmen chose La Manga as the ideal location for the development of a luxury residential complex incorporating multiple amenities, services and sports facilities. At the heart of their dream to build the best sports holiday complex in Europe were the two golf courses.

La Manga Club
Los Belones,
Cartagena, Murcia
◆
Location: 25km from
Murcia San Javier airport
off the N332
Tel: (34) 68 56 4511
Courses: North Course –
18 holes, 5873m, par 71;
South Course – 18 holes,
6268m, par 72;
Atamaria – 9 holes,
2559m, par 34
Visitors: Welcome at any time
Green fees: Ptas7000

Puttman's designs for both courses were built in record time and the complex was opened in October 1971. La Manga negotiated an agreement with the Spanish Golf Federation to sponsor and host the Spanish Open for five consecutive years from 1973. And it was this agreement that put La Manga on the international golfing map.

THE COURSES

Although the two courses were built at the same time, they are very different in character and offer completely different challenges. The North Course is just under 400 metres shorter than the South Course and puts the premium more on strategic play.

Both courses are typified by wide fairways, generous greens and vast bunkers of white sand which are generally more cosmetic than penal. Thousands of palm trees were planted during construction and they give La Manga a distinctly tropical feel.

But it is water that provides the key threat. Lakes were dug into both courses in profusion and come into play on many holes, particularly on the South Course. There are also numerous *barrancas* – deep

The 13th is an example of cultivated golf design. It's not difficult to see why many consider this to be one of the finest courses in Europe.

ravines lined with rough and filled with rocks – which present a major threat to any scorecard.

On the South Course, where water comes into play on more than half the holes, the 8th and the 9th are two of the toughest holes on the front nine.

The 8th is a long par 3 of close to 200 metres with a lake threatening on the right. It demands a very strong shot in any conditions but when the wind blows, as it often does at La Manga, it becomes particularly difficult.

The same applies to the 9th, which runs in the same direction. At very nearly 550 metres, the hole is a monster to start with, and very demanding. Add to the length the need to carry a *barranca* from the tee – not always easy with the wind against you – and a lake threatening the second shot on the right side, and it soon becomes clear that architect Puttman has concocted a recipe for golfing disaster.

There seems to be water everywhere on the back nine, never more so than at the final hole where it threatens this long par 5 left and right from the drive. It appears again in front of the green for those daring enough to attempt to get home in two shots.

Water hazards are not quite so obviously in play on the North Course but there are plenty of *barrancas*. Problems on the greens of several years ago have long since been overcome and they are now firm and fast and a match for any in Spain.

FACILITIES

It would be easier to list the facilities that La Manga Club does not have than those that it does. The concept of the Club was to provide guests with as wide a range of sporting facilities as possible. This has unquestionably been achieved.

The David Lloyd Racquet Centre is one of the best equipped in Europe with 17 tennis courts, most of them floodlit, plus two practice lanes. There are squash courts, a fitness and health centre with its own jacuzzi, sauna, Turkish bath and plunge pool and there are swimming pools throughout the complex.

La Manga Club has its own Equestrian Centre with horse riding across the unspoilt Murcian hills and with a purpose-built riding school to provide expert riding tuition.

The Club has its own Watersports Centre a few kilometres away on the inland sea known as the Mar

The 18th on the North Course and the magnificent clubhouse awaits. Here, you can relax with a drink or dine at one of the Club's own exclusive restaurants.

Menor. There you can dive for oysters or encounter seahorses, sail to one of the islands, windsurf or simply soak up the sun on the beach.

Children are very well catered for at La Manga Club with a wide variety of activities on offer.

And practice facilities are second to none which is why it has long been a favourite venue for teaching professionals running winter golf schools.

THE REGION

La Manga Club has gone to great lengths to provide as wide a range of facilities as possible on site. The main reason for this is because the area is quite remote.

Alicante is 90 kilometres from La Manga, and outside the complex itself there are relatively few counter-attractions. For those who wish to explore the region, however, there are interesting unspoilt villages and much local colour, but a car is a necessity.

ACCOMMODATION

There is no need to leave La Manga Club in search of accommodation. The Club has a comfortable, centrally-located hotel with a heated swimming pool. There are apartments and town houses around their own exclusive pools and luxury Andalucian style villas set in landscaped gardens with private pools.

The Club has a range of restaurants and bars to suit every taste from the golf clubhouse restaurant to the Hotel Terrace where there are two shows nightly featuring flamenco and ballet. Alternatively, enjoy fresh-grilled sardines at La Cala overlooking the Mediterranean, or savour a tropical fruit punch on the terrace of the nine-hole Atamaria course clubhouse and dine in style there. At the end of the day, the Piano Bar has its very own atmosphere and entertainment and has become something of an institution in European holiday golf.

La Moraleja Golf Club

F O U N D E D   1 9 7 6

Beware 'El Terror'

Not far from the centre of Madrid, La Moraleja Golf Club stands as another monument to the creative work of Jack Nicklaus.

Completed and opened for play in 1976, this is a classic Nicklaus design in a beautiful setting presenting a formidable test from the championship tees but a pleasant and interesting challenge from further forward.

La Moraleja Golf Club

La Moraleja, Alcobendas
◆
Location: 9km north of Madrid

Tel: (341) 650 0700

Course: 18 holes, 6075m, par 72

Visitors: Welcome on weekdays only

Green fees: Ptas7000

As with so many other Nicklaus designed courses, water comes into play on many of the holes at La Moraleja, and there is a high premium on careful consideration of the best tactical shot.

The club has been the venue for several major golfing events including the World Cup in 1992, when Fred Couples and David Love III took the title for the United States.

The first Benson and Hedges Mixed Professional event in which the top men and women professionals in Europe teamed up was played here in 1988 and produced some memorable golf. Mark McNulty and Marie Laure de Lorenzi fought off the opposition to take the title.

Former Ryder Cup player, Howard Clark, won the 1986 Spanish Open here with a score of 272, averaging 68 for each round.

The Course

Nicklaus sets out the challenge with a gentle opening dogleg left which has few complications. It is pleasant leisurely start. A bunker short and right of the green is the only troublesome factor before the player moves on to the excellent par 3 2nd.

At a fairly modest 176 metres, length is not the obvious challenge here, but there is plenty of potential trouble. A stream runs the length of the hole down the left side and the green is very well protected by trees and a nest of bunkers. From here the course swings uphill to the third with its elevated green protected by a deep bunker on the left.

It's back down the hill again at the next, a wonderfully challenging par 3 of 195 metres. The tee shot has to be carried all the way to the green.

The 5th – although it doesn't look it – is a difficult hole. Just out of shot, water awaits to ensnare the over-confident.

The drive at the dogleg 5th is critical. A cavernous bunker in the corner of the dogleg threatens the over-zealous who opt for too short a route, while three other bunkers threaten the overcautious on the other side of the fairway. Water behind the green completes the defences.

Only the very longest hitters will be able to reach the long 6th in two. Although it is only a relatively modest 472 metres on the card, it is played uphill

Possibly the best hole at La Moraleja. With the water to the left and two bunkers guarding the green, extreme circumspection at the 18th is necessary.

through a maze of attractive fairway bunkers.

The run from there to the 9th is fraught with danger with two tough par 4s, both doglegs which require long and accurate striking from the tee.

The 9th is more generous for the drive but trees on the fairway can be troublesome and often present an attack on the green with the second shot.

The first hole of the back nine is one of the best. Little imagination is required to understand why it has been named 'El Terror'. The fairway is extremely narrow and the green is surrounded by Spanish oaks making the approach very difficult indeed.

There is little respite at the next either where out-of-bounds threatens on the right and trees guard the long and very narrow green.

Water is a major threat at the 12th and 13th, although if you can avoid it from the tee at the latter, a short pitch will open up a birdie opportunity.

At only 288 metres, the 14th offers another birdie opportunity although the large bunker on the left has ruined many aspirations.

It is not unusual for Nicklaus to leave the best to last, and La Moraleja is a classic example of that. The 18th is a glorious par 5 with the lake prominent on the left for those launching a big drive along with their hopes of getting home in two.

FACILITIES

La Moraleja has a splendid modern clubhouse to complement Jack Nicklaus's course design. There is a bar and restaurant and, as with nearly all Nicklaus layouts, excellent practice facilities.

THE REGION

The non-golfer has much to see and do in the area around La Moraleja. The course is only a short drive from the centre of the Spanish capital with its long history and many fine examples of architecture.

Madrid is a spacious and beautiful city, although perhaps less distinctively Spanish than many towns of less importance. On the west side of the city, the river is overlooked by the magnificent royal palace, now a museum. It houses a notable collection of historic weaponry, while to the south of the palace the new cathedral, begun in 1881, stands in sharp contrast.

There are many museums and galleries with the Museo del Prado on the Paseo del Prado housing some the world's greatest art treasures.

ACCOMMODATION

There is a wide variety of hotels and other accommodation in and around the Madrid area for visitors to La Moraleja. However, for those who wish to be close to the course the Pamplona Hotel in San Sebastian de los Reyes is deservedly popular.

Real Club de la Puerta de Hierro

FOUNDED 1904

SPECTACULAR VIEWS AND A MIGHTY CHALLENGE
The Real Club de la Puerta de Hierro is not only the oldest club in mainland Spain, it also has in its championship layout one of the very toughest of all the great courses in the country.

Harris and Simpson laid out the original course in 1904 in rolling countryside just a few minutes from the centre of Madrid. It staged the first Spanish Open eight years later.

The venerable clubhouse stands elegantly on top of a hill commanding wonderful views across the valley and to the nearby Club de Campo. Beyond lie the mountains, covered in snow for much of the year.

Real Club de la Puerta de Hierro
28035 Madrid
◆
Location: 4km north of Madrid
Tel: (341) 316 1745
Courses: 18 holes, 6347m, par 72;
18 holes, 5273m, par 68
Visitors: By introduction only
Green fees: Ptas9000

THE COURSE

With fairways lined by trees and thick undergrowth, accuracy is everything at Puerta de Hierro.

Unusually for a truly championship venue, the course opens with a par 3 played across a valley in front of the clubhouse to a green heavily protected by three huge bunkers. The 2nd is a par 5 with trouble all the way down the left side. The fairway slopes towards the trees making the drive difficult while a double-level green adds to the problems.

From this point the course dives steeply downwards with the tee shot at the 3rd having to make a big carry to reach a fairway which then climbs steeply back up to a viciously fortified green.

At the next, care must be taken not to be blocked out by trees down the left side. The green is elevated, making fine judgement of distance extremely difficult. After a strong par 5 and a very picturesque par 3, the 7th demands a drive across the road to a fairway sloping quite smartly to the right.

There is a great temptation to 'have a go' at the short par 4 8th. At only 273 metres, the longer hitters can get home, but danger lies in wait for anything but the most accurate of drives. It is a big carry over the trees and often the carefully placed tee shot with an iron club, followed by a simple, short approach, will

Straight hitting is vital at the 12th where trees on both sides of the fairway threaten the errant driver. Beware the bunker to the right of the green.

prove more effective if you are after a birdie.

On the back nine the short 11th readily stands out as one of the toughest holes. At just short of 200 metres, it presents a very long carry to a green heavily protected by bunkers.

At the next there is more trouble around the green which is only accessible if the tee shot is struck particularly accurately. Trees threaten the drive, as

Not many greens are quite as closely fortified as the 3rd at Puerta de Hierro which is surrounded by a veritable army of bunkers.

does a dangerous bunker on the right, leaving very little room for manoeuvre.

The 13th might be lucky for some who attempt to drive the green on this 281 metres downhill hole. However, even those who do may find that the birdie often remains elusive because of the difficulties on the green. Three tiers on a putting surface with a wide array of possible and menacing hole placements needs a balanced judgement over the best tactical approach. Laying up safely and settling for a short pitch will produce the best reward.

Only two very fine shots will carry the two big cross bunkers at the long par 5, 15th but the rewards for success justify the risk of the attempt.

The longest hole is reserved until last and in

terms of pure length it is something of a monster at 550 metres. However, there is plenty of room off the tee to open the shoulders and the third shot approach is made to a large and generous green.

FACILITIES

The Puerta de Hierro Club has facilities as lavish as any to be found in Spain. Apart from the bar and excellent restaurant in the old clubhouse, there are superb tennis facilities and a polo ground which doubles as practice ground when major golfing events are held there.

There are of course more conventional practice facilities for everyday use, and the second 18-hole layout is an interesting diversion to its more famous bigger sister.

THE REGION

Like Club de Campo across the way, visitors to Puerta de Hierro naturally gravitate to the city of Madrid, the centre of which is just a few minutes' drive through the university campus. The nation's capital is rich in cultural attractions and has many fine restaurants and shopping facilities. The surrounding countryside is interesting, too, with the Sierra de Guaderrama to the north-west of the city providing a marvellous backdrop.

ACCOMMODATION

The choice of hotel accommodation to suit most pockets in and round Madrid is virtually limitless but, as is the case with Club de Campo, the Villa Magna in Madrid is one hotel within easy reach of the course that is worth consideration.

Valderrama Golf Club

FOUNDED 1975

THE AUGUSTA OF EUROPE

American golf course architect, Robert Trent Jones, was sitting on the veranda at the Augusta National Golf Club some years ago when he was approached by Severiano Ballesteros. The Spaniard had just won the US Masters and volunteered the opinion that he attributed his success in no small measure to two weeks' preparation at the new course at Sotogrande in southern Spain.

Trent Jones had designed and built the course, then known as Los Aves, in a spectacular location on a hill above the old village of Sotogrande. He had long maintained that the course was one of his finest achievements and that it truly belonged among the world's great courses.

In 1985 industrialist Jaime Ortiz-Patino and seven of his golfing friends acquired the course and formed the Valderrama Golf Club with the aim of making it an attractive and exclusive private club.

Trent Jones was brought in again to remodel the course and make some subtle but significant changes without altering the intrinsic character of the layout. He described it at the time as 'polishing the diamond to improve the shot values in some areas of the course'. The object was to make it a magnificent, challenging championship layout and there is no doubt at all that he succeeded.

Now the host club for the grand finale of the European Tour, the Volvo Masters, Valderrama has been widely acclaimed as one of golf's outstanding tests and is strongly tipped to host the Ryder Cup when it goes to Spain in 1995.

Ronan Rafferty, winner of the Volvo Masters and the Volvo Order of Merit in 1989, has described the back nine at Valderrama as 'probably more difficult than any other course in Europe'. Certainly, the final four holes are generally accepted among the players as the most punishing on the European Tour.

Valderrama Golf Club

Apto. 1, 11310,

Sotogrande, Cadiz

◆

Location: 15 minutes from Gibraltar off the N340 at Sotogrande

Tel: (34) 56 795 775.

Course: 18 holes, 6326m, par 72

Visitors: Welcome from 12-2pm by prior reservation

Green fees: Ptas9000

The beautiful Valderrama clubhouse blends in with its surroundings to contribute to the course's own unique brand of opulence.

Top American course design meets traditional Spanish architecture and natural terrain. The result – a championship golf course of the highest order.

Played from tees further forward, however, there is still immense enjoyment to be had for the mortal golfer on Trent Jones's creation. There are spectacular views all around the course, and there is an air of quiet elegance and charm usually encountered only in clubs of much greater age. Indeed, there are some who believe that Valderrama has now taken on the mantle of the Augusta of Europe.

There are few actual physical resemblances, but there is an aura about this wonderful creation in the Costa del Sol which would not be out of place at the home of the US Masters.

Yet, although it may not yet have become elevated to such a hallowed plane as Augusta, there is no doubt about Valderrama's commitment to excellence and jealously guarded privacy.

THE COURSE

Among many memorable holes on this wonderful course is the short 3rd which huddles into the hillside. It is severely bunkered to left and right making it an outstanding par 3. At 156 metres, it requires only a firm blow with a medium iron, but par is difficult to recover if the target is missed. The green has a tricky slope from back to front.

The long par 5 11th is one hole which came in for some attention from Robert Trent Jones in his course review. The fairway slopes from left to right from the tee, but not quite as viciously as it once did. A nest of bunkers to the right of the fairway in the landing area threatens the drive, while the approach is played up-hill to a green on the horizon, making judgement of distance very difficult. When you reach this green there is a truly magnificent view out across the sea.

All the single shot holes at Valderrama are spectacular but there is none more difficult than the 200 metre 12th. The tee shot is played from an elevated tee to a green set among cork trees. When the wind is blowing, it is a very difficult green to hit and anything off target is almost certain to find one of the fearsome bunkers which surround a green with many undulations and slopes from front to back.

A good drive from an elevated tee to a fairway which tends to gather the ball sets up a tricky pitch to the short par 4 14th. The green is surrounded by bunkers and has many subtle undulations. A delicate touch with the putter is essential.

Nothing is spared to make Valderrama as fine a course as it can possibly be. If it requires changes, Ortiz-Patino changes it regardless.

Some years ago, when it was felt that the new houses alongside the 3rd hole were beginning to intrude on the course, Patino planted several avenues of trees to block them out. And they were not saplings; at considerable expense, he brought in fully mature trees in six-tonne boxes ready for planting.

The houses were suitably obscured, although residents' comments have not been recorded.

FACILITIES

As with everything at this very special club, the

A deft touch with the putter is vital here at the 14th green, which may look as pretty as a postcard, but where the ground ducks and weaves like a featherweight boxer.

Sloping fairways, many trees and difficult bunkers make Valderrama a challenge for the best of golfers. To most players, a par here is a bonus.

clubhouse is quietly understated but provides every facility for members and those privileged to visit as guests. There is a fine restaurant and bar and an air of quiet, restrained opulence.

The practice ground in front of the clubhouse is excellent and must rank as one of the most expensive in existence. When Ortiz-Patino decided he needed a service tunnel and that in an ideal world it should cross the practice ground, he solved the problem by raising the practice ground by five metres!

The Region
Valderrama is set is quiet countryside well away from the tourist buzz of Marbella but is only a few miles along the coast from Gibraltar, the easiest airport access for this part of the Costa del Sol.

The bright lights of the Costa and the amazing excesses of Puerto Banus, with its boats, shops, bars and 'beautiful' people parading up and down the quayside, are within easy reach but there is peace and quiet here for those who prefer it.

Accommodation
There are many fine restaurants in the area serving local food, but few hotels close to the course. One exception is the Sotogrande Hotel which is small and friendly and offers horse-riding and tennis among its facilities for guests.

14

Sweden

Despite its relatively small population, Sweden has more golfers who play regularly than any other country in Europe. The game is immensely popular despite the northern parts of the country having a relatively short season.

The Swedes were one of the first European countries outside the British Isles to build a golf course and, with their commitment to structured development, the game has expanded rapidly throughout the country.

There are now more than 350 courses, most of them in the southern part of the country where the weather is milder and the season a little longer, but there are several notable courses in the north such as at the Ostersund-Froso Golfklubb which is very close to the Arctic circle. There is an annual Midnight Sun tournament played there in the height of summer when golf is playable 24 hours a day.

The benefits of a concerted and far-sighted junior coaching programme by the Swedish Golf Federation have been largely responsible for the immense advance in standards of play in the country since the early 1980s.

Swedish players have made a major impact on the European Tour culminating in Joakim Haeggman becoming the first Swedish player to win a European Ryder Cup place against the Americans at The Belfry in 1993. Haeggman has had more than ample support from others such as Anders Forsbrand and Per-Ulric Johannson, all products of the Swedes' very progressive attitude toward coaching.

Despite its long winters, Sweden offers a unique brand of hospitality with a surprise around every corner like this tiny fishing village at Kyrkesund.

In many ways golf in Sweden learned from the great success story of Swedish tennis a decade earlier. There is some disquiet internationally, however, about the Swedish attitude which makes little if any distinction between the amateur and professional game.

Sweden is a wonderful country for the visiting golfer, although the day to day living expenses are much higher than in other European countries. Against that can be laid the quality of the golf which, in some cases, is as fine as can be found anywhere in Europe.

The wonderful links course at Falsterbo near Malmo in southern Sweden is one of the world's great golf courses. There is a great affinity between the members at Falsterbo and several clubs in Scotland, including Prestwick and the Royal and Ancient Golf Club, and the club defends the great traditions of the game vigorously.

Access to golf in Sweden is extremely simple by ferry through Copenhagen in Denmark from where Falsterbo and its neighbours are a short drive away.

Falsterbo Golfklubb

FOUNDED 1909

CLASSIC LINKS FOR THE PURIST

Falsterbo is one of the classic links courses of Europe. Set in the very southernmost tip of Sweden, where the Oresund and the Baltic meet, this majestic course has all the ingredients of traditional Scottish seaside golf. It is golf for the purist on beautiful turf amid spectacular surroundings.

The club dates back to 1909 but it is not the oldest in Sweden. The Hovås club, south of Gothenburg, predates it by seven years reflecting the long-standing Swedish commitment to the game.

There are few places in the world which can boast a more hospitable membership than this fine old club where the old Scottish values prevail and are guarded jealously. Indeed there is a very strong affinity with Scotland. Several members are life members at Prestwick and play there regularly. One of their number, Bjorn Stenberg, was the first Swedish player to win the Prestwick club championship in 1986.

There are also strong connections with the Royal County Down Golf Club and the Royal and Ancient Golf Club of St Andrews as well as with Royal County Down in Ireland and Hoylake in England.

Falsterbo Golfklubb
Fyrvägen, S–23011, Falsterbo
◆
Location: 30km south of Malmo on the south-west tip of the peninsula at Falsterbo
Tel: (46) 4047 00 78
Course: 18 Holes, 6100m, par 71
Visitors: Reservations recommended. It's best to telephone and book in advance.
Green fees: SKr200-300

The original nine-hole course at Falsterbo was laid out in 1909 and the holes have changed very little in the intervening years. A further nine holes were added by Gunner Bauer in 1930 to make it one of the first full 18-hole golf courses in Sweden.

It is a striking place and an important nature reserve with its marshes at the northern end of the course a haven for rare and spectacular bird life. Set in the middle of the course is an old lighthouse, rather reminiscent of the famous Harbour Town Golf Links on Hilton Head island, South Carolina, home of the USPGA Tour's Heritage Classic.

The 7th is one of the finest holes on the course. And, with the clubhouse close by, some refreshment to fortify yourself for the remaining 11 holes makes perfect sense.

The 18th at Falsterbo is a great hole, a monster par 5 of over 500 metres with its fairway tight against the ocean and dunes of fine white sand.

THE COURSE

The toughness of the course is clear from the beginning. The tee shot at the first must avoid the out-of-bounds down the right side and trees on the other side of a fairway that swings slightly right. A par at this 410-metre opening hole represents a considerable achievement.

A shortish par 3 and a relatively benign par 5 follow, but when the player turns back alongside the marsh the going gets tougher.

Internal water hazards, as natural as they are unusual on a links course, present a dangerous prospect on the next three holes.

The first of them, the 4th, is one of the great two-shot holes in European golf. Usually played into the wind, this 400-metre par 4 has water camouflaged by tall reeds all the way down the right of the fairway, while the green is tucked into a corner of the marsh.

The second shot, which often requires a wooden club to make the long carry, must cross the corner of the marsh if it is to find sanctuary on the green. Water is also much in evidence at the next where it again threatens the approach shot, although this time on the other side of the fairway.

The lakes which dot this part of the layout are very unusual on a pure links golf course and give it both charm and distinction. The 7th is the shortest of Falsterbo's par 4s but it is one of the best and most interesting. It is a sharp dogleg left bringing the player back to the clubhouse where he, or she, can sample some of the club's renowned hospitality to fortify themselves for the onward journey.

The hole requires a good drive well to the right to open up the green for a short approach. The green,

On a clear day, you could play for ever. The 9th shows Falstelbo for what it is – one of the great European links courses. The famous old lighthouse is clearly visible.

which slopes away from front to back and is difficult to hold, sits in a hollow and is severely bunkered. Precision and care are paramount.

The same is true of the short 11th, the most notorious of Falsterbo's holes. It is modest in length, but the green is surrounded on three sides by water. Death or glory are the only alternatives here, particularly if there is a brisk breeze blowing from left to right across the hole as is usually the case. Access to the green is over a long footbridge built across the middle of the inlet. Some find that journey as perilous as the shot before it.

The holes around the central lighthouse are delightful in their variety, but from the 15th the golf is played alongside the sand dunes which are the stamp of this fine course.

The 16th, a beautiful 350-metre par 4, gently doglegs its way into the very corner of the peninsula where the waters of the Baltic and the Oresund meet. Here the views on the one hand to Denmark are unbelievably spectacular, while on the other there is nothing but the Baltic between the 17th tee and the former East Germany.

There are few better finishing holes than the 18th. From an elevated tee hard against the ocean, the hole doglegs right to follow giant sand dunes down the right side. Bunkers guard the corner of the dogleg and the green, some 500 metres distant from the tee, is tucked into an alcove beside the fine clubhouse which awaits you – but not quite yet.

The green can be reached in two strokes but they must both be truly struck for danger lurks in the rough to the left and even more so in the tough reed grasses and sand of the dunes.

It was here in the inaugural PLM Open of 1986 that a white piano was wheeled on to the green and some excellent twelve-bar blues was played by Englishman, Howard Smith, to the delight of the spectators awaiting the presentation of prizes.

FACILITIES

Falsterbo is very much a golf club in the traditional mould. A large practice ground with good practice balls available from a dispenser, and a first-class putting green, are very much in evidence.

If the wind is blowing at the par 3 11th, luck and a prayer may prove to be your best allies. The green is surrounded by water on three sides.

Inside, the clubhouse is comfortable and welcoming with a restaurant and bar and a patio which provides a popular rendezvous for a drink after the exertions of the round.

With strict drink driving laws in force in Sweden, the bicycle is the preferred mode of transport for the vast majority of Falsterbo members. The club has one of the biggest bicycle parks in world golf.

THE REGION

Southern Sweden has much to recommend it apart from several fine courses in the Malmo area. The summers are long and warm in this part of Scandinavia and golf can be played all year round at Falsterbo. There is very little snow, and often none at all, in winter at these latitudes.

Naturalists from all over the world find their way here to mingle with the golfers on a peninsula which is one of Europe's most important nature reserves. The lakes team with wildlife and rare species of birds.

Malmo is only a short drive from Falsterbo. From this major port, it is a very short ferry or hydrofoil trip across the Oresund to Copenhagen where Tivoli Gardens and the many attractions of the Danish capital are absolute musts for any Scandinavian visitor.

ACCOMMODATION

The area around the club is well served with a range of accommodation, although the village of Falsterbo has no hotels of its own. The golfer will have to look a little further afield.

A couple of kilometres along the road in the historic town of Skanör, the Hotel Spelabäcken is popular with golfers to the area. It is a small and comfortable, has a pool and solarium and always offers a warm welcome.

In Malmo the Hotel S T Jörgen has a renowned international piano bar, a fine restaurant and was the official hotel for the PLM Open before the event became the Scandinavian Masters.

There are several fine restaurants in Falsterbo and Skanör, with the Kaptensgarden particularly popular with locals and visitors.

Ullna Golfclubb

FOUNDED 1981

SWEDISH DELIGHT

There are some who say that Ullna Golf Club, an hour's drive from the centre of Stockholm, is the finest 17-hole golf course in Sweden. There is certainly no doubt that this project on a stunning site beside the Ullna Lake is one of the most talked-about courses in all Sweden.

Created by the Swedish architect, Sven Tumba, the layout was conceived as an unashamedly American-style golf course designed to attract major tournaments to Stockholm. Determined that the course would be a masterpiece, Tumba consulted several eminent players during the development stages, including Seve Ballesteros and Lee Trevino.

He chose the site beside the lake which is used in winter by the Ice Yacht Club of Stockholm and for skating. Across the lake, a man-made hill dominates the skyline and is used as a ski slope during the long winter months. The hill has its own ski lift.

The Ullna course was very expensive to build. Tumba followed the American trend for stadium-type courses and designed it to provide plenty of viewing hills for spectators. He also wanted it to be a permanent site for the Scandinavian Enterprise Open. The club did host the S.E.O. on several occasions and both Ian Baker-Finch and Ian Woosnam have won there.

Ullna Golfclubb
Rosenkälle, 18492 Åkersberga
◆
Location: 10km from Åkersberga
Tel: (46) 85 102 6075
Course: 18 holes, 5825m, par 72
Visitors: Welcome on weekdays. Weekend play with a member only. Course closed November to March
Green fees: SKr300

THE COURSE

The layout can best be summed up as a combination of many very fine holes and a few very ordinary ones. Lack of sufficient space

Perversely, Ullna gives its guests the choice of the devil or the deep blue sea. A par here is a treasure to be prized.

The Ullna lake dominates almost every hole. Here the sky and the green combine to present the course at its very best.

was the problem at the design stage and that is why Ullna is known as 'the best 17-hole course in Sweden'.

Much use has been made of water in the design and it comes into play very early in the round. The short 3rd is played to an island green and is one of the memorable holes.

The next is a par 5 and is even more daunting. Played alongside the lake, the tee shot must be carefully threaded to the right spot on the fairway. A one-iron or three-wood, cut slightly to follow the line of the lake, is the best play. Water and bunkers guard the front of a two-tier green; you'll need to decide whether to try to carry all the trouble or simply lay up.

The hole is not long and should be in range for most players, but it is a long carry and the penalty for failure is severe.

Great stands of birch and plenty of water combine to present the visitor with wonderful views all around, and this is without question one of the best maintained courses in the whole of Sweden.

Ullna in some ways saves the best for last with the 16th and 17th holes presenting a series of wonderful challenges.

The 16th is another par 3 played across water and is a hole that has ruined many a promising score. If it is safely negotiated, an even greater challenge awaits.

The 17th is played alongside and across water as well as over a hill. It is a stiff 400-metre test with the water threatening the drive on the left.

With the wind usually coming from the left, those who let the ball drift away to the right on the breeze soon find that the trees are as much of a threat as the water. The hole plays over a hill and drops down to a peninsula green with water close to the back. Par here is an achievement of which to be extremely proud and most visitors nominate the 17th as the outstanding hole on the this very fine golf course.

FACILITIES

The facilities in the Ullna clubhouse are first-rate, but they could certainly not be described as lavish. The club serves excellent food and there is a warm and friendly bar in which to analyse the dramas of the day.

There is a good practice ground and first-class tuition available from former European Tour player, John Cockin. The only criticism of this course is that it is only open from April to October.

THE REGION

Ullna is only 18 kilometres from Stockholm, Sweden's very beautiful capital city. It was developed from a small town built in the 13th century on an island which separates two stretches of water.

On the foundations of the old fortress which was built to guard the vital entrance to the trading centres of Lake Malaren, there now stands the imposing royal palace.

Stockholm is a city of splendid architecture with much to interest the tourist.

A fine old bridge leads northwards past the House of Parliament to Gustaf Adolfs Torg and the Royal Opera House. This marks the beginning of the Norrmalm area of the city where there are numerous cinemas, theatres and fine restaurants.

ACCOMMODATION

There is no shortage of excellent hotel accommodation in and around Stockholm. Within easy reach of Ullna is the Scandic Hotel in Upplands Väsby which offers comfortable accommodation as well as a first-class restaurant.

In Stockholm itself, the Sergel Plaza Hotel is an ideal base from which to explore the city and yet be within easy reach of the golf course.

The swans are probably the only creatures who can ever feel at home on such a challenging course. But the club in the background offers all its guests a warm welcome – whatever their score.

15

Switzerland

When the first golf course was built in Switzerland towards the end of the last century, the game was very much the preserve of the wealthy classes. Over the past hundred years little has changed, although the country is attracting more golfing visitors each year in search of an alternative destination to the more regularly travelled routes.

The great benefits of golf in Switzerland are the clear alpine air, the wonderful views and first-class facilities everywhere.

Switzerland was one country which the great golf boom of the 1980s carefully bypassed. During that period there was only a handful of new courses built, but it is not hard to understand, bearing in mind the very high cost of land together with the mountainous terrain.

A pretty bell tower, an alpine lake, with mountains and a deep azure sky behind – this is both the dream, and the reality, of Switzerland.

Golf here is essentially a summer diversion between winter sports seasons but there is, nonetheless, some very fine golf still to be enjoyed.

The majority of Swiss courses were built before, or soon after, the Second World War with the oldest club in the country, Engadine Golfclub north of St Moritz, dating back to 1898. The course is also the highest in the country at around 2000 metres although the layout itself is quite flat.

Today there are more than 30 courses in the country with the vast majority of them full 18-hole layouts. All have majestic settings in the mountains or the forest, and often the golf takes second place to the sheer joy and freedom of the surroundings.

Crans-sur-Sierre, set high in the mountains with stunning views across to the Matterhorn, is the annual venue for the Swiss Open, one of the classiest events on the European Tour. Often beset with weather problems as the cloud tumbles down the mountain it is, nonetheless, one of the most popular stops on the circuit.

Other fine courses in Switzerland are to be found at the Lucerne Golf Club, dating back to 1903, and in Zurich where the Zurich-Zumikon Golfclub is set in beautifully maintained parkland and has served the citizens of the city since 1931.

The Lausanne Golfclub is another of Switzerland's senior clubs dating back to 1921. It is not only one of the country's most important and fashionable clubs but also boasts one of the finest courses in all of Europe.

A summer visit to Switzerland to enjoy the thrill of the mountains and some very fine golf into the bargain should be high on any golfer's itinerary.

Crans-sur-Sierre

FOUNDED 1924

GOLF CAPITAL OF THE ALPS

Although the Golf Club Crans-sur-Sierre was not officially founded until 1924, golf has been played at Crans Montana, 1500 metres up on the high plateau, since 1905.

In that year Sir Arnold Lunn, proprietor of the Palace Hotel and one of the early pioneers of holiday skiing, was persuaded by his fellow directors to build a golf course on ground to the west of the hotel.

English golf course constructors, Freemantle and Gedge, were brought in to lay out the course. Nine holes were opened for play in 1906 and, two years later, the second nine were completed.

Until the outbreak of the First World War, golf at Crans was the exclusive preserve of the British gentry, but after the hostilities began the British left the Haut Plateau and the golf course was abandoned.

Two local hoteliers, Eysee Bonvin (Hotel du Golf) and Albert Bonvin (Beauséjour) resurrected the game in 1921 when they laid out nine holes with the start and finish outside the Hotel du Golf. Three years later, the Golf Club Crans-sur-Sierre was founded with René Payot as its first President.

Payot was an influential journalist and lost no time in publicizing his golf course and extolling its virtues of beautiful scenery and exceptional location. And it was not difficult to do, for the course is in one of the most magnificent locations anywhere in the world.

With its crystal clear air, views over the Rhône Valley to the Matterhorn and the circle of snow-clad peaks that surround it, Crans is quite simply one of the most spectacular sites in Europe.

As the demand for golf in this Alpine paradise grew so did the need to expand the course. In 1928 work began on a second nine holes. In July the

> **Golf Club Crans-sur-Sierre**
>
> *Case postale 296, 3963*
> *Crans-sur-Sierre*
>
> ◆
>
> Location: Off the N9 west of
> Crans-sur-Sierre
>
> Tel: (41) 27 41 2168
>
> Courses: Plan-Bramois
> Course – 18 holes, 6165m,
> par 72;
>
> Jack Nicklaus Course –
> 9 holes, 2667m, par 35
>
> Visitors: Welcome with current
> handicap certificate.
>
> Pre-booked starting times
> recommended in August.
>
> Course closed November to April
>
> Green fees: SFr80

The Grand Hotel du Golf, situated next to the course, offers a superb cuisine to its guests and a welcome to match.

following year, the full 18-hole course was inaugurated, starting and finishing on the same site as today.

Many changes have been made over the years with the most recent and major in 1954 when the old 6th hole was removed and the new 13th added. Greens have been remodelled, new bunkers put in and trees planted to create the course which has been the host of the Swiss Open – now known as the European Masters – since 1939.

THE COURSES

In some ways, Crans is an unlikely venue for a major European professional championship. It is not long by modern championship standards, particularly since the ball flies much further in the thin air at this altitude, and Crans is considered to be a relatively easy course for the top players.

However, the European Masters remains one of the most prestigious, and valuable, of the events in Continental Europe and this is very much thanks to its ambience and traditional location.

It is an exciting event if the weather is good, for scoring is always low. Italian professional, Baldovino Dassu, now retired from tournament golf, went round the mountain course in an historic 60 strokes in the Swiss Open of 1971.

The 11th gives even the top professionals trouble. The bunker – one of three defending the green – is more treacherous than it looks.

Spaniard José Maria Canizares had 11 birdies in a row in the 1978 event. He had five in a row at the end of his second round and six more at the start of his third. But he still lost out to his fellow countryman, Seve Ballesteros.

Although the course is unplayable for half the year when it is used as a nursery slope for beginner skiers, it does offer excellent conditions during the summer. The holes undulate gently across the plateau, with wide open fairways and very little in the way of rough. Great stands of beautiful pine trees and out-of-bounds fences close to the edge of the fairways are the course's main defences.

The 6th is a typical example. A modest par 4 at 295 metres, it is almost enveloped in pines and has out-of-bounds along the full length of the fairway on the left.

A scattering of bunkers around the green ensures that the approach shot has to be very carefully judged. The thin air puts the green in range for even players of moderate length, but it is a big gamble with a severe penalty for failure.

On the back nine, the short 11th gives even the top tournament players a great deal of trouble. It appears to be a relatively straightforward par 3 of 190 metres but the green is heavily defended by three dangerous bunkers. In the 1992 European Masters, it ranked as the second most difficult hole on the course at 94 over par for the field, a scoring average of 3.22.

By contrast, the long 14th, which has a beguiling lake short and right of the green to catch the wayward attempt to get home in two, was found to be one of the easiest despite its length. The thin air and a slightly downhill fairway undoubtedly help.

The club also has a nine-hole course laid out by Jack Nicklaus and

The alpine setting gives this, the 7th green, an innocent picture-postcard feel, however it is fortified by savage bunkers.

opened in 1988. It took several years to obtain the necessary permissions are this environmentally conscious country. Another nine are scheduled to be added to give Crans another full 18-hole course.

The nine holes of the current Nicklaus course are relatively short making it ideal for beginners.

FACILITIES

The club offers a wide range of facilities to its 1500 members and visitors alike. The driving range has 70 berths, there are three practice putting greens, two practice pitching greens and several practice bunkers.

There is a fine restaurant, a friendly bar and a terrace to enjoy the spectacular views.

THE REGION

Crans is set in the heart of the Alps, 190 kilometres from Geneva, in one of the world's best-known skiing regions. Built on the high plateau sown with fir trees and dotted with lakes, it opens out on to the Rhône Valley against a backdrop of Alpine peaks.

In the summer months, mountain walkers take advantage of the ski lifts to explore the upper slopes, or enjoy a choice of dozens of excellent restaurants dotted across the landscape.

There are boutiques and beauty parlours and a host of discotheques and clubs in the region which are as appropriate to après golf as to après ski.

ACCOMMODATION

Being a major skiing resort, there is no shortage of accommodation in the area around Crans. From relatively modest but well-appointed small hotels to the five-star Grand Hotel du Golf there is something to suit every taste, and almost every budget.

The gastronomic delights of this wonderful region are vast and legendary – from the local wines, which go so well with a traditional fondue to the most exquisite *nouvelle cuisine*.

Crans, it seems, has it all.

16

Wales

Although Wales is relatively small in comparison to its neighbours, the Principality is remarkably well adorned with fine golf courses. Well over a hundred await the visitor, from the great championship links of Harlech to charming little mountain courses such as Hollywell in Clwyd where the club dates back to 1906 and the sheep still keep you company while you play.

Although the Welsh were marginally behind the Scots and the Irish, they were not slow to get to grips with championship golf. The Welsh Amateur Championship predates the English equivalent by 30 years and there have been many fine Welsh players who have made their mark on the game.

It is a country hardly well blessed with many great seaside links courses by comparison with its Gaelic cousins to the north and west, but there are classic exceptions at Royal St David's Harlech and Royal Porthcawl. And there are courses with wonderful sounding names like Abergele and Pensarn, Vale of Llangollen and Pwlleli which dates back to 1900.

Who can resist wonderful Wales, with its dramatic landscapes and sporting traditions?

There is great antiquity among the golf courses of Wales and great traditions, too. The Amateur Championship, The Home Internationals, the Curtis Cup and the Ladies' Championship have all been played at Royal Porthcawl which celebrated its centenary in 1991.

Among the great spate of courses built just before and around the turn of the century was the famous Aberdovey Club in Gwynedd completed in 1892. This course is famous the world over as the favourite course of the doyen of writers on golf, Bernard Darwin. He once wrote of it: 'the course that my soul loves best of all the courses in the world.'

It was at Aberdovey that he learned to play, and he recalls in his book 'Historic Golf Courses of the British Isles' the very beginnings of golf there in the early 1880s.

Golf at Aberdovey and in Wales has come a long way since then, but what the visitor will find there is traditional golf played on well matured courses which have all stood the test of time.

He will also find courses of great charm in beautiful settings such as on the Isle of Anglesey where there are a handful of clubs dating back to before the First World War and beyond.

And, of course, there are also new courses to be explored in Wales. The famous Rolls of Monmouth club dates back only to 1982 and its fine 18-hole layout attracts many visitors to that part of Gwent.

Aberdovey Golf Club

FOUNDED 1892

DARWIN'S THEORY OF EXALTATION

Every golfer, said the learned Bernard Darwin, has a course for which he feels a 'blind and unreasoning affection'. His was Aberdovey.

In his *Historic Golf Courses of the British Isles* Darwin conceded that there were several very excellent courses in Wales, but he was quite determined to put Aberdovey at the very top of his list. 'Not that I make for it any claim that it is the best,' he wrote, 'not even on the strength of its alphabetical pre-eminence, but because it is the course that my soul loves best of all the courses in the world.'

Darwin could recall the earliest days of golf at Aberdovey from his uncle, Colonel Ruck. The Colonel, having played some golf at Formby, borrowed nine flower pots from a lady in the village and cut nine holes on the marsh near Aberdovey to put them in.

The clubhouse at Aberdovey has an excellent reputation – and, with a setting like this, it's not hard to see why.

Although the Colonel was the founder of the links, it was his brother, Major General R.M. Ruck, who was responsible for the development of golf at Aberdovey and was instrumental in the setting-up of the golf club itself in 1892.

Aberdovey Golf Club
Aberdovey, LL35 0RT
◆
Location: Three miles west of Aberdovey on A493
Tel: 0654-767210
Course: 18 holes, 6445yds, par 71
Visitors: Welcome but with minor restrictions
Green fees: £20-25

THE COURSE

The course is laid out on the north side of the Dovey Estuary on a narrow strip of land between the railway line and a range of hills on one side, and the sandhills and the seashore on the other.

From the normal tees it is played to just over 6000 yards and, stretched to its limit, it barely exceeds 6400 yards. But, as in all true seaside links courses, the wind is the arbiter of 'effective length' and Aberdovey is no different from dozens more like it perched along the shores of the British Isles.

The first four holes lie huddled against the sandhills with the sea beyond. The opening tee shot is to a fairway blind from the tee, but the pump house performs a useful secondary function here with the right edge indicating the optimum line to get the round underway.

It is not an easy start. From the back tee it is more than 440 yards to the green which, like most of the greens, is small and difficult to seek out.

The Trefeddian Hotel, sitting majestically above the course, is a popular resting place for visitors to the course at Aberdovey.

The 2nd hole offers a little respite with a short pitch for the approach after a drive from a pulpit tee to a narrow fairway.

The first of the short holes then presents itself. Surrounded by rough and sandhills, the 3rd green is reached with a fairly short iron if the wind is behind. It is a friendly green which tends to gather the ball and does much to help to lift the mood for the remainder of the round.

There are two more par 3s on the front nine with only one par 5, at the 7th. This is the middle hole of a trio where care must be taken to keep the drive to the left away from the dangers of the railway line. Downwind and in favourable dry conditions, its 482 yards can be covered easily in two good strokes.

If the wind is behind on the way out, it will almost certainly be in the face on the way home, and that presents a very difficult prospect indeed at Aberdovey.

The back nine is the longer by more than 600 yards, with two par 5s and only one par 3 to compensate for the extra length.

The 16th is the shortest par 4 on the course at only 281 yards, but it is fiendishly difficult. The railway threatens on the left side, while the fairway curves away with trouble on the right. Although the pitch to the green is not long, it has to be made to a small, undulating green protected by hills on the right and a sharp drop to the left.

A safe negotiation of the 17th requires a solid drive down the left side followed by an approach to the right side of the green from where the ball should be safely gathered home.

A dike runs across the front of the last tee and must be crossed on the walk from the 17th green. It then runs down the left side of the fairway towards the green. A good drive still mean a longish iron approach to the home green, and a two-putt par should leave a well deserved feeling of satisfaction.

It is not difficult to understand Darwin's love of this course which has hosted the Home Internationals and the Welsh Seniors' Championship.

FACILITIES

Aberdovey has a well deserved reputation for its hospitality. It is very popular with visitors and many golf societies and golf clubs from all over Britain make annual pilgrimages. There are first-class catering facilities available in the clubhouse and a warm and friendly bar. There is also a short practice ground.

THE REGION

The village of Aberdovey is no more than a ribbon of shops, houses, churches and pubs along the foot of the Welsh hills. If you are looking for a glittering night life, then you have come to the wrong place.

The area around Aberdovey is principally the domain of the hillwalker and climber, but for those interested in railways, there are two narrow-gauge railway lines which offer fascinating journeys. The Bala Lake Railway puffs its way along the shores of the lake from Llanuwchllyn to Bala, while the Tal-y-llyn Railway travels inland from Tywyn to Nant Gwernol. Much of this track runs through the Snowdonia National Park and some truly spectacular scenery.

ACCOMMODATION

The Trefeddian Hotel in Aberdovey is a popular base for visitors to the course. It offers excellent value and is very convenient to the club.

An alternative is the Hotel Plas Penhelig which enjoys fine views over the Dovey estuary.

Although the sheep are perfectly at home beside the 2nd, with its heavily fortified green, it remains a constant challenge to any other visitors who venture out here.

Royal Porthcawl Golf Club

F O U N D E D 1 8 9 1

AMONG THE BEST IN THE WORLD

The great links course of the Royal Porthcawl Golf Club in Mid Glamorgan is indisputably one of the best of all the championship courses of the British Isles. Indeed, there are some, the noted golf writer Tom Scott among them, who place it very high on any list of the world's top courses.

It is not difficult to understand why. Laid out in a triangular shape, which is considered to be the ideal arrangement for a course subjected to the seaside winds, Porthcawl is a stiff and yet very fair examination.

A mixture of linksland close to the sea and moorland with bracken, heather and gorse in the rough on its upper level, the course hugs the shore hard by the Bristol Channel.

It commands fine views across to the hills of Devon and Exmoor and along to the Gower Peninsula. It also has the rare claim to fame that, from some point on each hole, the sea is in view.

Despite the fact that it celebrated its centenary in 1991, the course is a relative newcomer to the championship rota. It was 1951 before it was invited to stage the Amateur Championship when Dick Chapman won an all-American final. That event undoubtedly confirmed Royal Porthcawl's credentials because the R & A took the Amateur back there again in 1965, 1973, 1980 and 1988. Indeed the present R & A secretary, Michael Bonallack, won the second of his five Amateur titles there in 1965.

The Home Internationals, the Curtis Cup and the Ladies' Championship have all been played at Royal Porthcawl as well.

The original course of nine holes was laid out in 1891 on a stretch of land known as Lock's Common. Seven years later, the club moved to the present site.

Over the years some improvements have been made but the course has altered very little. Harry Colt made some changes in 1913, Tom Simpson made a few others in 1950, and T. H. Cotton was the last golf

Royal Porthcawl Golf Club
Porthcawl, CF36 3UW
◆
Location: 22 miles west of Cardiff. M4 junction 37
Tel: 0656-782251
Course: 18 holes, 6691yds, par 72
Visitors: Welcome but with weekend restrictions.
Handicap certificate required
Green fees: Midweek £25-30; weekend £40-45

The wall of photos in the clubhouse at Porthcawl provide ample evidence of the Club's illustrious 100-year history.

The beach which runs alongside the fairway at the 2nd at Porthcawl can act as a magnet to those who select a 'club too far'.

course architect to leave any mark on the course with some modest alterations in 1950.

THE COURSE

This is a classic seaside course with not a tree to break the skyline. The triangle of land has its base parallel to the sea and its apex about 10 metres above sea level. Here the turf is more akin to moorland than the pure links, but is pleasantly keen and crisp to play from nonetheless.

Unless the wind blows strongly – which it frequently does on this exposed part of the Bristol Channel – length is not the major obstacle here.

At under 6700 yards, the longer hitter has little advantage unless he can ally that element of the game to accurate play from the tee.

Porthcawl relies for its defences on tightly bunkered fairways and small greens which are hard to seek out. Like the Old Course at St Andrews, there is always a way round at Porthcawl – if you can find it.

Driving accuracy is the key to success. The player who can consistently thread the ball between fairway hazards and leave good position for the approach is the one who will succeed.

The humps and bumps of pure links golf add to the problems of the approach shot as well as on the greens which are undulating and very fast, even during the winter months.

The first three holes run along the shore to the west, with the last of the trio so close to the water that you can drive on to the shingle all too easily. The course then swings inland via the short 4th, a demanding par 3 of almost 200 yards.

The climb up to the higher part of the course begins at the next. It is a long pull up to the 5th green

The bunkers which guard the 18th are not there for show. But whatever your score, a genuine Porthcawl welcome awaits you in the clubhouse.

on a hole which is just a par 5 for length, but plays much longer because of the rise in the ground.

On the upper plateau there are shades of Ganton perhaps, with heather in the rough and gorse aplenty. But that is hardly surprising since, at one stage in its existence, the ground upon which that great Yorkshire course was built was covered by the sea.

The 7th is almost a toy-like hole of only 116 yards, but do not be fooled. It is heavily bunkered and the green has huge slopes.

The best of the front nine holes, and perhaps even of the entire course, is the 9th itself. A medium length par 4 of 368 yards from the medal tee, the drive is played across a big dip followed by a medium iron to a very small and well guarded green.

The back nine is marginally longer than the front with three demanding par 4s of more than 400 yards, and two very fine and memorable short holes.

Of the two par 5s, the 17th is the only one of genuine three-shot value, but again it very much depends on the wind. Legend has it that when the late autumn mists descend upon the course, the ghost of the Maid of Sker appears on the fairway.

Whether you catch her or not, the finishing hole at Porthcawl is one which certainly befits this great championship links. The tee shot is downhill from a plateau tee straight towards the sea. A rough hollow around 270 yards out only troubles the longest players. From there, great care must be taken with the approach shot.

The green is long and narrow and anything overhit will run through, and straight on to, the beach immediately behind.

A lasting memory of the course is the quality and pace of the greens. They are the perfect example of what can be achieved in the never-ending quest for genuine year-round golf in the British Isles.

This is the masterpiece of Welsh golf where great history and tradition permeate a clubhouse which has barely altered in a hundred years and where the visitor is assured of a warm welcome.

FACILITIES

A friendly bar and a new dining room serving first-class food are just exactly what the player wants after his or her round at this venerable club.

Clubs are available for hire and caddies are occasionally available by prior arrangement, usually during the school holiday period. There is also an excellent full-length practice ground.

THE REGION

The coast of South Wales remains largely unspoiled and undiscovered by the travelling golfer. And yet there is great golf to be found here and much to enjoy away from the challenge of the links.

The Principality retains a glow of an earlier, gentler age when standards were paramount and traditions carefully preserved. The visitor can wander the rugged coastline with its coves and deserted beaches or head north to the mountains and valleys for which Wales is much better known.

For those who stick by the coastal route and choose Porthcawl as a base, a visit to Tenby at the western end of Carmarthen Bay should certainly be on the itinerary. The town in many ways sums up the appeal of this coastline of Wales. Its most famous son, Augustus John, who spent his boyhood there, said of it: 'You may travel the world over, but you will find nothing more beautiful. It is so restful, so colourful and so unspoilt.'

Little has changed in the interim. The medieval walls surrounding the town and the cobblestone streets have remained the same for centuries. The ruined castle is a reminder of its long history as a fortress town and Tenby's harbour, with its painted boats, presents as pretty a picture as can be found anywhere in the British Isles.

A windswept landscape with the sea closing in. For lovers of links golf the course at Porthcawl is as close to perfection as you can come.

The town also claims another of South Wales's great links golf courses.

ACCOMMODATION

Visitors to Royal Porthcawl will find the four-star Coed-y-Mwstwr Country Hotel in Bridgend ideal for their purposes. This Victorian mansion has stunning views and 24 en-suite bedrooms with every amenity.

Entries in bold face indicate a chapter/section for individual clubs and countries.

Entries in italics indicate an illustration.

Picture Credits

Courtesy Aberdovey Golf Club 227
Jackum Brown 60 inset
Malcolm Campbell 18, 22, 26-28, 134
    top, 135-141
Courtesy Club de Golf El Prat 196, 198
Danish Tourist Board 21, 24 top
Grand Hotel Huis ter Duin 113
Courtesy of La Grande Motte 71
Gruppo Marcegglia 134 bottom
Courtesy Gut Altentann 14
Matthew Harris 230
Hobbs Golf Collection 58, 149
Courtesy Hotel Copthorne Stephanie
    19 bottom
Courtesy Hotel Excelsior, Florence 147
Courtesy Hotel du Golf, Crans 223
Courtesy Hotel Koldingfjord 28,
    29 bottom
Courtesy Hyatt La Manga Club Resort 203
Irish Tourist Board/Brian Lynch 114 inset,
    116 bottom /Pat Odea 114 background,
    122
**Courtesy of Kennemer Golf and Country
    Club** 107
Ulrich Kerth 83-86
Courtesy of Manor House Golf Club
    36/Tracey Elliot-Reep 35
Brian Morgan 2, 4, 7, 9, 10 background,
    12 top,13, 15, 16 background, 19 top, 20
    background, 24 bottom, 25, 29 top, 30-33,
    37, 39-44, 47-51, 53-56, 59, 60 back-
    ground, 62, 63, 65-69, 72-80, 82
    background, 87, 88, 90-92, 94, 95, 96, 97,
    98, 105, 106, 107-110, 112, 116 top, 117-
    121, 124, 125-131, 132 background,
    143-146, 148, 150-161, 164-165, 167, 169
    top, 171-176, 178-191, 192 background,
    193-195,197, 199-202, 204-209, 211-213,
    214-221, 222 background, 224, 225, 226
    background, 229, 231-233
Courtesy VVV Noordwijk Promotie 104
    background, 111
Courtesy of Palheiro Golf 162-3
Platinum Travel Services 100 background,
    102, 103
Royal Birkdale Golf Club 38
Courtesy of Royal Dornoch Golf Club 177
Royal Liverpool Golf Club/J.E.Behrend 45
Courtesy of St-Nom-La-Bretêche 81
Phil Sheldon 52, 123, 210
Spectrum 10 inset, 16 inset, 20 inset, 64, 70
    inset, 82 inset, 100 inset, 104 inset, 132
    inset, 142, 168, 192 inset, 214 inset, 222
    inset/G.R.Richardson 89, 93
Courtesy Sporthotel IGLS 12 bottom
Courtesy Talyllyn Railway 226 inset
Courtesy Trefeddian Hotel 228
David J. Whyte 169 bottom

Course Graphics by Strokesaver 95, 97, 99,
    122, 124, 129, 166, 170, 175, 178, 185,
    191

Multimedia Books Ltd have endeavoured to
observe the legal requirements with regard
to the rights of suppliers of photographic
materials.

*While every effort was made to ensure that
all information was correct at the time of
going to press, opening hours, prices etc
are subject to change.*

SAVE £S ON HOTELS AND GREEN FEES

Seven vouchers for some of the finest Hotels and Golf Courses in Europe give you the opportunity to receive discounts of up to 50% from a normal green fee or a third night free in a participating hotel. Simply tear off the voucher and use according to the rules and conditions on the reverse.

Discount — DE VERE — THE BELFRY *Voucher*

THE BELFRY, WISHAW, NORTH WARWICKSHIRE B76 9PR
Tel: 0675 470301. Fax: 0675 470178
(also applicable to other De Vere hotels, see overleaf)

This historic venue of Ryder Cup victories needs no introduction. A first class hotel with excellent facilities set in the heart of the Warwickshire countryside.

**20% discount from published price of standard residential Winter golf packages
(1 November–31 March)**

10% discount from published price of standard residential August golf packages

Voucher expires 31 March 1996

Voucher only valid if printed in blue

Discount THE MANOR HOUSE HOTEL & GOLF COURSE MORETONHAMPSTEAD *Voucher*

MANOR HOUSE HOTEL AND GOLF COURSE
Moretonhampstead, Devon TQ13 8RE
Tel: 0647 40355. Fax: 0647 40961

Devon's most prestigious Hotel & Golf Course – set within the Dartmoor National Park – offers comfort, luxury and splendour combined with "one of England's finest inland courses".

20% discount from regular midweek green fees for the voucherholder on presentation of this voucher.

Voucher expires 31 December 1995

Voucher only valid if printed in blue

Discount ST. MELLION INTERNATIONAL *Voucher*

ST MELLION GOLF AND COUNTRY CLUB
Saltash, Cornwall PL12 6SD
Tel: 0579 50101. Fax: 0579 50116

A remarkable course designed by Jack Nicklaus, in an idyllic West Country setting.

**£7 discount from regular green fees on the Nicklaus Course or £4.50 discount
from the Old Course for the voucherholder on presentation of this voucher.**

Voucher expires 31 December 1995

Voucher only valid if printed in blue

RULES AND CONDITIONS OF USE

1. All vouchers are offered subject to availability from the hotels and golf clubs concerned. Early reservations are recommended.
2. Vouchers are non-refundable, non-exchangeable and may not be used in conjunction with any other offer.
3. Make advance reservations directly with the hotels and golf clubs concerned. The voucher must be mentioned on initial reservation.
4. The voucher must be presented at check-in.
5. All discounts apply to prices in hotels and golf courses at the time of booking.
6. MULTIMEDIA BOOKS LTD will not be responsible for any loss or damage incurred as a result of a reader making use of this offer. MULTIMEDIA BOOKS LTD will not be responsible in the event of acts of God, fire, casualties, strikes or other events beyond its control.

Offer for residential golf packages as overleaf also applies to the following two De Vere Hotels:
Mottram Hall, Wilmslow Road, Mottram St Andrew, Prestbury, Cheshire. Tel: 0625 828135
Belton Woods, Belton, Nr. Grantham, Lincolnshire. Tel: 0476 593200

RULES AND CONDITIONS OF USE

1. All vouchers are offered subject to availability at the hotel concerned. Early reservations are recommended.
2. Vouchers are non-refundable, non-exchangeable and may not be used in conjunction with any other offer.
3. Make advance reservations directly with the hotel concerned. The voucher must be mentioned at initial reservation.
4. The voucher must be presented at check-in.
5. All discounts apply to prices applicable at the time of booking.
6. MULTIMEDIA BOOKS LTD will not be responsible for any loss or damage incurred as a result of a reader making use of this offer. MULTIMEDIA BOOKS LTD will not be responsible in the event of acts of God, fire, casualties, strikes or other events beyond its control.

RULES AND CONDITIONS OF USE

1. All vouchers are offered subject to availability from the hotels and golf clubs concerned. Early reservations are recommended.
2. Vouchers are non-refundable, non-exchangeable and may not be used in conjunction with any other offer.
3. Make advance reservations directly with the hotels and golf clubs concerned. The voucher must be mentioned on initial reservation.
4. The voucher must be presented at check-in.
5. All discounts apply to prices in hotels and golf courses at the time of booking.
6. MULTIMEDIA BOOKS LTD will not be responsible for any loss or damage incurred as a result of a reader making use of this offer. MULTIMEDIA BOOKS LTD will not be responsible in the event of acts of God, fire, casualties, strikes or other events beyond its control.

RULES AND CONDITIONS OF USE

1. All vouchers are offered subject to availability from the hotels and golf clubs concerned. Early reservations are recommended.
2. Vouchers are non-refundable, non-exchangeable and may not be used in conjunction with any other offer.
3. Make advance reservations directly with the hotels and golf clubs concerned. The voucher must be mentioned on initial reservation.
4. The voucher must be presented at check-in.
5. All discounts apply to prices in hotels and golf courses at the time of booking.
6. MULTIMEDIA BOOKS LTD will not be responsible for any loss or damage incurred as a result of a reader making use of this offer. MULTIMEDIA BOOKS LTD will not be responsible in the event of acts of God, fire, casualties, strikes or other events beyond its control.

Discount  *Voucher*

COED-Y-MWSTWR HOTEL
Coychurch, Near Bridgend, Vale of Glamorgan, Wales CF35 6AF
Tel: 0656 860621. Fax: 0656 863122

This Victorian mansion hotel with stunning views and every amenity is the ideal place to stay when playing the great links course of Royal Porthcawl Golf Club.

Three nights for the regular price of two (room only) at Coed-y-Mwstwr Hotel any time of the year.

Voucher expires 31 December 1995

Voucher only valid if printed in blue

Discount  *Voucher*

MARINE HIGHLAND HOTEL
Troon, Ayrshire, Scotland KA10 6HE
Tel: 0292 314444. Fax: 0292 316922

A spectacular hotel which overlooks the 18th fairway of the championship course of Royal Troon Golf Club – the perfect place to stay to play this historic course and explore the beautiful coastline of Ayrshire.

Three nights for the regular price of two (room and breakfast) at the Marine Highland Hotel except 24-26 December, 31 December–2 January.

Voucher expires 31 December 1995

Voucher only valid if printed in blue

Discount Voucher

CORFU HILTON
Nafsikas Street, Kanoni, 49100 Corfu, Greece.
Tel: (30) 661 365 40. Fax: (30) 661 365 51

As owners of the Corfu Golf Club, the Corfu Hilton makes sure its guests are particularly well catered for with standards renowned in Hilton hotels throughout the world.

With every week's stay at the Corfu Hilton, a 50% discount from green fees for unlimited rounds of golf for the voucherholder at the Corfu Golf Club.

Voucher expires 31 December 1995

Voucher only valid if printed in blue

Discount  *Voucher*

GOLF D'HARDELOT – HOTEL DU PARC
111 Avenue Francois 1er, 62152 Hardelot, France.
Tel: (33) 21 33 22 11. Fax: (33) 21 83 29 71

14km south of Boulogne. This wonderful complex offers a wide range of attractions in addition to excellent golf and the Hotel du Parc is a firm favourite with visiting golfers.

Three nights (room only) for the regular price of two, at the Hotel du Parc situated near the golf courses to include a Sunday night, any time of the year except August or public holidays.

Voucher expires 31 December 1995

Voucher only valid if printed in blue

RULES AND CONDITIONS OF USE

1. All vouchers are offered subject to availability from the hotels and golf clubs concerned. Early reservations are recommended.
2. Vouchers are non-refundable, non-exchangeable and may not be used in conjunction with any other offer.
3. Make advance reservations directly with the hotels and golf clubs concerned. The voucher must be mentioned on initial reservation.
4. The voucher must be presented at check-in.
5. All discounts apply to prices in hotels and golf courses at the time of booking.
6. MULTIMEDIA BOOKS LTD will not be responsible for any loss or damage incurred as a result of a reader making use of this offer. MULTIMEDIA BOOKS LTD will not be responsible in the event of acts of God, fire, casualties, strikes or other events beyond its control.

RULES AND CONDITIONS OF USE

1. All vouchers are offered subject to availability from the hotels and golf clubs concerned. Early reservations are recommended.
2. Vouchers are non-refundable, non-exchangeable and may not be used in conjunction with any other offer.
3. Make advance reservations directly with the hotels and golf clubs concerned. The voucher must be mentioned on initial reservation.
4. The voucher must be presented at check-in.
5. All discounts apply to prices in hotels and golf courses at the time of booking.
6. MULTIMEDIA BOOKS LTD will not be responsible for any loss or damage incurred as a result of a reader making use of this offer. MULTIMEDIA BOOKS LTD will not be responsible in the event of acts of God, fire, casualties, strikes or other events beyond its control.

RULES AND CONDITIONS OF USE

1. All vouchers are offered subject to availability from the hotels and golf clubs concerned. Early reservations are recommended.
2. Vouchers are non-refundable, non-exchangeable and may not be used in conjunction with any other offer.
3. Make advance reservations directly with the hotels and golf clubs concerned. The voucher must be mentioned on initial reservation.
4. The voucher must be presented at check-in.
5. All discounts apply to prices in hotels and golf courses at the time of booking.
6. MULTIMEDIA BOOKS LTD will not be responsible for any loss or damage incurred as a result of a reader making use of this offer. MULTIMEDIA BOOKS LTD will not be responsible in the event of acts of God, fire, casualties, strikes or other events beyond its control.

RULES AND CONDITIONS OF USE

1. All vouchers are offered subject to availability from the hotels and golf clubs concerned. Early reservations are recommended.
2. Vouchers are non-refundable, non-exchangeable and may not be used in conjunction with any other offer.
3. Make advance reservations directly with the hotels and golf clubs concerned. The voucher must be mentioned on initial reservation.
4. The voucher must be presented at check-in.
5. All discounts apply to prices in hotels and golf courses at the time of booking.
6. MULTIMEDIA BOOKS LTD will not be responsible for any loss or damage incurred as a result of a reader making use of this offer. MULTIMEDIA BOOKS LTD will not be responsible in the event of acts of God, fire, casualties, strikes or other events beyond its control.